D0628613

THE INCREDIBLE
Power of
PRAYER

**David W. Balsiger, Joette Whims,
& Melody Hunskor**

Tyndale House Publishers, Inc.
Wheaton, Illinois

Visit Tyndale's exciting Web site at www.tyndale.com

Designed by Brian Eterno

Edited by Kathryn S. Olson

ISBN 0-8423-1579-9

Printed in the United States of America

03   02   01   00   99   98
7   6   5   4   3   2   1

CONTENTS

THE EVANGELICALS

ACKNOWLEDGMENTS

This book and its companion video series–television special have been in the making for nearly fifteen years. On more than one occasion, I thought God had assembled the right team to bring this message about the incredible power of prayer to the public. I was wrong again and again as our "team efforts" produced only false start after false start. More than twenty book publishers showed disinterest in the project, while over two hundred potential financiers of the video series–television special also declined participation. I finally came to the realization that I couldn't personally make this monumental project happen. All I could do was pray that God would bring the project to fruition in his timing. When I prayerfully left the project in God's hands and quit trying to make it happen by my own means, that's when God started to move, bringing together the team he wanted involved.

My special appreciation goes to the new team: to God for showing me the way on this project and for the personal ministry to me as a result of doing it; to Thom and Joani Schultz of Group Publishing/Productions for producing the video series–television special; to my longtime friend and television producer-director Charles E. Sellier for his superb directing on this most unique video-television special; to my screenplay cowriter, Barbara Lowe, for her contribution; to Carolyn Wing Greenlee and Paul Woods for their spiritual input and support; to Meg Diehl and the other editors at Tyndale House for catching the vision for this book; to my cowriters, Joette Whims and Melody Hunskor, for their sacrifices and talents in helping to make this book a powerful message for this generation and for those who will guide America through the twenty-first century; to Rev. Peter Marshall and Stephen McDowell for their historical research and consultation; to television hosts/commentators Richard Blair, Ralph

Baker, and Jane Chastain for their special efforts and contributions in making a successful video-television production of this book; to my wife, Nancy, for her patience and often hands-on participation in this project; and to all the production crew members and Christian organizations who contributed to the project—plus the countless number of people who have been praying for all our efforts.

—David W. Balsiger

The four-part companion video series is available from Group Productions, P.O. Box 508, Loveland, CO 80539.

ONE

The Transforming Power of Prayer

What do you think about when you hear the word *prayer?* Of course, the simple response is "talking to God." But beyond that definition, what do you feel deep down when you hear the word? Be honest.

Does it make you feel guilty because you know you should spend more time in prayer?

Do you think of elderly Christians or clergy you greatly admire who make a daily practice of extended prayer?

Or does your mind picture grace at a meal or long-winded stretches of prayer during church services?

Prayer means so many different things to so many people. We have all struggled with understanding how prayer affects our lives and how much we can rely on it in times of difficulty. Most of us have wondered whether or not God's response to our prayers has played a key role in altering daily events and changing our life. Do you ever wonder if it can also play a role in society at large?

In *The Incredible Power of Prayer*, we will take a deeper look at prayer. We will ask the hard questions and search for concrete answers. Our purpose is to search the depths of how

God moves among us in response to our pleas for his mercy, grace, and forgiveness, both as individuals and as a society.

One of the central questions we will consider is, Is prayer a key to changing the situation in which we find ourselves today in America? If so, then how do we pray for change in our homes, our communities, and our nation?

THE ROLE OF PRAYER IN A FRIGHTENING WORLD

All of us will readily admit that we live in a frightening world. Many indicators suggest that America—indeed, the whole world—is in the midst of a vast spiritual decline. You can probably name some looming problems in your own community, even your own neighborhood.

Our schools—the institutions that we attended with pride and anticipation not so many years ago—have become armed camps, with teachers being threatened and assaulted. We fearfully watch our children go to school. And these fears are not unfounded. According to a recent Gallup poll, 63 percent of our students will experience assault during school hours.[1] Each month in 1984, 125,000 teachers were threatened, and one thousand needed medical attention because of in-school assaults.[2] Today the problems are even worse.

But this decline doesn't affect just schoolchildren. Millions of marriages will end in divorce, leaving adults and children with deep emotional scars. Many schoolchildren will become latchkey kids who must fend for themselves.

All across our country, churches and synagogues are being desecrated and burned. Movies, books, and videos that assault our sensibilities with the most vile language and visual scenes imaginable are not only readily available but are part of the so-called mainstream media and are widely applauded.

So what do we do? The problems we face are undoubtedly too big for any one of us to handle alone. Are they unsolvable? Or is it possible that prayer can help? Will God really influence or even change events in response to our prayers?

In 2 Chronicles 7:14, the Lord says, "If my people who are called by my name will humble themselves and pray and seek my face and turn from their wicked ways, I will hear from heaven and will forgive their sins and heal their land." This verse is often quoted to encourage Christians to pray for their country. Still, many of our friends and neighbors wonder if the United States of America, the only nation on Earth to boldly claim, "In God we trust," is now beyond that hope.

If Americans are truly a praying people, then the answer to whether or not God will intervene in our society in response to prayer might be found in our past, in the range of our nation's experiences with prayer from the earliest colonial days. Can we find evidence from our past that God responds to the simple act of praying, actually changing the destiny of our nation? In other words, is there really incredible power in prayer?

A WALK THROUGH HISTORY

Power is an interesting word. Our dictionary lists no fewer than twenty-eight separate meanings; chief among them is "a great or marked ability to do or act; strength; might; or force."

In the following pages, we will discover that this definition aptly describes the incredible results of beseeching God. We will see how the power of prayer led to the discovery of our land. Through prayer the colonies were established and preserved.

Power was also demonstrated by the strength and might of the ragtag Continental army that broke the back of the most formidable military power on Earth—the British Empire—

3

during the 1700s. Most of us probably don't know that the real power that forged a great nation out of thirteen bickering colonies began with one man, George Washington, as he humbly prayed on his knees at Valley Forge.

We will walk with the Founding Fathers as they write the documents that have guided our country through two centuries. Their reliance on prayer is astounding—and a little-known fact. We will experience the prayer revivals that shook the spiritual lethargy and coldness from our land like a mighty earthquake. All of our national conflicts, from the Revolutionary War to the Persian Gulf War, were won through the incredible power of prayer!

But we can't forget to examine one of the most controversial questions of recent decades. Ever since the Supreme Court ruled on the separation of church and state, the debate has raged over what the Founding Fathers intended. In courtrooms and legislatures, the questions are raised again and again. Did the framers of the Bill of Rights really mean to say that it is wrong to post the Ten Commandments in public buildings? Is it wrong to have prayer in schools? Should we eliminate God from all public proceedings?

The answers to these questions may surprise you.

Let's start, then, where we are right now—in our individual, everyday lives. That's where the power of prayer really begins—in the hearts of Christians who humble themselves before God. We must determine if prayer really can change us, one life at a time. We must be sure that we can depend on God's power to direct us, guide us, and move us.

Sometime ago, we heard about the experience of a Loveland, Colorado, resident, Roger Morrison, a technical engineer for a computer-related firm. Roger had a best friend—alcohol. When he married his wife, Benji, he brought his best friend into her life and expected her to live with it. But Benji had a best friend, too—the Lord Jesus Christ. Benji's best friend didn't get along well with Roger's. In fact, Roger considered himself an atheist, and he hated the church that Benji attended because he believed that religion had brainwashed his wife. But Benji just prayed for him and asked her church to pray for him, too. She prayed for more than twenty years.

The Morrisons' lives set up the dilemma. Whose power is greater? Is the power of prayer able to conquer a spirit of addiction like alcoholism? The way God worked in the lives of Benji and Roger will show you the incredible power of prayer!

A NEW BEST FRIEND

Roger was furious. Every day as he drove to work, he had to pass the huge, wooden freeway sign, the one that advertised Benji's church, Resurrection Fellowship, and had *JESUS* written on it in huge letters. Each time he sped by those words, he hated that sign more deeply.

Finally one night after he had been out drinking, he decided to do something about that sign. Taking a chain saw, he drove out to the flat Colorado countryside and parked on the side of the road. Reaching the sign, he cut through the four huge, wooden telephone poles that held it up and watched it topple. It fell with a glorious crash. Now he could gloat as he drove past that spot. It seemed as if he had dealt the church a serious blow.

Not too long after his battle with the sign, however, he was arrested for driving drunk. As he sat alone in his jail cell, he realized for the first time that his best friend, alcohol, had become his worst nightmare. All along, he had thought he could control his drinking. Now he admitted that he needed help. He began to pray as his wife had urged him to do if he ever came to a crossroads with his addictive friend. Immediately, the Lord took away Roger's desire to drink. He was a free man!

From that moment, the Morrison home changed drastically. Roger began attending church with Benji, and he threw away all his alcoholic beverages. But there was one problem. The issue of the sign continued to haunt him. He had to make it right with the church.

One day he knocked on the door of the pastor's office. The pastor cordially invited him in. Roger began talking about his new life and how he had been an alcoholic. The pastor seemed excited to hear his testimony of God's power in his life. How could Roger ever admit to what he had done? Finally, gathering up his courage, Roger confessed to being the "sign assassin."

To Roger's surprise, the pastor just laughed. "God bless you, Roger," he said, and Roger felt the glow of being loved unconditionally. Roger had not lost a best friend when he gave up his alcohol and received Jesus Christ into his life. He had found a greater power that helped him conquer his old enemy, drinking.

Today, Roger has a new best friend—Jesus Christ. Roger realizes that the change in his life is due to the faithful prayers of his wife, who brought him before the Lord for twenty-seven years, and to the unconditional love and prayers of the church members![3]

AMAZING STORIES OF GOD'S POWER

This is only one example of how God intervenes in people's lives today. He works uniquely in each individual's life. As he transforms us, we begin to change our neighborhoods, and changed neighborhoods lead to transformed communities. Transformed communities in turn exert influence to change our society and nation. Through the prayers of his people, God works in miraculous ways, above and beyond the power of any one person or any group of people.

As the example of our ancestors will demonstrate, when the darkness hovers so thickly that the way seems lost, God's light shines brightest. In the following chapters, we'll learn about

★ ordinary people who became extraordinary through the incredible power of prayer;

★ amazing stories of ordinary people who changed history through prayer;

★ astounding accounts of how prayer altered nearly one hundred past and present events in the world;

★ stories of miraculous prayer interventions that will prove the power of God in our national history;

★ prayer renewal, signaling that a Fifth Great Awakening may be coming to America in this generation.

In each section of the book, we will not only present historical facts about our prayer heritage, but we will also bring you to the scenes of powerful prayer interventions through fictionalized re-creations. You can experience what it must have been like at specific times in our nation's past when God moved among his people. Together, we can relive the times when

★ the Pilgrims saw a miraculous life-and-death deliverance from devouring grasshoppers;

★ our Constitution was resurrected just in time by the power of prayer;

★ George Washington's life was miraculously protected during battle; and

★ a mysterious seagull saved a group of starving World War II airmen adrift in the ocean.

But prayer miracles are happening today, too. We will also discover the many grassroots prayer movements beginning to take shape in our own century that could bring us into a new and revitalized spiritual period in our national history.

This book isn't just an inspiring collection of stories about God's work. You will also learn how you can pray as powerfully as our predecessors did. In the concluding chapters, you will discover steps you can take to bring renewal into your private life and, as God wills, into our society. We're sure you will find that becoming a part of the incredible power of prayer today will be the most adventurous and awesome experience you could have.

Let's begin our journey into our nation's prayer heritage by looking at the prayer life of Christopher Columbus and other early explorers, a little-known aspect of this world-famous period. We will see how God moved them to change their world for Christ.

THE EXPLORERS

★ ★ ★

TWO

The Impossible Proposal

What do you remember about your days in elementary school? Chalkboards with black-and-white erasers? Desks with hinged tops? And playing kick ball in the school yard during recess?

In the third or fourth grade, you probably learned that Christopher Columbus discovered America in 1492. But most of us were taught three fallacies about his explorations.

First, you learned that Christopher Columbus discovered America. Now you probably know that the Americas had been "discovered" long before he landed here. The American Indians discovered this land when they migrated through the Bering Strait near Alaska. But Columbus should get the credit for being the explorer who made Europeans aware of this rich land, which touched off the exploration of the Western Hemisphere.

Second, you may have learned that fifteenth-century European scholars believed the world was flat and that Columbus set out to prove that it was round. His terrified sailors were convinced that their ships would sail off the edge of the earth. That, too, is incorrect. All well-informed individuals of the period knew that the world was round. Thomas S. Giles, editor of *Christianity Today,* writes, "Contrary to legend, Columbus

11

did not sail to prove the earth was round. Most educated Europeans and mariners already knew that."[1] The debate was over the size of the earth. Most mapmakers estimated its size as much smaller than it really is.

The textbooks in our children's classrooms today have corrected these first two fallacies, but they still hang on to a *third* misconception: Educators teach that Columbus's main purpose for coming to America was secular. What *was* his original intent for exploration? This is the most significant part of the discovery of America.

Columbus believed his mission was to take God's message of salvation to those who had never heard it. Although history books make no mention of Columbus's strong faith or God's miraculous hand in that great discovery, Columbus himself takes great pains to tell the world who deserves the credit. His personal diary is very explicit:

> It was the Lord who put into my mind (I could feel His hand upon me) the fact that it would be possible to sail from here to the Indies. . . . There is no question that the inspiration was from the Holy Spirit, because He comforted me with rays of marvelous illumination from the Holy Scriptures. . . . For the execution of the journey to the Indies, I did not make use of intelligence, mathematics, or maps. . . . No one should fear to undertake any task in the name of our Savior, if it is just and if the intention is purely for His holy service. . . . The fact that the gospel must still be preached to so many lands in such a short time, this is what convinces me.[2]

It seems clear that God chose Columbus, an ordinary man of prayer and vision, to lift the curtain on a new world. And prayer was the guiding force. Kevin A. Miller, editor of *Christian History Magazine,* writes:

Columbus's deep Christian faith still causes academic bewilderment. Some scholars attribute his recurring encounters with a heavenly voice to mental instability, illness, or stress. Others complain that Columbus's biographers described him as more religious than he really was. Some protest that Columbus was greedy and obsessively ambitious, so he couldn't have been truly religious, as if competing qualities cannot exist in one person.

But why explain away his intense religious devotion, when it was obvious to those who knew him and persistent throughout his writings?

Concludes Pulitzer-Prize-winning biographer Samuel Eliot Morison, "There can be no doubt that the faith of Columbus was genuine and sincere, and that his frequent communion with forces unseen was a vital element in his achievement."[3]

Let's take a closer look at the life of Columbus to see how God led Columbus to America through miraculous answers to his prayers.

HUMBLE BEGINNINGS

What kind of a person do you think would be most likely to discover a new world? A duke or a prince? Someone in the center of power? Hardly someone with the background of Christopher Columbus. Born in 1451 to a humble weaver named Domenico Columbus in Genoa, Italy, he had no formal schooling and probably learned his family trade. The name he was given—Christopher—means "Christ Bearer," which was significant since he would spend much of his life "bearing" Christ's name to people across the Atlantic.

As he grew into a young man, Columbus set his sights on sailing. He hired out on several ships and may have even engaged in sea battles against Muslim Barbary pirates. At the age of twenty-five, he was shipwrecked off the coast of Portugal. He remained in Lisbon for several years and became a mapmaker.

Many historians believe Columbus became convinced that God had given him a special mission during his thirty-third year, when he spent time seeking God for a revelation. He became convinced that God wanted him to carry the light of Christ to undiscovered lands and bring the native people to the holy faith.

Let's join Columbus in his workroom. . . .

Columbus unrolled his maps on the heavy, wooden table in the center of the small, dusty room and stared at them. His broad forehead creased deeply as he etched a few lines with his quill pen.

The door squeaked on its leather hinges as Bartolomeo, his brother and partner in the mapmaking profession, slipped into the room. As Bartolomeo quickly closed the solid door, the rush of fresh air rustled the corners of the maps. "Christopher, you won't believe this!" he announced.

"What is it?" Columbus asked, not taking his eyes from the map.

"Sailors came in this morning with wooden carvings they found floating in the sea. And you know what's so interesting about the carvings? They aren't like anything we've seen before."

A flash of excitement flitted across the intense eyes of the explorer. "I *can* believe it! Don't you remember the bodies those sailors discovered in Flores? They had very strange features. They weren't from any nation we know of. Think of how short a time those bodies must have been in the water. They must have come from somewhere close. And how about

14

those strange reeds and pine branches we saw on our voyages? They make me even more sure of my calculations. Look, Bartolomeo." He jabbed his finger at a section of the uppermost map. "I've plotted out all the information from Marco Polo's last journey to the East. Here are Cathay, Chiambra [India], and the islands of Cipangu [Japan]. Polo says Cipangu is only 4,700 miles from here." Columbus pulled out another large, hand-drawn map. "This is Toscanelli's latest map. See how he's plotted the route to the East."

Then Columbus brought out the most important map, the one he had drawn with his own quill pen. "I think they're both wrong," he said firmly as he pointed to a line drawn to the uncharted West. "By my calculations, if we drop down to the twenty-eighth parallel and follow it straight west, we will find a shorter route to Cipangu. We won't have to travel down around the African coast. I figure our journey will be only 2,760 miles."

Bartolomeo laughed. "I've never known anyone else with a dream like yours. We can't command ships like royalty!"

Columbus bristled. "It's not a dream. I am sure that God has given me a mission to carry out. I must take Christ's message to people who have never heard his name."

"But where will you get the money for such a trip? You'll need several ships." Bartolomeo rolled up one of the maps and waved it in the air. "You sure won't make enough money as a mapmaker!"

Columbus took the map from his brother's hands and unrolled it gently. "I have asked God to send someone who will finance my explorations. God has assured me that he will answer. Have you seen the rock formation of a horseman on the island of Corvo?"

"Oh yes, I remember it clearly."

"The horseman is pointing west across the ocean. It's a sign that we must sail west. God wants me to find the western route."

Bartolomeo looked down once more at the map Columbus had drawn. "You are the best navigator and mapmaker I've ever seen. I do believe you can do this. I believe you have heard from God and that he has given you this mission. I'll help any way I can. . . ."[4]

THE TRIP TO SANTA FE

Over the next four and a half years, Columbus presented his plan to several European kings, but none of them took him seriously. The last monarchs he contacted, King Ferdinand and Queen Isabella, who were well known for their devotion to God, also turned him down.

At this point Columbus's faith wavered. His situation seemed futile. Perhaps he questioned whether God had really given him a special revelation. As he trudged back home from the Spanish court, he spent the night at La Rabida, a Franciscan monastery. The man in charge was Father Juan Perez, and his main task was to guide the spiritual lives of the monks and missionaries in the area. Father Perez was known for his godly wisdom and for helping those in spiritual despair.

God led Columbus to Juan Perez exactly when he needed encouragement. We can only imagine the prayers offered by these two men, but we do know that the next day Father Perez sent a letter to Queen Isabella, telling her that he believed God's hand rested upon Columbus and that she would be wise to reconsider his proposal. Columbus waited at the monastery for her reply. Would his prayers be answered?

The queen replied quickly, asking Columbus to come to

Santa Fe, the city of Holy Faith, where a battle with the Muslim Moors was being fought. She even sent him money for his journey!

What a difference a fortnight can make in a life! Have you ever been in a position like Columbus's, where you have exhausted your last hope and are tempted to give up? When every path becomes a dead end and we lose our hope and give in to despair, prayer opens the doors. One providential event occurs, and despair evaporates. Then we wonder why we didn't trust God a little more. Perhaps that's what Columbus felt. He must have been ecstatic as he entered Santa Fe. But what a sight met his eyes. . . .

As Columbus rode among the throngs of excited Spaniards, people were celebrating everywhere. Women were hanging pennants and bunting from tents and houses. He smelled roasting meat and the dust of flying feet. He heard singing and laughing inside the homes and in the streets. The Moorish king was about to surrender!

That afternoon, he followed the crowds to the heart of the city, where the walls of the citadel stood basking in the hot sun. At one end of the street, a royal pavilion had been erected. Crusaders in full burnished armor lined the road to the grand gate. Their white surplices emblazoned with red crosses hung in perfect order. Each soldier held his lance proudly.

As Columbus watched, the Moorish banner came down and the huge gate swung open. The defeated Moorish king rode out at the head of a column of noblemen. He slowly made his way to the pavilion in the distance. Under the awnings waited King Ferdinand and Queen Isabella in all their royal splendor.

When the Moorish king reached the pavilion, he dismounted. Columbus could see the press of defeat written in the king's exaggerated motions and in the curve of his neck. The king slowly walked up to the royal couple on their thrones. The crowd hushed in anticipation. Then the Moorish king knelt and kissed the hands of Ferdinand and Isabella.

Pandemonium broke out. The crowd cheered; soldiers wept and gave thanks to God.

Columbus walked away with joy in his heart. The time seemed perfect for presenting his request. He was calculating what he would say to the royal couple when they summoned him. *Thank you, almighty God,* he prayed. *You have provided just the right circumstances for my proposal. . . .*[5]

The timing for Columbus's request was just right. Because Ferdinand and Isabella believed that God had given them the victory over their fierce enemies, the Moors, they were open to expressing their gratitude by spreading the gospel to other lands. Did these events come together as a coincidence, or was Columbus seeing the miraculous answer to his prayers? God had planned it all!

But Columbus almost defeated his own plans to sail west. When the king and queen asked what he wanted in return for his services, he asked for three things: one-tenth of all the riches he brought back, the rank of admiral of the ocean sea, and the chance to serve as both viceroy and governor of all the lands he discovered. The king and queen were aghast and almost dismissed him once again.

Sadly, the outlandish demands were an early indication of a weakness Columbus harbored in his soul. In spite of his devotion to God, he coveted material wealth, worldly acclaim, and authority. With these demands, he planted seeds that would grow into choking weeds of sin and dishonor just when his dreams were being fulfilled. How easily we all let our mission for God be misdirected by other desires! Later we will see how Columbus's greed thwarted some of the good he could have accomplished for his Lord.

But Ferdinand and Isabella did commission him to sail in command of three ships! In the next chapter, we'll discover the essential part prayer played in each step of that famous ocean voyage of the *Niña,* the *Pinta,* and the *Santa María.*

For Discussion and Reflection

Adult Discussion

Before your discussion, tape two large pieces of paper to a wall. Form two groups, and give each group a marker. Say: "You have three minutes to complete your mission. I'll be right back." Then leave the room and return after three minutes. Say: "OK, you should have completed your missions by now."

Collect the markers, smile at people's protests, and have groups show you what they've done. Then ask:

  ★ What was unusual about the mission I gave you?
  ★ What did you think about that?
  ★ Why was not having your mission defined a problem?
  ★ What was Columbus's mission in life?
  ★ What part did prayer play in Columbus's mission?
  ★ What's the importance of knowing your mission or spiritual goals in life?
  ★ What part does prayer play in your mission?

Have someone read aloud Matthew 28:18-20. Ask:

  ★ What does this passage say about the mission God has given us?

★ In what specific ways can you seek to fulfill this mission in your daily activities?

Youth Discussion

Say: "As we read in this chapter, when Columbus felt like giving up, he received encouragement and help from Father Juan Perez. Encouraging and helping one another is an important biblical concept."

Ask:

★ When have you experienced encouragement or help from someone older than you are?
★ What did the help or encouragement do for you?
★ How was your experience like that of Columbus?

Form groups of two or three and give each a three-by-five-inch index card on which is written one of the following pairs with its reference: Eli and Samuel (1 Samuel 3); Mordecai and Esther (Esther 4); Elijah and Elisha (2 Kings 2:1-14); Ananias and Saul (Acts 9:1-22); Peter and Cornelius (Acts 10); Paul and Timothy (Acts 16:1-5).

Have the groups read their passage and write on the reverse side of the card one or two qualities of the spiritual advisor and one or two qualities of the younger friend. After a few minutes, have one person from each group share the group's answers. Then discuss the following questions as a large group:

★ How are the experiences of these biblical people similar to Columbus's experience? to your experience?
★ How important is it to have a spiritual model or mentor? Why?

Say: "Think about who might be your spiritual model, advisor, or mentor." Have people form pairs to discuss the final three questions:

- ★ How might that person help you live your Christian life better?
- ★ What part can prayer play in a caring relationship such as those we've discussed from the Bible?
- ★ How is this study going to affect your prayer life?

THREE

The Lure
of Gold

At last Columbus could begin the thrilling task of equipping the three ships he would take on his journey. He planned for eight months at sea, so he secured two experienced sailors, Martín and Vicente Pinzón, to captain the *Pinta* and the *Niña*. Then he hired a crew of handpicked veteran sailors from among the bravest and best seamen in Spain. But the truth is that the best seamen had never been more than three hundred miles offshore. This would be a journey that would test the faith and courage of all of them. Finally, on August 3, 1492, the ships were ready to sail. The last thing Columbus did before he left dry ground was to kneel in the name of Jesus and pray for the success of the dangerous journey he was about to undertake. As we will see, a miraculous event would make the difference between success and failure for those three tiny ships so far from home. Let's join Columbus during the last few moments before he heads out to sea. . . .

THE HISTORIC JOURNEY BEGINS

Streaks of light glinted off the small waves lapping on the beach. Gulls swooped over the gentle sea as the breeze spread the salty aroma of fish drying on the piers. The three ships waited proudly in the harbor, their high masts reaching toward the distant, wispy clouds.

Sailors carrying heavy loads ran up and down the docks, dropping their burdens into several small boats that were then rowed out to the ships. A crowd of people dressed in their Sunday best gathered on the shore.

Then a magnificent train of couriers, soldiers, and priests made its way to the piers. In the midst of the train was a heavily ornamented carriage drawn by superb horses. The carriage stopped. The door opened, and Queen Isabella, dressed in a white gown with her head draped with a flowing royal scarf, descended. A pair of young pages picked up her train before it was soiled on the ground. King Ferdinand descended after her.

Christopher Columbus stepped out of the crowd, his head bare, revealing his graying hair. When the entourage reached the end of the pier, a priest in robes and headdress joined the royal group. "We are here," he intoned in his steady voice, "to offer a last confession, along with absolution and Holy Communion, to these voyagers who will journey so far in the service of our Lord and Savior, Jesus Christ."

One by one, the sailors knelt before him, confessing their sins, receiving absolution, and tasting the bread and wine. In turn, each boarded the small boat and waited.

Finally, Columbus came forward and knelt before the queen. He kissed her outstretched hand. "In the name of our Father in heaven, I thank you and King Ferdinand for sponsoring this trip. God has ordained our travels. I know that he will reward you for your faithfulness to our mission."

He turned to the priest and bowed his head meekly as the sacred words were intoned. When the ceremony was complete, he stood and stared across the expanse of water now golden with morning's light. He raised his arms. "In the name

of Jesus Christ our Lord, I ask for safety on our dangerous journey. In his glorious name I command the sails to be set for the
first voyage to and discovery of the Indies!"

The crowd gave a huge shout, cheering and waving as Columbus stepped into a small boat and the sailors began to
row. As the light sea spray moistened their faces, they
watched the great, white sails unfurl, revealing huge red
crosses.

When the rowboat reached the *Santa María,* all aboard
were swallowed into the hull of the ship. Then the *Niña,*
Pinta, and *Santa María* headed out for sea. The historic journey had begun. . . .[1]

TWO MONTHS OF SAILING

This journey would prove to be one of the greatest moments in
history. Have you ever wondered what went on aboard those
three ships during those long, uncertain months? How does
Hollywood portray life aboard a Spanish sailing ship? Sailors
drinking and cursing, men fighting and even committing murder? Have you ever seen a movie where the sailors take time
for personal devotions every day? That's exactly what the crew
on those three ships did. Samuel Eliot Morison, a Columbus
historian, writes:

> In the great days of sail, before man's venture and gadgets had
> given him false confidence in his power to conquer the ocean,
> seamen were the most religious of all workers on land or sea.
> The mariner's philosophy he took from the 107th Psalm:
> "They that go down to the sea in ships and occupy their busi-
> ness in great waters; these men see the works of the Lord, and
> his wonders in the deep. For at his works the stormy wind
> ariseth, which lifteth up the winds thereof."[2]

The ship's daily schedule helped the sailors remember God. At daybreak, the crew sang a hymn and recited the Lord's Prayer. At the close of day, everyone on board, including Columbus, sang a hymn and retired for private devotions.[3] Kevin A. Miller cites a respected historian: "Columbus was visibly and verbally 'an exceptionally pious man,' writes historian Delno C. West. 'Throughout his journals and letters, we find him constantly in prayer.'"[4]

Day after day of empty horizons passed. Can you imagine what the seamen must have thought as their homes slipped farther away? The weather was gorgeous, but the sailors were skittish. While they went through the accepted religious ritual of their day, they did not necessarily share Columbus's personal faith in God, and they were superstitious.

After two months and more than three thousand miles of sailing, suspicion and fear began to unnerve the crews. After all, hadn't Columbus predicted that land was only about twenty-seven hundred miles away? The ships had passed that point, and they were still sailing west into the unknown. Talk of mutiny spread. The situation became threatening. Considering Columbus's habit of evening prayers and his dependence on God as revealed in his journals, his cries to God must have been filled with great passion at that point. The answer God provided was no less than miraculous. . . .

TROUBLE ON THE SEA

When Columbus came out of his cabin, he noticed the small boat heading toward the *Santa María*. He recognized the jaunty hats of the Pinzón brothers. "Now what?" he muttered to himself.

As the two men clambered aboard, they had scowls on their

faces. "Captain!" Martín called out as both men approached. "We have some real problems aboard our ships. There's talk of mutiny."

"Yes," Vicente agreed in his slow manner. "The sailors are determined to turn back. If we continue to sail west, you'll have a mutiny on your hands for sure."

Columbus shook his head. He thought of the miraculously good weather they had had so far. He was sure land was close. "We must keep going." He pointed to the stiff westward winds that were billowing the sails. "God's given us winds to speed us on our way. Surely he'll provide the easterly winds for our return—but only at the right time."

The brothers just shook their heads.

"Three more days," Columbus urged. "Just give me three more days. If we haven't sighted land by then, I'll order the ships to turn around."

Martín and Vicente looked dubious, but Martín said, "All right. Three more days. But we can't hold the men back after that."

With that, the two headed for their boats. With a sinking heart, Columbus returned to his cabin. After his eyes adjusted to the dim light, he stared at all the paraphernalia scattered over his table. What good did his maps do now?

"I staked everything on this trip. I will not go back because I know God has led me here." He knelt in front of a hard chair next to a candle that had burned so low it was almost out. "O Lord God almighty," he pleaded. "This is an impossible journey. I was so sure of my calculations. Now how can I find land within three days when we've been sailing for months?"

The candle began to send up a thin stream of smoke. It flickered, then burned strongly again. "Only a miracle can save us," Columbus admitted to his God. "Only you can make it possible to bring your gospel to these lands. And I know you will."

Columbus continued pouring his heart out in prayer as the candle stub flickered erratically. Then the light drowned in its own wax, leaving Columbus in semidarkness. . . .[5]

MIRACULOUS WIND

During the next twenty-four hours, a miracle occurred. A strong wind came up and began to push the *Santa María* forward at an alarming speed, rapidly widening the distance from their homeland. In fact, the ships sailed so fast that they equaled the greatest speed of the entire trip. The crew panicked. They knew if they didn't do something right away, the distance would be too great to make it back home safely. They attempted a mutiny, but Columbus controlled the uprising.

God was at work through the wind. During that first day, the sailors on the *Pinta* sighted a reed and a piece of carved wood. On the *Niña,* crewmen spied a small branch with roses on it. Yet no one sighted land. During the second day, the wind continued. Despite sailing at record speeds, there was still no sight of land.

Before dawn on the third day, Columbus began pacing the deck. Would his prayers be answered, or would he suffer defeat without achieving his mission?

He leaned his bare head into the wind and peered into the darkness. Soon, the first few streaks of dawn flitted over the heavy waves, tipping them in gold. The *Pinta* neared, its bow easily slipping through the waves.

Suddenly, a voice high on the *Pinta's* mast rang out, *"Tierra! Tierra!"*

"Land! Land!" Columbus shouted with joy. The cry began echoing throughout the ship as sailors picked up the good news. Soon everyone who was available came onto the deck to peer into the graying darkness.

As the morning light became stronger, Columbus got his first glimpse of the low, white cliffs on the horizon. The beauty took his breath away. The hostile atmosphere aboard ship changed dramatically as fear dissipated in the salty air.

When the sun finally marched over the horizon, an incredible sight met the sailors' eyes. An island thick with foliage, surrounded by crystal-clear water shimmered in the distance. It seemed like a mirage.

As the crew readied one of the small craft to take a group to shore, the ship's officers ran to the cabins to change into their finest clothes. In his cabin, Columbus opened a trunk and carefully unfolded a scarlet doublet he had brought just for this occasion. His hands trembled as he pulled on the rough cloth. This was his moment. He was now admiral of the ocean sea!

The crew had already lowered the boats by the time Columbus emerged. He and his officers entered the craft and rowed toward the white coral beach that shone in the bright sunlight. Once the boats were grounded on the sand, Columbus stepped into the shallow water. He waded ashore, carrying the royal standard. His was the first foot to make an imprint on dry land. He firmly planted the standard.

Martín and Vicente followed, carrying a huge white banner with a green cross and the Spanish royal initials. They knelt in the pristine sand. Immediately, Columbus erected a cross. "I christen this island as San Salvador—Holy Savior." Then he prayed, "O Lord, Almighty and everlasting God, by thy holy Word, thou hast created the heaven and the earth, and the sea; blessed and glorified by thy Name, and praised by thy Majesty which hath deigned to use us, thy humble servants, that thy holy Name may be proclaimed in this second part of the earth. . . ."[6]

THE LURE OF GOLD

This was the beginning of a new era. Although Columbus didn't realize the significance of his discovery, he had set foot on continents unknown in the Old World.

For the next three months, Columbus explored the islands he had discovered, always erecting a cross as "a token of Jesus Christ our Lord" and claiming the land for Christ and for Spain. During this time, he had peaceful contacts with the Native Americans. In his journal, he recorded his intentions for the new citizens of Spain:

> So that they might be well-disposed towards us, for I knew that they were a people to be delivered and converted to our holy faith rather by love than by force, I gave to some red caps and to others glass beads, which they hung around their necks, and many other things. . . . At this they were greatly pleased and became so entirely our friends that it was a wonder to see.[7]

But it was during this time that the lure of gold began to overpower the sailors, most of whom did not share Columbus's devotion to his Savior. Many of the native people had gold jewelry, so at every stop, Columbus and his men searched for the source of that gold. This greed led to much heartache for the native peoples and for the Spaniards. Atrocities perpetrated by the Spanish caused the Indians to revolt.

In four subsequent expeditions, Columbus discovered many more islands, as well as Central and South America. The king and queen sent along priests and clerics to teach "the principles of the Holy Faith" and to treat the Native Americans with love. They directed Columbus to

> force and compel all those who sail therein as well as all others who are to go out from here later on, that they treat the said Indians very well and lovingly and abstain from doing them any injury arranging that both people hold much conversation and intimacy, each serving the others to the best of their ability. Moreover, the said Admiral shall graciously present them with things from the merchandise of Their Highnesses which he is carrying for barter, and honor them much; and if some person or persons should maltreat the said Indians in any manner whatsoever, the said Admiral, as Viceroy and Governor of Their Highnesses, shall punish them severely by the virtue of the authority vested in him by Their Majesties for this purpose.[8]

But the New World was so far away from the Old World that the settlers ignored the king and queen's command to treat the Indians with love and respect, especially when the possibility of great wealth presented itself. Misfortune plagued Columbus throughout the remainder of his life. Much of it stemmed from the weakness he had displayed early and had never grappled with—his desire for wealth and power. Although he never strayed from his mission to evangelize the Indians, his efforts to gain more and more wealth and power brought him grief. He was eventually replaced as viceroy, or governor, and sent back to Spain in chains. What a humiliation for the "admiral of the ocean sea."

God had answered the prayers of a man who had the faith to set out on a humanly impossible journey and enabled him to become one of the greatest explorers in history. But God did not bless him when he began mistreating the Native Americans in an attempt to gain wealth and power. Eventually, Columbus, a sick man, retired to his Spanish home. Two years after he retired, he received the Lord's Supper and last rites. He died on May 20, 1506.

On the heels of Columbus's discovery, Spain sent many conquistadores to the New World. Although they came in the name of the Lord, the thirst for gold consumed many of them. They found Indian empires that practiced human sacrifice and cannibalism, yet these so-called Christians were no more humane. They slaughtered, raped, and looted the natives. But along with the proud conquistadores came another breed of men, humble and wearing robes. These priests and friars quietly did a work that deserves notice. In the next chapter, we'll see how they carried on the legacy of prayer and evangelism that Columbus had begun—and saw miraculous answers to their prayers.

For Discussion and Reflection

Adult Discussion

On a piece of paper, write the words to "Twinkle, Twinkle, Little Star." Set three chairs in a semicircle in front of the group, and have three volunteers sit in them. Instruct the two people sitting across from each other to alternate saying a number as they count by twos to one hundred. While they are counting, have the third volunteer read the words to the song to distract the counters. Have the group help the song reciter distract the counters.

When the demonstration is finished, ask the counters: "How did it feel to try to count while others were trying to distract you?" Ask the distracters: "What was it like to try to distract the counters?" Ask everyone: "How was this activity like real life? How was it different?"

Form groups of four to discuss the following questions:

★ What things tend to distract you from your mission in life?
★ How can prayer help you keep your focus on that mission?
★ Columbus never realized the significance of what he had discovered—the New World. How fully do we realize the significance of what we've discovered in Christ? Explain.

After the groups have discussed the questions, have them report on their discussions. Then discuss the following questions with the whole group:

★ How do our lives change as we more fully understand what Christ has done for us?
★ Read 1 Corinthians 3:10-15. How can the principles contained in these verses help us stay true to what Christ wants for us?

Youth Discussion

Form two groups. Tell kids in Group 1 that when you say, "Go!" they are to run in place as fast as they can. Tell kids in Group 2 that they are to run in place at a comfortable pace. Say, "Go!" and allow the groups to run in place until the fast group begins to tire. Then have the groups sit down. Discuss the following questions together:

★ Group 1, how did you feel when you started your run and when you ended your run?
★ Group 2, how did you feel at the beginning and at the end?

Have someone read aloud 1 Corinthians 9:24-27. Form groups of four, and have them discuss the following questions:

★ How does our running activity illustrate the message of this passage? How is the message different?
★ How did Columbus begin and end his race?
★ What problem hampered Columbus's race?
★ What problems do we face that are similar to Columbus's?

Have groups report on their discussion; then wrap up your discussion with the whole group:

★ When a runner trains, what part does the coach play in his training?
★ How is this like the part God wants to have in our lives?
★ How does having a daily time for prayer and Bible reading help us run the Christian race?

FOUR

Poverty, Prayer, and Service

One of the greatest movements in history began to occur as Europeans crossed the Atlantic to get their piece of the pie in the New World. Spain, Portugal, and France all rushed to get what they could. Caravans of ships loaded with weapons and soldiers sailed across the ocean. The Spanish conquistadores were gripped with so much greed that they raped, murdered, and looted throughout Central America. Spanish explorers blazed trails through unmapped wilderness, claiming the land for Christ but acting as unscrupulous and ambitious conquerors.

How could there be any good in this clash of people and cultures? Yet in the worst of times, God has his people. Sometimes they go unnoticed, but they always carry through, bringing his love with the power of prayer. This was also true of those dark days.

The priests and friars who accompanied the explorers lived a sacrificial life totally devoted to God. Whereas the conquistadores subdued the Indians by force, the men in drab robes befriended the natives and lived alongside them. They established orphanages, schools, and places of refuge. These religious men were very successful at establishing settlements—while for the most part the soldiers failed miserably.

The outcomes of the lifestyles of the two groups contrasted sharply. In fact, even the Spanish rulers in the New World acknowledged that "one friar could accomplish peaceably what it might take a thousand soldiers to do forcibly."[1] The difference? The incredible power of prayer and the part that godly devotion plays in an individual's goals and actions.

What was it about these simple people that made them so different from their countrymen? A person who took on holy orders agreed to a life of poverty and service to Christ. Although the Catholic church had by this time fallen into practices such as holding inquisitions, hawking religious relics, and selling indulgences, these devout men kept their focus on serving their God. One reason for their single-minded objective was the hours they spent in prayer. Many were known for kneeling four to five hours each day to seek the Lord's face. Most had thick calluses on their knees.

Where did these priests and friars come from? Some were highly educated sons of noble families. But others were simple peasants. Once they put on the religious robes, they put off the distractions and advantages of their former lives and practiced a discipline that included few personal goods, simple food, and, of course, hours of prayer.

JERONIMO DE AGUILAR

In recent years, one conquistador—Cortés—has received much negative press for his bloody march across what we now call Mexico. He is one of the most controversial figures in the history of the Americas. With a few hundred soldiers, he conquered hundreds of thousands of Indians and the highly developed Aztec civilization. He was a devout Catholic who treated friendly native tribes with kindness and always presented the message of Christ—sometimes even to the detriment of his cause. At the same time, he was a ruthless military man who used his military wiles to subdue the natives. It's hard to understand how he could combine those two opposite qualities. But the religious men who traveled alongside Cortés didn't share his ruthlessness. They had a genuine love for the people they met.

One fascinating event that shows the power of one person's prayer happened early in Cortés's journey across Mexico. When Cortés and his soldiers arrived at the island of Cozumel in southeastern Mexico (a famous cruise/resort destination today), they discovered what they thought was a large cross that had been erected to honor God but was actually used for idol worship. The Spaniards quickly decided that the cross was a sign that they were to preach Christ to the people. One morning, they gathered in a courtyard containing many temples and idols where Indians were burning incense and offering sacrifices to their gods. As the Spaniards watched, an old pagan Indian priest climbed to the top of the central worship area and delivered a sermon.

Cortés, through his interpreter, tried to convince the people to tear down their idols and build a Christian altar. But the interpreter didn't know the language well, and the message didn't get through. The Indians refused to turn away from their idols.

Cortés ordered his soldiers to destroy the idols, and they smashed the main ones in the courtyard, leaving many smaller ones intact. Then the Spaniards erected an altar and a chapel and performed a Mass while the Indians watched. It seemed as if the Indians were determined to worship in their own way. Then the answers to several prayers converged to change the entire situation. . . .

Several soldiers stood along the narrow beach watching the waves come in. The lush vegetation crowding the shore made the place seem lonely and isolated. Then one of them pointed across the waves. A lone canoe was making headway against the currents to shore. As the craft slipped through the gentle waves, the soldiers peered closely at the people inside and saw several men in Indian dress. Within moments, the canoe slid onto the sand and came to a stop. One man in the canoe waved his arms wildly. "Gentleman, are you Christians?" he shouted in Spanish as he clambered out of the boat. Shocked at hearing their own language coming from an Indian in this isolated place, the soldiers noticed that this man had lighter hair and a lighter complexion than the other canoeists.

"Yes, we're Spaniards," one soldier answered hesitantly.

The man burst into tears. "Is this Wednesday?"

"Yes, it is," the Spaniards replied.

"Oh, God has saved me," he exclaimed. "I always devote several hours to prayer on Wednesday. How wonderful that this is the day God led me here. Please join me." And he sank to his knees. While the soldiers watched in amazement, he prayed with his head bowed over the hot sand. "Thank you, loving heavenly Father, for your mercy in liberating me from my slavery. Thank you for bringing me here and restoring me to the men of my own nation."

When he finished his prayer, he stood to his feet. Before anyone could say anything, he announced, "I'm Jeronimo de Aguilar, Catholic priest and citizen of Spain!"

A clamor of voices followed his announcement. "How did you get here?" "Why are you dressed like that?" Before he could explain, the soldiers led him to the place where they had built the chapel. Someone ran to get Cortés.

As the sun went down, a chill spread through the air. Someone built a lively fire, and the men all sat in a semicircle, giving Jeronimo a flat rock as a seat. Cortés joined the group, and Jeronimo introduced himself to the leader.

"Tell us your story," someone insisted.

Jeronimo sighed. "Yes, I must tell you what has happened." He took a moment to compose himself before he went on. . . .[2]

GOD HAD A PLAN

Eight years earlier, Jeronimo said, he and several companions had begun a great journey into the unmapped wilderness to bring the gospel to the native people. But they ran into severe storms and were blown off course. Their ship began to break up, and they were in danger of perishing in the sea. All they had were their prayers.

Their boat damaged, for thirteen days they floated wherever the currents carried them. Finally they sighted a thickly overgrown shore and drifted in. The moment their boat landed on the beach, they knelt and thanked God for saving their lives.

One by one, the men began to get ill and die. Then a local chief discovered the survivors, took them back to his village, and made them his slaves. More of the company died until only one other man and Aguilar were left.

But Aguilar was a man of prayer. Every Wednesday he devoted several hours to prayer, asking God to deliver him from his captivity. But how was he to find his way home when he was lost so far from any settlement?

God was answering his prayers—even if he didn't realize it. In time, the chief noticed Aguilar's learning and promoted him by giving him more freedom and responsibility. Eight long years of hopes and prayers passed. Then, that very week, the chief had allowed him to leave. And that's how he ended up meeting Cortés's soldiers.

The soldiers were astounded. What was even more amazing was that Cortés and his group had actually left the island several days earlier. But one of the ships had developed a leak, and contrary winds forced them to return. If these difficulties had not detained Cortés and his soldiers, Father Aguilar would have missed them completely!

Realizing that Aguilar was a valuable man because he had learned the Indian language during his captivity, Cortés invited him to serve as interpreter. Aguilar was happy to accompany Cortés. Let's pick up the story once again. . . .

SHATTERED IDOLS

The next morning, as the sun came up over the chapel in its bright fury, the Indian people began to gather once again. The broken pieces of their idols lay at their feet. But many more undamaged idols were scattered over the clearing. The soldiers stood at attention behind the Indians, waiting for any unexpected move.

Then Jeronimo climbed the steps to the altar built by the Spaniards. A gentle breeze stirred his long hair and wispy beard. He began to preach in the Melchorijo language, first softly in his rich voice, then building in intensity. As the Indians listened to the gospel message in their own tongue, their faces reflected wonder at hearing such strange ideas.

Aguilar's sermon was powerful, stirring the hearts of the people. When he finished and walked back down the steps, they began bringing the undamaged idols and smashing them on the stones. The sounds of shattered pottery and the crack of heavy stones echoed through the forest surrounding the courtyard. As the idols were taken from the temples, the Spaniards erected crosses. Finally, the idols were only pieces scattered everywhere. Their power over the people had been shattered!

From that moment, the Indians began worshiping Jehovah God. As the sun went down that night, many crosses were silhouetted in the sky—for the first time in history.

As Cortés prepared to leave them, the people begged him to leave a missionary to teach them about Christ. But Cortés didn't trust the people and was afraid they might kill the man he left behind. So the company moved on. But the Indians kept their faith, begging anyone who traveled their way and knew God's truth to come and teach them. . . .[3]

As Aguilar accompanied Cortés farther inland, his prayers to reach the Indians with the gospel were answered again and again. Instead of reaching just a few scattered tribes with the gospel, he was able to travel with Cortés and go farther inland than any Christians had ever gone before!

FATHER JUNÍPERO SERRA

As the Spanish pushed farther and farther inland, they began hearing about a great island to the west and north. Cortés heard about this rich island when he reached what is now Mexico City and conquered the Aztec ruler, Montezuma. That mystical "island" was actually what we now call California. Eventually, the explorers, along with many Jesuit priests, built settlements along the coast into Baja California. Other priests pushed northward into what is now New Mexico, bringing the gospel to the Indians.

Then on June 24, 1767, Marquis de Croix, viceroy of New Spain, expelled the Jesuit priests from the missions they had established. Who would take their place? The Franciscans. The authorities in Spain selected fifty-four-year-old Father Junípero Serra as the new president. Where did he come from? How would he handle the new responsibilities? Let's go back a few years and visit him in his position as professor at the Convent of San Francisco in Palma, Spain. . . .

Father Serra could hardly believe the honor he had been given. He had been chosen by the faculties of the university to preach the most prestigious sermon of the year in the gorgeous Palma cathedral! As he waited on the sidelines to do his part, his eyes drank in the colors of the flowers and banners hanging all over the ornate church.

With the sound of trumpets and drums, the viceroy, bishop, mayor, aldermen, professors, students, and guests paraded into the sanctuary and found their seats. When they were seated, the Mass began. Serra's ears were caressed with the familiar recitations and the Gregorian chants, but his mind was going over what he would say in his sermon. *I have achieved so much for a frail child born in the little forgotten Spanish village of Petra,* he thought. *God has given me so many privileges—becoming a Franciscan father, studying in the finest universities, and now teaching in this sacred school. Many say that one day I may even become the rector of the university—or even a bishop.* As he quietly waited, he thanked God for all he had been given.

Then it was his turn to speak. He climbed into the pulpit, which sat high above his audience. Instead of looking down, he gazed up at the rich ornamentation of the vaulted ceiling. Then he introduced his sermon. His words fell like golden rain, refreshing and rich and inspiring.

Later, when he was alone in his austere cell, he thought

back over that tremendous day. It had been all he had expected it to be. He began praying. Not a sound disturbed his time with God inside the thick walls of the monastery, but his heart was disturbed by his own thoughts. "My Father in heaven," he cried out, "you have blessed me greatly. But I have heard of a land called the Americas. They say there is great wealth in this land, but I think of the people who have never heard your name. They are a flock without a shepherd. They worship strange idols and practice abhorrent rituals."

As he meditated, Father Serra's mind took him back to when he had first entered the service of his Lord. He saw himself at sixteen, small and sickly. The Franciscans had turned him down at first. But finally he had been accepted into the Franciscan order. His mother and father had been so proud that a boy from Petra, their son, could become a priest and study at the university. He saw himself studying diligently so long ago. What was that book he was holding? Yes, it was *The Little Flowers of Saint Francis,* his favorite book. How he loved those tales of Saint Francis and his missionary journeys. But best of all, he loved to read about Saint Francis's closest friend, Brother Juniper, who was known as the "jester of the Lord" because of his humor. Juniper followed Saint Francis everywhere, so zealous in the service of the Lord that he disregarded his own needs.

That's why Father Serra had taken the name Junípero. "It's those missionary journeys," he prayed. "That's what I desire. My studies have distracted me for a while, but that's my deepest yearning—to tell others of your Son's name." After a long time of prayer and meditation, he finally fell asleep on his bare cot.

As Father Serra went about his daily routine over the next few weeks, he kept his longing to himself. Almost no one knew of his prayer to go to the New World and of his dream to have companionship like that shared by Saint Francis and Brother Juniper. Soon a rumor started circulating through the sacred halls that one of the fathers in the university wanted to travel to the New World. Serra was just glad the rumor didn't include his name.

One day, Serra visited his pupil and closest friend, Palou, in his monastic cell. Palou had a serious expression on his face.

Serra sat down on the cot next to his friend. His gray robe fell gently around his knees. "What is it, my friend?" he asked.

Slowly Palou told his mentor, "I have a desire that is so strong, I know it must come from God. I have prayed many hours about my desire, but I know I must follow it. I wish to become a missionary and travel to the West. I want to bring the message of Christ to the farthest reaches of the world."

Serra was stunned into silence.

"What do you think?" Palou asked his friend, afraid that Serra's silence meant disapproval.

Tears filled Serra's eyes, then spilled down his cheeks.

"Oh, don't be sad," Palou insisted. "We shall part, but our Lord will comfort our hearts. And we shall be reunited one day, even if it must be in eternity."

Then Serra's face broke into a huge smile. "I'm sure you heard the rumor about this professor who wants to journey to the Indies. The rumor is true. I am the one who intends to make the long journey. But I have been sad because I had no one to go with me like Saint Francis had Brother Juniper. I pleaded with God to touch someone's heart. And it is you he has spoken to. Let's keep praying, together now, that the Lord will send us. . . ."[4]

Two men, praying alone in separate cells but with the same heart cry. God heard each of their pleas and gave them the desire of their hearts—an opportunity to serve him in the New World. That's how Father Serra came to the Americas and received the honor of establishing missions up the coast of California. As a boy he had been sickly. As a teen he was considered too small to join the Franciscans. But he overcame all that through the incredible power of prayer and through his dedication to that call.

Accompanied by Spanish soldiers, the Franciscan father—already in his fifties and suffering from a chronic ulcer on one leg—established a series of missions up the California coast as far north as San Francisco. One of these, San Juan Capistrano Mission in southern California, is world famous today as the mission where the swallows reputedly return to nest on the same day in March every year.

Father Serra offered the Indians eternal life as well as what he considered a better life on this earth. He taught them farming and trade crafts and brought in cattle and sheep. Father Serra and his companions never asked anything of the Indians that they didn't ask of themselves. The missionaries lived in austere cells, prayed for hours at a time, and loved the people they had come to serve.

Father Serra remained in his adopted land until he died at the age of seventy. His last days were spent in prayer and meditation and in talking with the many people who visited him—their dying leader. He was buried in his simple habit at the Mission San Carlos Borromeo. During the fifteen years he served as president of the missions, he saw six thousand baptisms and five thousand confirmations at the missions. What an incredible answer to the prayers of a simple man with the faith to ask God to send him across two continents!

Anyone visiting the National Statuary Hall in our nation's Capitol will find Father Serra's statue, one of two statues contributed to the hall by the state of California. Each state is allowed to contribute two statues representing the most outstanding individuals from that state's history. These honored people represent the best in that state's leadership and character.

ISAAC JOGUES

Spain wasn't the only Catholic nation to send men of prayer and dedication to the New World. The French sent Jesuit missionaries farther north into what we now know as Quebec. These men practiced the same life of prayer and austerity as did their southern brothers in the faith. Some conducted explorations that went down in history. Many became martyrs for their faith as they tried to reach hostile Indian tribes in North America. All of them lived a life of prayer to their Father in heaven, who sustained them throughout their ordeals.

Isaac Jogues, a Jesuit priest, was one of these Frenchmen. In 1642, Jogues and his party were ambushed by the fierce Iroquois, but he escaped their grasp. His companions were dragged off. As he hid in the forest, he must have thought about the possibility of a horrible death at the hands of the Indians. Surely he prayed deep in the forest, asking for strength to do what he knew he must do. Then he surrendered himself to the Indians. He later wrote:

> Could I indeed abandon [these people] without giving them
> the help which the Church of my God has entrusted to me?
> Flight seemed horrible to me. If it must be, I said in my heart,
> that my body suffer the fire of earth, in order to deliver these

46

poor souls from the flames of hell, it is but a transient death, in order to procure for them an eternal life.[5]

For the next year, only prayer would bring him through his ordeal. First he was tortured by having his fingernails pulled out and his fingers mangled or cut off. Then he was kept as a slave for intermittent torture. At times the pain was so unbearable that he pleaded with his Savior to take him home to release him from the torment. But in each instance, the incredible power of prayer sustained him.

After a year, he escaped and eventually made his way back to France. Can you imagine what it must have been like for him as he made his way to the Jesuit College of Rennes? The French people, who had heard of his bravery, lined the roads, hailing him as a hero. What would you have done in his position? Enjoyed the well-deserved fame and rested for a while? That's not how Father Jogues reacted. Imagine what it must have been like the day he met with royalty. . . .

Servants ushered the father into the presence of the French queen, Anne. The crowded room had become so quiet that he could hear his robes swish around his legs as he walked. He looked around, amazed at the number of people who had gathered to see him.

As he walked up the thick carpet to the exalted chair, he glanced up at the woman in the satin gown and the long train. Then he knelt, bending his head to the floor. "My queen," he said, "I am at your service."

"Come to me." She beckoned, and one of the servants helped him to his feet. The father stared at the queen, unsure why she would want him to approach her mighty throne. The servant gently pushed him from behind, and Father Jogues found his feet taking the steps to the hem of her gown. He bowed low again, embarrassed at being singled out.

She stood and reached down to him. Then she took his hands in hers and lifted him up. With her hands, she spread out his mangled fingers, holding them as a mother would caress her baby's tiny fingers. Her smooth, white skin contrasted sharply with his reddened, ugly flesh. Then she bent her head and kissed his malformed hands. Her lips lightly pressed against the scarred flesh.

A deep flush spread over Father Jogues's face. "I do not deserve this honor," he stammered. "I am only in the service of my Lord."

"Just tell me what you want and need," the queen said as she gently released his hands. "You have proven your devotion to God. Now we must see to your comfort and well-being."

Father Jogues knew exactly what he wanted. He had not forgotten his prayers for the Iroquois people. Without hesitation, he said firmly, "I have only one desire—to go back and complete the sacrifice the Lord has begun. I want to see the Iroquois nation find their Savior and turn from their savage ways. Please assign me as a priest to the Iroquois nation. . . ."[6]

Once again God answered the prayers of his devoted child in a miraculous way. France had just signed a peace treaty with the Iroquois nation, and Father Jogues was commissioned as the French ambassador! What an amazing "coincidence." Imagine what the Indians must have thought when he returned. They were in awe of a man who would still love them after all he had been through at their hands. What an awesome example of someone who served the Lord sacrificially—and lived by the power of prayer!

The Spanish and the French are both notable for having

sent godly people who asked God to do the impossible in the New World. In the next section of this book, we will go back a few years to pick up the thread of another story that had an even more profound influence on the history of America. This time we will hear of the prayers of the British settlers. They, too, lived by the power of prayer. We'll learn how their prayers began a mighty work that is still influencing our lives today.

For Discussion and Reflection

Adult Discussion

Form groups of three or four. Have each group list accomplishments and recognition Father Serra would list if he were writing a contemporary résumé. For example:

★ Chosen to give the keynote speech at a prominent function at San Fernando University
★ Chosen as president of the Franciscans in New Spain
★ Established many missions in New Spain

Then have groups list what they think Father Serra would have listed as his most important spiritual accomplishments. After a few minutes, have groups report. List their answers on a chalkboard or large piece of paper. Then have someone read aloud Acts 11:19-21. Ask:

★ How is what happened in this passage similar to Father Serra's ministry?
★ How would it feel to have such an impressive list of personal and spiritual accomplishments?

Next hand out paper and pencils. Allow time for people to reflect on and write out their spiritual résumés. When most have finished, form pairs to discuss the next two questions:

* How do you feel about your own personal and spiritual accomplishments?
* How can you follow Father Serra's example in your own life?

Have pairs pray together, seeking God's help in serving him.

Youth Discussion

Form groups of three. Have the students in each group write a page about their lives, listing the major events that have happened to them. Some examples are birth date, first day of kindergarten, learned to ride a bike, got an A in algebra, helped a friend decide to quit smoking. Have students put a star by the event in their lives that touched the most lives or changed someone for the good.

After three minutes, ask volunteers to share the events they starred within their small group. Then ask the whole group:

* How does it feel to know you've made a difference in someone else's life?
* How did Father Serra's decision change his life?
* How did it change the lives of others?
* How can our decisions and actions change the course of our lives?
* How can our decisions and actions change the course of another's life?

Have kids return to their small groups and give each group paper and a pencil. Ask: "What makes it hard for us to follow God's purpose in our lives today?"

After groups have listed several things, have them call out suggestions. List their suggestions on a chalkboard or large piece of paper. Examples may be watching too much television, sleeping in instead of having personal devotions, getting wrapped up in making money, or trusting in ourselves instead of asking God for help.

Have groups read Acts 11:19-21. Ask:

★ What did the early church focus on?
★ How was their focus similar to that of Father Serra?

Next have groups list ways to overcome these distractions or to see the future from God's perspective. After groups each have a list, have them share their lists with the class. Write their suggestions next to the obstacles the students called out.

Give students a few moments to silently reflect and pray about the things in their lives that are getting in the way of following God's will. Encourage them to ask God to help them keep the right focus.

The Colonists

★ ★ ★

FIVE

Jamestown Colony

John White impatiently tapped his fingers on the ship's wooden rail. He could hardly wait to catch sight of land. Turning his face toward the wind, he let the sea spray moisten his warm face.

"Are you just a bit anxious, John?" a seaman teased as he walked by with arms full of thick tarry rope.

John nodded absently. He could still see the scene he had left when he sailed away four years ago. His daughter, holding her tiny new daughter, Virginia Dare, had waved to him until the longboat in which he was sitting reached the ship. Then she and the other well-wishers had turned and trudged back to the fort. At that moment, his heart had tightened. He wished he could stay and help build the settlement, but he knew he had to get back to England to buy emergency supplies for the struggling settlement.

John absentmindedly rubbed the rough wood on the ship's rail. A small splinter slipped under his nail, but he didn't even feel it. He visualized how each person in the group of colonists had looked as they boarded the ship for the last time before they sailed from England in 1587. They were a hardy group: almost a hundred men, seventeen women, and several children.

He had been so proud of his daughter. She had not only survived the trip but also delivered little Virginia on the new soil.

John's mind snapped back to the present when he heard gulls calling in the distance. *The ship must be close to land,* he thought. He strained his eyes toward the horizon. Sure enough, within a few minutes he spied the thin wisp of Roanoke Island shimmering in the distance.

The brisk wind soon deposited the ship close to shore, and the crewmen dropped anchor. Several ran to lower the longboat into the waves. When it was steady, John gingerly climbed down the rope ladder and settled himself into the front of the boat. Within minutes, the boat began to cut through the waves as the crew pulled hard on the oars.

As the longboat slid onto the beach sand, John paused for a moment to listen for sounds of life. All he heard was the call of birds and the waves as they danced along the shore.

Everyone must be working in the fields, he decided. Eagerly, he waded through the shallow water and stepped onto the shore.

The small fort stood proudly in the distance, the sharp ends of the hand-hewn posts spearing the blue sky as the fragrant breeze tossed the heads of the beach grasses. John began to trot up the slope to the entrance of the fort. Then he stopped in his tracks, causing the other men to stop abruptly behind him. He stared at the main gate. It was leaning off its posts. Behind it, the small thatched huts gaped wearily, and weeds sprouted on the pathways.

Where is everyone? Where is my family? he worried. As he noticed the weed-infested fields nestled behind the fort, the silence turned eerie.

John began running through the fort, calling out names in a desperate attempt to find someone. But not a voice answered;

no little bare feet pattered on the hard earth; no smoke curled from the crude chimney stacks made of sticks and clay. It was as if everyone had vanished into thin air.

With despair clutching his heart, he kept searching for signs of life behind each building. Had he come too late? He'd spent four long years in England waiting for the war with Spain to end so he could come back. Finally the way had cleared for him to return. He had expected the colonists to be alive and well. He had even bought a lacy bonnet for his granddaughter and tucked it into one of his trunks.

He jumped as one of the sailors shouted, "Over here! Over here!"

The men all ran to a huge tree. Four letters were etched into the bark: C-R-O-A. What did those letters mean? John felt a cold shiver run through his arms and down his back. . . .[1]

THE MYSTERY OF ROANOKE

That was the beginning and tragic end to the Roanoke colony, one of the first settlements planted by the English in the New World. Whatever happened to the Roanoke colonists? Historians aren't sure, but in the eighteenth century, settlers arriving along the Lumber River found a tribe of gray-eyed Indians whose native language was similar to English. The Lumber River is just two hundred miles from Roanoke Island. Although no one knows the heritage of the Lumbee Indians, some historians believe they intermarried with the lost colonists of Roanoke Island. In fact, there was an island south of Roanoke, called Croatoan, inhabited by the Hatteras Indian tribe. In 1650, many Hatteras migrated to the mainland, settling in the Lumber River Valley.[2] Is this the answer to the puzzle of the lost settlers?

The Roanoke tragedy burst the bubble for those in Britain who had believed they could obtain easy riches in the New World. The harshness of settling an untamed land became all too real. The New World was a wild place, unfamiliar and deadly to those who didn't understand its ways.

Would the English ever establish a thriving settlement? Not until the power of prayer intervened. In this chapter, we will look at English colonists who had interests other than godly ones for settling on the East Coast—the Jamestown Colony, settled in 1607. In the next chapter, we will meet another group of English settlers who supported every move they made with fervent prayer—the Pilgrims.

THE EARLY EXPLORATION OF JAMESTOWN

A recent Disney film brought to life a segment of American history—the legendary story of John Smith and Pocahontas. We watched with delight as the fair and kind John Smith met the beautiful Indian maiden Pocahontas. What a tranquil and idyllic scene as they courted each other in the pristine forests. But the media had it all wrong. There was nothing tranquil about the early exploration and settlement of Jamestown. In fact, this was one of the most dismal examples of early American settlements.

The story began early in the seventeenth century when the Virginia Company was formed in England and a charter was written. The charter said that the main reason for settling the New World was "propagating of the Christian religion."[3] The official statement also said:

> The principle and main ends of the settlers . . . were first to preach and baptize into the Christian religion, and by propagation of the Gospel, to recover out of the arms of the Devil, a number of poor and miserable souls, wrapt up into death in

almost invincible ignorance; to endeavor the fulfilling an accomplishment of the number of the elect which shall be gathered from all corners of the earth; and to add our mite to the treasury of Heaven.[4]

Although the rhetoric of this era of European history sounds strange and perhaps even a bit arrogant to us today, the intent of the charter was basically honorable and godly. But as we will soon learn, they were just words penned by insincere men. Preparations were never made to accomplish the purpose of spreading the gospel to the Indians. The prayers the colonists said may have been lofty and eloquent, but God knew their hearts. It's clear that the real goal of the partners of the Virginia Company was to gain wealth.

The Jamestown expedition attracted all types of people. English gentlemen, poor from the streets, adventurers, and criminals were part of the 105 who boarded the first ship to Jamestown. Does it strike you as odd that only one of them was a minister? If the colonists' primary goal was spreading God's Word, one minister seems a disproportionately small number to accomplish that end.

From the beginning, the Jamestown Colony was known for its bickering and disunity. Even as the ship set sail, arguing began. It continued until the colonists landed on May 14, 1607, at what is known today as Jamestown, Virginia. Just imagine what the conditions were like when the ship finally reached the James River. Let's take a look at the scene. . . .

The ship, anchored off the river, bobbed sleepily as a small crowd gathered in a meadow near the shore of the low, marshy land. An important gathering was taking place, but only the

English gentlemen were invited. The women and men from the lower classes were in the distance unloading the cargo.

One man who was richly dressed held a box in his hands on which was the official stamp of King James I.

"Open it!" commanded a short man at his elbow. "Let's see what it says."

"Hold on," the other said. "Is everyone here?"

"Yes, everyone's here," another impatient voice cut in. "Get on with it."

The gentleman gently broke the seal on the box. Inside was a piece of paper on which seven names were written. The men named would comprise the new ruling council for the colony. The gentleman took out the letter and read the names to himself.

"Read them out loud," the short man demanded.

The gentleman slowly announced each name. As each member of the ruling council was announced, groans went up from others who hadn't been chosen. As soon as the last name was announced, arguing broke out over who should be the rightful leader of the group. Voices began to get heated.

"I should be president!"

"You? Who'd listen to you? I think it should be me."

After some time of arguing, someone suggested, "We've got to elect someone."

The men huddled, trying to jockey for position in the seven-member ruling group. Finally, after about an hour of wrangling, Edward Maria Wingfield was chosen president.

Grumbling once again floated through the group of men.

"I'll read the rest of the document," Wingfield announced, grabbing it. "These are our directions for establishing a fort." He read, "Select a site on an island in a navigable river. Avoid marshy or heavily wooded ground."

"What?" one of the council members spoke out. "We're here now. I'm not moving another thing."

"What are they going to do about it in England?" a man with a pockmarked face sneered. "Are they coming out here to see where we settled? I say let's do what we want to do."

"Right," the richly dressed gentleman agreed. "Look, they're unloading the cargo now. We'd have to put it all back on the ship to find another spot. This looks as good as anything."

"Not at all!" interjected veteran explorer Bartholomew Gosnold, who had been elected as a council member. "This place is too marshy. You know what happened to other colonists who settled in low places. They died of disease. We need to find higher ground, where the water is fresh and drains properly. We've got to move on."

After sharp argument, the group couldn't reach an agreement, so the only answer was to stay. "Let's put up some shelter. It'll be night soon," someone suggested.

Some of the gentlemen moved off to oversee the work. They commanded the workers to put up a tent of rotten sailcloth for a nightly shelter. "Hey, I'm not going to work," one of the gentleman exclaimed, then walked down to the shore and began picking up oysters and opening the shells to look for pearls. Others followed him and also picked up the numerous oysters. Once the men had poked through the soft flesh inside the shells, they disdainfully cast them aside. . . .[5]

Does it look as if God's will was the central focus of this group? Certainly not. Self and ego reigned. Right away, doubts about Edward Maria Wingfield as president began to spread. Many of the colonists wondered if he was an atheist since he never carried a Bible and wouldn't even allow preaching. A short time later, he was arrested for stealing food from the common stores and was consequently sent back to England for trial.[6] This inauspicious beginning was the start of years of idleness and a fruitless search for easy wealth.

THE LEGEND OF JOHN SMITH

The first six months of the settlement were disastrous because most of the men spent their time panning for gold. Since the murky water was a breeding ground for malaria-carrying mosquitoes, panning led to countless deaths. Food became scarce, but no one would abandon the search for gold in order to farm. The colonists kept from starving by trading for corn with the nearby Indian tribes. Soon half the men had died, and the settlers were embroiled in a war with the natives.

Eventually all seven council members either fled to England or died. Once Wingfield was gone, John Smith proclaimed himself president of Virginia. He fortified the Jamestown post and took charge of the fort. Surely John Smith, the Jamestown hero, would lead the colony to success. Unfortunately, history says otherwise.

What kind of man was John Smith? Before this expedition he had been a soldier, a slave, and a pirate. When he first arrived in Virginia, he was imprisoned because of his plans to wrest control of the colony. He was divisive and untrustworthy and was known for boasting. He had a very sharp tongue and was constantly handing out cutting remarks, which made him very unpopular.

The encounter with Pocahontas shows him in action. Because the colony's food supply was depleted, Smith and nine other men went to trade for corn with the Indians. Smith became impatient, and the trading changed to raiding. In one of the attacks, Smith killed two Indians and was captured and brought before Chief Powhatan.

The Indians decided his penalty—to dash his brains out on two boulders. Smith pleaded his case, explaining that the "white chiefs" across the sea would come to avenge his death. But this did not move Chief Powhatan. The death penalty would be carried out.[7]

According to Smith's account, Pocahontas, the chief's twelve-year-old daughter, pleaded for leniency and laid her head on Smith's. He wrote, "Pocahontas, the King's dearest daughter, when no entreaty would prevail, got his head in her arms and laid her own upon his to save him from death; whereat the emperor was contented he should live." Smith described Pocahontas as "next under God . . . the instrument to preserve this colony from death, famine and utter confusion."[8]

According to Smith, the chief then changed his decision and even gave Smith a gift of corn. But because of John Smith's character, the accuracy of the story is very much in doubt. We do know that six years later Pocahontas married John Rolfe, changed her name to Rebecca, and sailed to England, where she eventually died of smallpox.

Curiously, the Indians continued to feed the colonists even when they were treated badly in return. When the food supply ran short, the colonists often attacked an Indian village. Things kept deteriorating until by the fall of 1607, only thirty settlers were left.

Back in England, the Virginia Company policy makers mounted a major propaganda attack. Their theme was the noble goal of reaching lost souls with the gospel. But their real aim was to raise financial backing to boost their own wealth. So they painted Jamestown as a place of harmony and beauty. Not a word was mentioned about the deaths, the poor leadership, the Indian attacks, and the lack of spiritual work.

Because of these motivating presentations, many people invested in the Virginia Company and some volunteered to make the long journey to America. So the ships brought more people to Jamestown. What a shock it must have been for these new settlers to see the quagmire of Jamestown for the first time and then to fall sick with malaria or starvation! Most of the settlers died during their first year.

TERRIBLE CONDITIONS AT JAMESTOWN

As the winter of 1607–1608 set in, the situation was very dismal. Fire had destroyed all but three houses. While new shelters were being built, many more lives were lost. By April, food ran out. Again the Indians stepped in and helped the colonists.

Wouldn't you think that when spring came the settlers would realize the importance of planting crops? But just like us, they found lessons hard to learn and habits hard to change. The elusive search for gold was still the top priority, and another planting season was wasted.

In December 1608 the food again ran out—even earlier than the year before. Because he believed the Indians were trying to starve the colonists, John Smith devised a plan to kidnap Chief Powhatan. Smith met with the chief, asking him for kindness, knowing that his men were planning to ambush Powhatan in their second meeting. Wise Chief Powhatan said:

> Captain Smith, having seen the death of all my people thrice, and not anyone living of those three generations but myself, I know the difference between peace and war better than any in my country. . . . Think you I am so simple as not to know it is better to eat good meat, lie well, and sleep quietly with my women and children, laugh and be merry with you, have copper, hatchets or what I want, being your friend, than be forced to fly from all, lie cold in the woods, feed upon acorns, roots,

and such trash? Let this, therefore, assure you of our love, and every year our friendly trade shall furnish you with corn—and now, also, if you would come in friendly manner and not thus, with your guns and swords as if to invade your foes . . . if you intend to be friendly as you say, send hence your arms that I may believe you, for you see the love I bear you doth cause me thus nakedly to forget myself.[9]

John Smith promised to come back unarmed but instead arranged for a secret signal to send his men in to ambush the chief. The chief became aware of what was about to happen and slipped away. Finding himself in the midst of many hostile warriors, John Smith escaped downriver, then continued to raid smaller Indian villages for food.

Back in England, word finally got out about the terrible conditions in Jamestown. The Virginia Company reorganized and appointed a new governor to replace John Smith. They also made another religious appeal to the English people, telling them of the great opportunity to share the gospel with the Indians in America. As a result, nine ships and eight hundred settlers sailed in June 1609. John Smith was deposed and sent back to England. In his book *Description of Virginia,* he tried to repair his ruined reputation by describing the greediness of the other colonists. He wrote:

We did admire how it was possible such wise men could so torment themselves and us with strange absurdities and impossibilities, making Religion their color, when all their aim was nothing but present profit, as most plainly appeared by sending us so many refiners, goldsmiths, jewelers, lapidaries, stonecutters . . . so doting on mines of gold and the South Sea, that all the world could not have devised better courses to bring us to ruin than they did themselves.[10]

The winter of 1609 was called the "starving time." To stay alive, the colonists ate everything they could find, including dogs, cats, rats, and shoes.[11] Corpses were dug up and devoured. Many people froze to death in their beds. Nine out of every ten settlers perished.[12]

As the years passed, living conditions eventually got better. The reason? Pocahontas introduced a very profitable cash crop—tobacco. The plant was soon popularized in Europe, and the demand for it rose. By 1622, twelve hundred settlers were in the process of developing plantations. Slavery was first introduced to North America on these estates, and Virginia eventually became a stronghold of a practice that would cause untold suffering for generations.

REVEREND ROBERT HUNT

The true hero of Jamestown was not John Smith but the Reverend Robert Hunt, the only minister on the first voyage. He was a powerful preacher who called the settlers to repent and made church services mandatory. He tended the sick and performed last rites. His selfless attitude was a contrast to the selfish attitudes of the majority. On his memorial at Jamestown is written:

> He was an honest, religious and courageous Divine; he preferred the service of God to every thought of ease at home. He endured every privation, yet none ever heard him repine. During his life, our factions were oft healed and our greatest extremities so comforted that they seemed easy in comparison with what we endured after his memorable death. We all received from him the Holy Communion together as a pledge of reconciliation, for we all loved him for his exceeding goodness.[13]

But the Virginia settlers didn't follow Robert Hunt's example. In fact, it would be twenty years before the colony actually planted a crop that produced enough to feed all the people. For the most part, they continued panning for gold until they sent a whole ship full of their panned gold back to England. What an embarrassment to find that their precious treasure was only iron pyrite—fool's gold!

A TRAGIC LEGACY

What can we learn from the experiences of Jamestown Colony? *First,* God knows our hearts. The partners of the Virginia Company wanted everyone to think that their intentions were righteous. But God knew the truth, and soon most of England knew their real motives. By the end of the business venture, the colonists gave up their holy facade and their attempts to have England's churches financially support their expeditions. Instead, the Virginia Company raised its money through public lotteries and a mail campaign to small towns that invited people to invest money taken from their town's treasuries.

Second, our adventures should be God controlled, not man controlled. If the settlers had focused on a godly goal, their plans would have been guided by righteousness. But instead they spent years working on futile tasks such as panning for gold, which resulted in disaster. Many lost their lives because of greed. But before we criticize their actions, we should ask ourselves how often we do the same things in our churches. Many of us spend an enormous amount of time working on our own agenda and are easily distracted from godly goals such as building up believers and seeking the lost. We too are susceptible to greed and selfishness.

Third, we need to build on godly principles rather than

worldly desires. God allowed the colonists to do things their own way, but their decisions resulted in many lost lives and tragedy. The effects were far-reaching—even to the extent of hundreds of years of heartache resulting from the great evil of slavery and the addicting habit of tobacco use.

But let's look at the next chapter in the story—the colonists who arrived in 1620 and who built their settlement on prayer. Their story is one of the great miracles of America's history—and we remember and honor these colonists every year on Thanksgiving Day.

For Discussion and Reflection

Adult Discussion

Prepare ahead of time slips of paper with a simple sentence on each. For example, you might write, "The dog walked through the forest."

Form groups of three or four. Give each group one of the slips of paper you prepared. Have each group make up a long, wordy sentence that says the same thing. For example, for the sample sentence given above, a group might write: "The canine mammal set one foot in front of the other in a progression through trees and undergrowth covering a large area." When groups finish, have them read their sentences to the class to see if other groups can come up with the simple meaning.

Then ask:

- ★ How did you respond to the other groups' statements?
- ★ How is what we just did like the way we sometimes use lofty words and hard-to-understand statements to make ourselves sound smart?

★ When have you used a lot of words to say very little or nothing at all?
★ In what situations are words twisted to change meanings or make ideas easier to swallow?

Have people return to their small groups to discuss the following two questions. Ask:

★ The Virginia Company had commendable goals written into their charter for Jamestown Colony, but the settlers never followed through on them. What similarities can you see in churches today?
★ What similarities might exist in your personal life? in your prayer life?

Read aloud James 1:22-25. Ask:

★ How did the Jamestown colonists fail to live up to the command in this passage?
★ How do we fail to live up to this command?
★ How does this passage relate to our prayer lives?
★ What can we do to be more faithful to this passage in our daily actions?

Youth Discussion

Bring in everyday items like a hairbrush, sunglasses, a book, a telephone, or breakfast cereal. Form groups of three or four, and give each group one of the items. Have each group examine their item and think of a use that was not originally intended for it. For example, the book could be a doorstop. Have each group then create a commercial to try to sell the idea to the other groups. After the groups have presented their commercials, ask:

★ How did you feel promoting a somewhat phony advertisement?

★ How is this like the way the Virginia Company published a spiritual-sounding charter while never intending to fulfill it?

Have groups read 1 Samuel 16:7 and discuss the following questions. Ask:

★ Where did the Jamestown colonists go wrong, according to this passage?

★ What are ways we do the same things with our families, friends, teachers, or employers?

★ In what ways do we sometimes put on a false outward appearance toward God?

★ How can having a vital personal prayer life combat this tendency to put on a false front?

As you wrap up your session, ask everyone to silently think about the following question and consider making a commitment to God. Ask: "How will you personally change your prayer life to help you become more truthful in your relationship with God?"

SIX

An Unlikely Beginning

Pilgrims. The name conjures up images of poor, uneducated refugees fleeing England for religious freedom. But many of them started out with college educations, nice homes, vast amounts of wealth, and promising futures. They gave it all up to seek God's will in their lives. They lived by a simple plan—making prayer the most important part of their daily lives. That's how they could cheerfully give up the things dear to their hearts like their earthly goods and the respect of other people. Because of their uncompromising faith, they were despised throughout England. In the end, they also had to leave behind their loved ones and homeland. What caused the Pilgrims to suffer all this deprivation for their faith?

THE BEGINNINGS OF THEIR DISSENT

Imagine a huge windstorm that begins in the Atlantic Ocean and whips its way across our country all the way to the Pacific. It is so powerful that it hits every state, every city, and every town. In its wake, people are unsure how to rebuild their lives.

That's a picture of what happened in Europe during the sixteenth and seventeenth centuries. On October 31, 1517, Martin Luther nailed his famous ninety-five theses to the door of

Castle Church in Wittenberg, Germany. Although that event was not singularly reponsible for the Protestant Reformation, it did begin a great shake-up in the Christian church. People began to question the authority of the pope and greedy practices within the Catholic church. They began to examine what faith and salvation really were according to God's Word. Great thinkers such as Calvin, Wycliffe, and Luther wrote and preached about salvation by faith, not works. All over Europe, people began to leave the Catholic church and worship in independent congregations.

In time, the Protestant Reformation jumped the English Channel to instigate the development of the Church of England, also called the Anglican church. But many people were not satisfied with the Anglican church. Two groups, specifically, wanted to follow the teachings of the Bible more closely. One group—the Puritans—tried to purify the Church of England from the inside. The other group—the Separatists, or Dissenters—felt that reforming the church was hopeless, so they left the church.

Many of the colonists (known as the Pilgrims) who established Plymouth Colony in 1620 were Separatists. The colonists who came nine years later and established the Massachusetts Bay Colony were Puritans. In the next few chapters, we will see how these two groups laid the foundation for our early American government. Let's begin with the Pilgrims. Their story is one of lives built around communion with God and thanksgiving for all he did for them—in spite of significant hardships.

ORDINARY MEN, EXTRAORDINARY FAITH

God used three men to form a Separatist congregation in Nottinghamshire that would help lay the Christian foundation for our country. They were probably not the kind of leaders we would choose to head up a movement today. They were a village postman, a young farm boy, and a disgraced pastor.

William Brewster started his career as a confidential secretary to William Davison, a prominent member of Queen Elizabeth's court. Brewster was at the prime of his career when Davison fell out of favor at the court and was removed. William Brewster lost his position, too, so he moved to the quiet, obscure village of his roots called Scrooby. Since his father was ill, William took over his job as postmaster. Eventually, Brewster separated from the Anglican church and began meeting secretly with local Christians. In time he became the leader of the congregation.

Another person who joined the small group of dissenters was a young man named William Bradford. A childhood illness had prompted him to start searching the Scriptures. In his teens, a friend took him to an Anglican church where Reverend Richard Clyfton preached from the Bible. Bradford sat under this man's teaching until Clyfton withdrew to become the preacher at the Scrooby congregation. Now Bradford faced a decision. Should he stay in the Church of England or withdraw and join the Scrooby congregation? Cotton Mather, a well-known early American preacher, had a deep admiration for William Bradford. In his biography of Bradford, Mather wrote:

> To withdraw from the communion of the parish-assemblies, and engage with some society of the faithful that should keep close unto the written word of God, as the rule of their worship . . . although the provoked rage of his friends tried all the ways imaginable to reclaim him from it . . . his answer was . . . "Nevertheless, to keep a good conscience, and walk in such a way as God has prescribed in his word, is a thing which I must prefer before you all, and above life itself."[1]

Bradford stood up for his faith and joined this loving group of believers who made prayer their lifestyle. From the beginning, he had a wonderful relationship with Brewster. In describing his friend, Bradford talked about how the Pilgrims lived:

> They originally met at his house on the Lord's Day (which was a manor of the bishop's) and with great love he entertained them when they came, making provision for them to his great charge. . . . And when they were to remove out of the country he was one of the first in all adventures.[2]

Another key figure in the early Pilgrim movement was John Robinson, a young pastor who had been dismissed from his church for not conforming to the Church of England. Because of his dismissal, he was forced to return to Scrooby and stay with relatives. There he became involved in a dissenters group, which would become part of the Pilgrim group. Robinson spent twenty years preparing his congregation to start a new colony in America by teaching them about Christian self-government and unity. William Bradford wrote:

> His love was great towards [his congregation], and his care was all ways bente for their best good, both for soule and body; for besides his singuler abilities in devine things (wherein he excelled), he was also very able to give directions in civill affaires, and to foresee dangers and inconveniences; by which means he was very helpful to their outward estats, and so was every way as a commone father unto them.[3]

These men followed Paul's admonition in Romans 12:2: "Don't copy the behavior and customs of this world, but let God transform you into a new person by changing the way you think. Then you will know what God wants you to do, and you will know how good and pleasing and perfect his will really is" (NLT). Their choice would lead to hardships, persecutions—and, for some, death.

Although they didn't seek trouble and even informed King James that they didn't want to interfere with the Anglican church, the king became increasingly bothered by this small congregation. He called them religious fanatics, "ever-discontented with the present government and impatient to suffer any superiority, which maketh their sect unable to be suffered in any well-governed commonwealth."[4] He issued an ultimatum: they must either conform to his wishes or be driven from the land. When they didn't obey, he ordered the police to hunt down the Separatists.

People began hunting them with enthusiasm. Neighbors spied on them and watched roads to inform on their whereabouts. Brewster, Bradford, and Robinson feared for the safety of the women and children in their congregation. After much prayer and discussion, they decided that they must leave England. But how would they do it? It was against the law—under penalty of death—to leave England without permission.

SAD FAREWELL

Can you imagine how difficult it must have been for the Pilgrims to consider leaving their homes in England? Besides breaking the law, they had to say good-bye to many friends and relatives and embark on a dangerous journey. Through all of this, they relied on prayer to calm their souls and to seek God's guidance.

It was a challenge to find a boat to take them out of the country. Most ship captains, naturally, were afraid to help people who were hated by the king. But finally the Dissenters found a Dutch shipper who agreed to take them to the Netherlands. He accepted their money and arranged to load their cargo on a preappointed day. They had finally found a friend and ally. The men quietly sold their farms and bought provisions for starting over in another land. The women, children, and men packed all they could carry. . . .

The night was cold and crisp, and the countryside was quiet as the people gathered and started walking. They carried heavy bundles and children who were too small to walk. No one said a word, afraid that any noise would alert their enemies to their escape.

Mile after mile, hour after hour they walked. Their homes soon faded into the distant shadows. Feet began to blister and legs ached. Occasionally, a child whimpered. Sixty miles was a long way to travel with such heavy burdens.

When daylight came, the group rested and ate the food they had prepared for the trip. As the sun came up, they gathered to pray. Then they slept fitfully until they could walk again under cover of darkness. Finally, after a long and difficult journey, they saw the sparkle of blue water and the rugged shore. But where was the ship they had come to meet?

"Don't worry," William Brewster said. "The ship will come. God hasn't brought us this far to abandon us. Our trust is in him."

The others nodded in agreement, and they settled down to wait. They arranged a little camp and settled the children. But time seemed so heavy on that windy shore. A little one cried, "Mama, I want to go home."

"Not now," his mother comforted. There was no home to go back to.

Then, late one night, a lookout ran back to the little group to whisper the news. "The Dutch ship has slipped into the harbor. It's time to go." There in the moonlight lay the ship, her hull glistening with salt water. Everyone began rolling up blankets and shouldering bundles.

The people cautiously made their way to the shore. The men began throwing cargo into the small boats that met them at the water's edge. The boats made trip after trip, oars dipping musically into the calm water. Then the women and children boarded the boats. Some had tears in their eyes as they felt English soil under their feet for the last time. Finally the men, too, made their way to the ship until everyone was safely on board. Some of the Pilgrims gathered to quietly thank God that they were safely on their way to new homes in the Netherlands.

One little girl began jumping up and down near the ship's rail. "Daddy, look! More boats!" Many eyes turned in the direction she was pointing. Several boats were headed toward the ship.

"What is it?" a fearful voice whispered in the chill air.

Suddenly one of the men cried, "I see uniforms. It's the king's officers!"

Brewster ran to tell the captain to set sail before the boats could surround them. But the ship didn't budge from its moorings. Waves gently lapped against the unmoving hull as Brewster came back with pain etched on his face. "The captain has betrayed us," he informed the startled group. "He planned this from the beginning." Sobs and prayers broke out in the huddled group as the officials' boats came closer.

Then a tall, stately woman spoke up. "Our men must escape. If they are captured, they will be executed for leaving England!"

"Yes, yes!" the other women agreed.

When the men began to object, a small, slight woman answered, "God will protect us. We must stay with the children, but all of you must go!" They quickly gathered for prayer, then the men began to slip away as the king's officers boarded the ship.

When they climbed aboard ship, the British officers grabbed the women and the remaining men, pushing them over the side of the ship into the open boats. The children were roughly handed down. Then the officers began searching the men and women's clothing for money and valuables. The Pilgrims could hear sailors ransacking their belongings aboard the ship as the boats headed for the nearby town of Boston. In the confusion, the remaining Pilgrim men slipped over the sides of the boats until all of them managed to escape.

As the sun came up, the officers herded the women and children through the dusty streets of Boston. The townspeople were stirring as the sad line of refugees was paraded down the narrow streets. Townspeople flocked to see the sight. The officers shoved the onlookers back as the little group trudged by. The women bowed their heads, and the children walked quietly beside them, their sad eyes wide with fear. Several women clutched babies tightly in their arms. Finally, the human train reached the dull stone steps of the dungeon. The now huge crowd held its breath as the small figures of the women and children disappeared one by one into that dank, dark prison. . . . [5]

How could God let this happen to such devout men and women? Had they misread the will of God? Had they given up everything for nothing? William Bradford later described the tragedy that had fallen upon his people:

> After long waiting, and large expenses he [the shipper] came at
> length and took them in. . . . But when he had them and their
> goods aboard, he betrayed them, having beforehand plotted
> with searchers and other officers . . . who took them, and put
> them in open boats, and rifled and ransacked them, searching
> their shirts for money. [The police] then carried them back to
> town and made them a spectacle and wonder to the multi-
> tude.[6]

Wouldn't this disaster cause you to wonder if you were traveling down the wrong path? Would your faith waver if the
women and children in your congregation were thrown into
dungeons where most prisoners died from lack of necessities?
This is how Bradford described the scene:

> Pitiful it was to see [these] poor women in this distress. What
> weeping and crying on every side, some for their husbands . . .
> others not knowing what should become of them, and their
> little ones, others again melted in tears seeing their poor little
> ones hanging about them, crying for fear, and quaking with
> cold.[7]

But God was working through the prayers of his people.
Through the imprisonment of these women and children, the
British people became aware of their cause and noticed their
godly example, and the situation became a political embarrassment for King James. To save face, he let them go, saying again
that they must conform or leave England. They chose to join
their husbands and fathers, who had escaped to the town of
Leyden in the Netherlands. God had answered their prayers,
and they were all able to leave England—men, women, and
children—with the consent of King James, although not in the
way they had originally planned.

The Pilgrims remained in Leyden for eleven years. Because they were immigrants in Holland, they were allowed to do only menial labor. Although they worked from dawn until night, it barely paid enough for them to eke out a living. It was a hard life, and many died an early death. But these godly people did not complain and carried on cheerfully, worshiping God in freedom for the first time.

THE CENTER OF GOD'S WILL

The Pilgrims still had their dream. They wanted to move on for several reasons. First, the hard life the Pilgrims led caused Separatists in England to remain there, under the persecution of King James. The Pilgrims also began to fear that they'd soon be too worn out to move again. But perhaps the greatest fear was for their children. Many of their children and young people were being drawn away by the "evil examples" of the Dutch. Some even thought it would be better to endure England's prisons than to risk seeing their children fall away into the decadent lifestyle of the Dutch.

The Pilgrims began considering a move to the New World. Having heard about Jamestown Colony and its "starving time," they wondered whether they could survive in such a harsh wilderness. Another possibility was a settlement in a warmer climate, such as Guiana in South America. They had heard great reports of the land, but it was controlled by Catholic Spain. The leaders asked God for his guidance. Bradford described the decision:

> It was answered that all great and honorable actions are accompanied with great difficulties, and must be enterprised and overcome with answerable courages. It was granted that the dangers were great, but not desperate, and the difficulties

were many, but not invincible . . . and all of them, through the help of God, by fortitude and patience, might either be borne or overcome. . . . [But] their condition was not ordinary. Their ends were good and honorable, their calling lawful and urgent, and therefore they might expect the blessing of God in their proceeding; yea, though they should lose their lives in this action, yet they might have comfort in the same, and their endeavors would be honorable.[8]

Although most of the leadership felt at peace about *where* they should go, John Robinson wanted to be sure about *why* they were going. He began praying for a deeper revelation. He wrote:

Now as the people of God in old time were called out of Babylon civil, the place of their bodily bondage, and were to come to Jerusalem, and there to build the Lord's temple, or tabernacle . . . so are the people of God now to go out of Babylon spiritual to Jerusalem . . . and to build themselves as lively stones into a spiritual house, or temple, for the Lord to dwell in.[9]

Financing the trip, of course, presented a significant obstacle. Robinson and Brewster approached Sir Edwin Sandys, a treasurer to the Virginia Company, which had sponsored the Jamestown Colony, and asked for financial backing. They gave the following reasons that the company could have confidence in them:

1. We verily believe and trust the Lord is with us, unto Whom and Whose service we have given ourselves in many trials, and that He will graciously prosper our endeavors according to the simplicity of our hearts therein.
2. We are well weaned from the delicate milk of our mother country, and inured to the difficulties of a strange and hard land, which yet in a great part we have by patience overcome.

81

3. The people are, for the body of them, [as] industrious and frugal, we think we may safely say, as any company of people in the world.

4. We are knit together as a body in a most strict and sacred bond and covenant of the Lord, of the violation whereof we make great conscience, and by virtue whereof we do hold ourselves straitly tied to all care of each other's good, and of the whole by everyone and so mutually.

5. Lastly, it is not with us as with other men, whom small things can discourage, or small discontentments cause to wish themselves at home again.[10]

Unfortunately, the Virginia Company was almost bankrupt and turned them down. Shortly thereafter, the Pilgrims were approached by a London merchant, Thomas Weston. He assured them he had only their best interests at heart and that he would finance a ship if they would agree to a seven-year period of indentured servitude. That meant that each of them would work as servants of the owners, who would provide food and supplies. The owners would receive all profits during those years. At the end of the seven years, each person would be given one share of the company, two shares if they equipped themselves at the beginning of the journey. Also, at the end of the seven years, the profits would be divided by shares.

With some reservations but no other options, the Pilgrim leaders agreed to this plan. Weston went back to England to confer with his backers and to secure a ship to take them to the New World.

A DAY OF FASTING AND PRAYER

You can imagine the excitement and sadness of the small congregation as they prepared for the journey. Only two hundred of the six hundred members would be able to go. Deciding who would remain was difficult. John Robinson agreed to stay behind and shepherd the remaining flock.

Before the departure date, the entire congregation spent a day of fasting and prayer to prepare the travelers for the hard journey. At the end of the day, the Pilgrims ate dinner and sang their favorite psalms.

Think of the life-changing decisions we make today, like moving to a new city, changing jobs, getting married, or buying a new home. How often do you hear of Christians spending a day in fasting and prayer to prepare spiritually for the challenges of their decisions? As a congregation, how often do we consider each major decision by setting aside a day of fasting and prayer? Often we spend much time in prayer *before* our decision but very little *after* the decision. What an example these Pilgrims are for us!

On July 22, 1620, with all their provisions loaded into their ship, the *Speedwell,* they said their last farewells. On the dock, John Robinson knelt to pray, and his congregation followed his example. He asked God's blessing on the undertaking. Tears flowed. Last hugs and kisses were given. Then the travelers boarded the ship and the crew cast off. Would this journey end in disaster like the one to Holland did? Or would prayer make the difference for this little band of godly men and women? Little did the Pilgrims know what lay ahead of them on this long journey over miles and miles of ocean.

For Discussion and Reflection

Adult Discussion
Give the following survey to each adult in your group.

VALUE SURVEY

Rank the following items in order from one to eleven, with one being the most important and eleven being the least important to you:

____ A comfortable life (having what you need)

____ A sense of accomplishment (making a lasting contribution)

____ Evangelism (telling others about your faith)

____ Family security (safety for the people you love)

____ National security (protection of the country from attack)

____ Pleasure (a fun life)

____ Respect (recognition by others, having others like you)

____ Eternal life (a relationship with God through Jesus)

____ Friendship (close companionship)

____ Happiness (having what you want)

____ Wisdom (knowing a lot and understanding life)

When everyone is finished with the survey, discuss the following questions:

> ★ What thoughts went through your mind as you filled out this survey?
> ★ Which things on this list did the Pilgrims give up for their beliefs?

Form groups of four or five and discuss the following questions:

> ★ After eternal life, what are the three most important values on this list?
> ★ What are the three least important values on the list?

Have the groups report on their discussions; then have them read Matthew 10:37-39 and discuss the following questions:

> ★ What does it mean to lose your life for Jesus' sake?
> ★ What would be the hardest things for you to give up for the sake of Christ?

Bring the class back together, and have them report on the first of the two questions above. Then ask:

> ★ What aspects of our spiritual and daily lives would change if we had to give up the things that the Pilgrims had to give up?
> ★ How would our prayer lives change?
> ★ What positive things do you think would result from those changes?

Youth Discussion
Before class, fill small baby-food jars halfway with cooking oil and the rest of the way with water tinted with food coloring.

Put lids on the jars, and make sure they seal tightly. Form groups of four, and have the kids try to mix the liquids in the jars by shaking them. Ask:

* ★ What happened in the jars? Why?
* ★ What went through your mind as you tried to mix these liquids?
* ★ How were the Pilgrims in this chapter similar to the colored water?

Form pairs and have them read Romans 12:1-2 and then discuss the following questions with their partners:

* ★ How did the Pilgrims practice being nonconformists?
* ★ What power did the Pilgrims rely on to help them?
* ★ What are your biggest struggles in the fight to not conform to this world?
* ★ What things help us in this fight?
* ★ What part does your personal prayer time play in helping you stay away from sinful things? How could it do more?
* ★ What are you going to do this week to stand up for your faith?

SEVEN

The Incredible Journey

The Pilgrims were a people of prayer. It was their spiritual bread and butter, the staple from which the rest of their lives was nourished. Because prayer was so much a part of everything they did, their lives reflected holiness and love for God and each other. Among the early colonists of North America, the Pilgrims' prayer life and resulting love and steadfastness were unequaled. The trials they endured in England and Holland produced in them a deep dependence on God and a minute-by-minute walk with him. And the voyage over rough seas in crowded conditions further developed their reliance on prayer.

The Pilgrims' journey differed from the first journey of Columbus in several ways. The time and circumstances were different: The Pilgrims prepared to leave Holland more than one hundred twenty years after Columbus set sail from Spain; they headed for a shore one thousand miles north of where Columbus first landed. Their reasons for leaving were different: Columbus had the blessings of the king and queen of Spain and was heralded when he returned; the Pilgrims were refugees from their land and hated for their religious stance. And their expectations were different: Columbus expected to find gold and riches; the Pilgrims knew of the deaths and hardships suffered by the British colonists who had preceded them. Fleeing religious persecution, they hoped to establish a government based on biblical principles.

A SHAKY START

The Pilgrims left the Netherlands in the *Speedwell,* which joined the *Mayflower* at Southampton, England. The *Mayflower* held passengers who were not part of the Pilgrim congregation, and some of them did not have similar religious beliefs. They had paid for their passages hoping to make profits in the New World.

The captain, Christopher Jones, who was part owner of the *Mayflower,* had been hired to take them just south of the Hudson River, which was part of the northern lands of the Virginia Colony. He planned to stay with them long enough to see them settled in.

As the group prepared to leave Southampton, they experienced their first test. Thomas Weston, the London merchant who was financing the trip, tried to change the original contract. He wanted the Pilgrims to leave all property in the ownership of the company even after their seven years of indentured service. He felt that since the Pilgrims were inexperienced businessmen they would sign the contract. Much to his dismay, the Pilgrims refused to sign the new agreement. Their refusal enraged him so deeply that he stormed back to London without settling their final debts.

Not willing to delay their journey, the Pilgrims sold off all food and supplies they didn't absolutely need. They sent a letter to the other London merchants promising that if the settlement was not profitable after seven years, they would work until every cent was repaid. Then Brewster assembled the congregation and read John Robinson's farewell letter. It said:

> Loving Christian friends, I do heartily and in the Lord salute
> you all, as being they with whom I am present in my best affection, and most earnest longings after you, though I be constrained for a while to be bodily absent from you. . . . We are
> daily to renew our repentance with our God, especially for our
> own sins known, and generally for our unknown trespasses, so
> does the Lord call us in a singular manner upon occasions of
> such difficulty and danger as lies before you.
>
> Your intended course of civil community will minister continual occasion of offense, and will be as fuel for that fire, except you diligently quench it with brotherly forbearance. . . .
> Store up therefore patience against that evil day, without
> which we take offense at the Lord Himself in His holy and just
> works.[1]

He also advised them to form a democratic government:

> Whereas you are to become a civil body politic, using amongst
> yourselves civil government, and are not furnished with any
> persons of special eminence above the rest, to be chosen by
> you into office of government, let your wisdom and godliness
> appear, not only choosing such persons as do entirely love and
> promote the common good, but also in yielding unto them all
> due honor and obedience in their lawful administrations.[2]

These words of wisdom reflected the Pilgrims' godly focus, which came from their deep prayer life.

Now the moment came to start their long journey. Years of prayer and planning were finally realized! But it was only three days before their faith was tested again. The *Speedwell*'s masts caused her seams to open while in full sail. Their only choice was to turn around and repair her. A week later, they tried again. Once again the *Speedwell* began taking on water. The two ships turned back. This time the sailors searched every crack of the ship for the open seam but could not find it. At last it was decided to leave the *Speedwell* behind.

God was testing the inner character of each person aboard. Already they had gone through two weeks of a trying ordeal. As they combined the cargo and passengers onto the *Mayflower,* some began to wonder if this trip was worth it. Twenty of them decided to drop out. By the time they left for the last time, the small company of Pilgrims included sixteen men, eleven women, and fourteen children. They made up about one-third of the passengers, but their influence far outweighed their numbers. Bradford wrote: "Like Gideon's army this small number was divided, as if the Lord, by this work of His Providence, thought these few were still too many for the great work to do."[3] Instead of getting angry at the circumstances or blaming someone, these few adventurers took their difficulties to God and laid them in his care. This was the pattern the Pilgrims followed with each difficulty.

PSALM-SINGING PUKE-STOCKINGS

Finally, the remaining Pilgrim band and their traveling companions were all aboard one ship—all 102 passengers crammed into a space no larger than a volleyball court! They would spend the next two months in these cramped, close quarters. Imagine living in this small space with one hundred people, many of them strangers. You would get to know each person's habits and nature very well. The Pilgrims had already found a unity needed to build a nation, but in the next two months, these small quarters would become a melting pot that would cause the other passengers to form a bond with the Pilgrims as well.

Can you see yourself living in those quarters for two months? One hundred two people huddled in a stifling, dark area. The hatches could not be opened because of the storms. The boat constantly rolled and pitched, causing seasickness. Most of us would whine and complain and fall into depression. Instead, the Pilgrims prayed together through it all. God brought them peace instead of despair.

Not only was the living space less than desirable, but the Pilgrims also faced torment and ridicule from members of the crew. The leader of these tormentors took an intense dislike to these religious zealots. He led the crew in calling them "psalm-singing puke-stockings." He said he couldn't wait till they died and he could sew them into shrouds and feed them to the fish.

Suddenly, at the peak of one of his tirades, the sailor fell to the deck with some mysterious illness. He died that day and was the first to be thrown overboard. No one else caught this mysterious disease, and the crew never mocked the Pilgrims again.[4]

Then, about halfway through the trip, a near catastrophe occurred. A continuous series of miraculous prayer interventions proved the power of the Pilgrims' prayers!

CRISIS EN ROUTE

Mary shivered as she felt the cold blast of icy wind. Low clouds were scurrying across the horizon as if they were running from something fierce. Master Jones emerged from his chart room, his hair flying in the wind. He faced the stiff gusts, then turned to the passengers on the quarterdeck. "There's a big one brewing," he announced. A spear of despair pierced Mary's heart. She knew what that meant.

"Furl the sails!" the captain commanded, and the sailors scurried to obey. "Passengers, you must stay on the tween deck below!"

Mary gathered her three children and headed for the gloomy hold. She looked at eight-year-old Bartholomew and her two younger daughters, Remember and Mary. The little one was coughing again. As she handed down her little Mary into someone's waiting arms, the smell belching from the lower deck made her stomach churn.

Father, you are so gracious to keep us from harm, Mary prayed as she too climbed down to the crowded deck. So many people, cold food, and soiled clothing and bedding. She crawled over many legs until she found a small corner next to the ship's hull for herself and her children. Already she could feel the huge waves crashing against the planks. She would never get used to the way the ship shuddered.

Her husband suddenly towered over her. "Here you are!" he exclaimed.

"Where have you been, Isaac?" she asked automatically, knowing he couldn't have gone far.

"The men were praying on the capstan. Master Jones says we're only halfway to the Virginia Colony, but he's never seen a storm bear down like this. We were praying for safety." He sat down next to her and cradled little Mary in his arms.

Hour after hour they sat in the cramped corner, elbow to elbow with their neighbors. Sometimes Isaac prayed. Other times, they joined in the singing of psalms that broke out now and then. Isaac's rough, tuneless voice was so comforting to Mary.

The ship was tossed like flotsam. Mary heard someone getting sick near her. Thank goodness her children had inherited her iron stomach.

Suddenly, a loud crack resounded through the deck. Every human noise stopped instantly. All Mary could hear was the pounding of the waves against the ship.

Then Mary felt a drop of water hit her arm. The drops became a steady stream.

"We're sinking!" a woman screamed in the darkness.

"I must go see if I can help," Isaac whispered, then disappeared. Mary tucked in her children and quickly followed him. The fetid smell in the air thickened as seawater and rain seeped in.

Soon she slipped into the soft glow of a lantern. Several men were trying to fix a cracked beam above them.

"What happened?" she asked.

Isaac noticed her and explained, "A crossbeam that holds up the mainmast broke in the storm. The sailors tried to lever the crossbeam back onto the mast, but it wouldn't stay. Only God can save us. The ship looks doomed."

Mary could barely breathe, thinking of her three little ones sleeping so soundly. She noticed a few of the Pilgrim men gathered in the shadows, praying. Their whispered words were so comforting to Mary's ears. She prayed, too. Even some of the sailors were muttering prayers as they worked.

"Master Jones wants us to turn back," Isaac said a few minutes later. "He says there's no way to fix the beam."

Then William Bradford spoke up. "We have that great iron house jack we brought from Leyden. Perhaps we can use it to repair the beam."

Hope lit the shadowed faces of the men. Bradford left his post and crawled back toward the main hold. With seawater pouring in all around them, the men waited many long minutes. Then he appeared with the jack in hand. The sailors pushed with their backs to straighten the beam, and several men fixed the jack onto the beam. When they finished, everyone stepped back and held their breath. The seawater had stopped flowing into the hold. The beam held!

Master Jones exclaimed, "I do believe the *Mayflower* is as seaworthy as ever!"

Mary laughed with relief. "Surely God is our helper!" she whispered. Then she listened to the sweet sound of the squeaking and groaning of the mast as it strained against the wind. . . ."[5]

LAND HO!

Finally on November 9, after sixty-six days at sea, the two words those weary travelers were waiting to hear sounded: "Land ho!" Everybody ran up to the deck to drink in that long-awaited sight! Going through everybody's mind was the question, *Where are we?* One of the crewmen identified the place as Cape Cod. They were hundreds of miles off course!

The captain steered the ship southward, heading for the Virginia Colony. But the strong shoals and riptides made their progress treacherous. Finally Captain Jones, fearing for their safety, headed back to sea to wait a day or so to try again.

How disappointing this must have been for those weary travelers. Surely they wanted to be on solid ground as soon as possible. But they also began to wonder if maybe God was trying to tell them something. He had blown them off course, and now it seemed as if he was preventing them from getting to their original destination. So they spent hours in prayer and discussion. Finally, they decided that God must have brought them here for a reason, and they instructed Captain Jones to turn around and head for the northern tip of the Cape.

After anchoring, they realized the new problem they faced.

They had chosen to settle outside the boundaries of Virginia, which made their patent invalid. Their ship was under no one's jurisdiction. Some of the men who didn't belong to the Pilgrim group began to take advantage of the situation and revolt against the leadership.

Without a doubt, a rebellion would destroy the expedition, so the Pilgrim leaders acted quickly. They formed a quick huddle and drew up the famous Mayflower Compact. This document would become a cornerstone of American democracy. This is what they penned in the chart room of that ship:

> In the name of God, Amen. We whose names are under-written, the loyal subjects of our dread sovereign, Lord King James, by the grace of God, of Great Britain, France, Ireland, King, defender of the faith, etc., having undertaken, for the glory of God and advancement of the Christian faith, and honor of our King and country, a voyage to plant the first colony in the northern parts of Virginia, do by these presents solemnly and mutually in the presence of God, and one of another, covenant and combine ourselves together into a civil body politic, for our better ordering and preservation and furtherance of the ends aforesaid; and by virtue hereof to enact, constitute and frame such just and equal laws, ordinances, acts, constitutions and offices from time to time, as shall be thought most meet and convenient for the general good of the colony, unto which we promise all due submission and obedience. In witness whereof, we have hereunder subscribed our names at Cape Cod, the 11th of November, in the year of the reign of our sovereign lord, King James of England, France, and Ireland the eighteenth, and of Scotland the fifty fourth. Anno Domini. 1620.[6]

What would have happened if the Pilgrims hadn't listened to the Holy Spirit guiding them to stay at Cape Cod? What if they had been too busy to keep tuned in to God through prayer? They might have kept going south and sailed to their intended destination, and this important document would never have been written. But they stepped out in faith and settled outside the protection of the Virginia Company.

God had many reasons to put them in this very place, and he was clearly looking out for them. As we shall see, their survival through the harsh winters can be explained only by God's providence.

But for now, their journey had ended and its trials were over. William Bradford wrote:

> Being thus arrived in a good harbor and brought safe to land, they fell upon their knees and blessed the God of heaven, who had brought them over the vast and furious ocean, and delivered them from all the perils and miseries thereof, again to set their feet on the firm and stable earth, their proper element. And no marvel if they were thus joyful.[7]

As always, the Pilgrims fell to their knees thanking and praising God. They trusted him and his providence. The Pilgrims would face their severest tests over the next few years, but their character would prove pure, as a result of their faithfulness in prayer.

For Discussion and Reflection

Adult Discussion

Form groups of three or four. Have each group make a pie chart representing a twenty-four-hour day in the life of the average Christian. Have them include sleeping time, TV watching, reading, prayer, family time, church activities, and anything else they care to add.

When groups have finished, have each make a pie chart representing what might have been a typical day for a Pilgrim on the *Mayflower*. Then have groups compare the two charts and discuss the following questions:

★ How did it feel to compare the average Christian to the Pilgrims?
★ Why are these two charts so different?

Reconvene as a large group, and discuss the following:

★ Many people today are talking about the breakdown of the American family. Based on the charts, what changes could we make to strengthen the family today?

Read James 5:13-16. Ask:

★ How closely do you think the Pilgrims followed these verses?
★ What things in the Pilgrims' lives helped them to weave prayer so strongly into their daily activities?
★ What prevents us from following these verses in our lives?

Give each person a sheet of paper. Say: "Make an 'ideal' pie chart for yourself. Before you start, ask yourself how you could make prayer a more prominent part of your life." When people have finished, allow volunteers to share their charts. Then form pairs and wrap up your session by having partners pray together for their families.

Youth Discussion

Bring in squares of fabric, about eight inches by eight inches. Have people form pairs, and give each pair a fabric square. Say: "Each fabric square represents the lives of the Pilgrims." Have each partner grab a side of the fabric square and pull to try to tear the fabric. When all have torn their fabric or have given up, ask:

★ How did you feel when your fabric tore (or didn't tear)?
★ What made it difficult to tear the fabric?
★ What made the lives of the Pilgrims strong?
★ How is prayer in our lives like the weave of the thread in the fabric?

Read James 5:13-16. Say: "The Pilgrims' spiritual lives were strong because of prayer. They built their lives on it, demonstrating what this passage talks about." Have kids form pairs to discuss the following questions:

★ What are some things we tend to build our lives on?
★ How much time have you spent in prayer in the last twenty-four hours?
★ What weaknesses does this passage point out in your prayer life?
★ What are ways you could strengthen your prayer life?
★ What do you commit to do to seek to strengthen your prayer life this week?

EIGHT

The Plymouth Settlement

If the Pilgrims thought the journey across the Atlantic was hard, they would soon find out that the difficulties they had faced in the ship were nothing compared to the hardships of the winter ahead. Only two people died on the *Mayflower,* but over half of the group would die that first winter. Would their faith waver? Would they give up their dependence on prayer?

The Pilgrims were not about to turn away from God now. And they would find that he was there, providing for their needs and guiding them through the rough spots. In the next couple of years, God's hand of provision would be evident in many ways. But it was especially seen in three remarkable events that clearly illustrate the Pilgrims' dependence on prayer. Let's look at each one.

THE RIGHT SETTLEMENT
The Pilgrims' approach to starting a settlement was the opposite of that of the Jamestown colonist. Remember how the Jamestown colonists rushed to shore at the nearest harbor and began unloading cargo as fast as they could? Their goal was to get settled and search for gold.

The Pilgrims, on the other hand, did not start their settlement at the closest and easiest place. The Pilgrims always started out with prayer. They had brought along a thirty-foot sailing boat called a shallop, with which they could explore the shoreline for the best place to land. It took the ship's carpenter three weeks to assemble the shallop.

In the meantime, several men rowed ashore to look around. The Pilgrims called this trip "The First Discovery." While there, they found a vegetable they had never seen before. The food, of course, was corn, the main staple of the Indian diet. Corn would become a lifesaver for the Pilgrim band. God had shown them the first step in the answer to their prayers for food during the winter that had already descended on the countryside.

As soon as the shallop was caulked and trimmed, Miles Standish, ten of the men, and a few sailors headed out to explore the coastline. During this exploratory trip, they encountered a group of Indians. In a journal written by William Bradford and Edward Winslow, they described the encounter:

> Presently, all of the sudden, they heard a great and strange cry, which they knew to be the same voices they [had] heard in the night, though they varied their notes, and one of their company, being abroad, came running in and cried, "Indians, Indians!" and withal, arrows came flying in amongst them . . . two muskets were discharged at them, and two more [men] stood ready in the entrance of their rendezvous, but were commanded not to shoot till they could take full aim at them. . . . The cry of the Indians was dreadful. . . . Yet by the especial providence of God, none of [their arrows] either hit or hurt us, though many came close by us and on every side of us, and some coats which were hung up in our barricado were shot through and through. So, after we had given God thanks

for our deliverance . . . we went on our journey and called this place "The First Encounter" [a name it bears to this day].[1]

They continued on their journey in search of a good harbor that Robert Coppin, the pilot, had seen in a previous journey to the New World. Again God intervened. He had a better site prepared for them. He guided them to it by sending a storm. Bradford writes:

> The sea became very rough, and they broke their rudder, and it was as much as two men could do to steer her with a couple of oars. But their pilot bade them be of good cheer, for he saw the harbor. But the storm increasing, and night drawing on, they bore what sail they could to get in, while they could see. But herewith they broke their mast in three pieces, and their sail fell overboard in a very grown sea, so as they had like to have been [wrecked]. Yet by God's mercy, they recovered themselves, and having the [tide] with them struck into the harbor.[2]

To avoid running ashore, everyone began rowing as fast as they could. Finally, they found shelter on a small island that seemed to appear out of nowhere. Everyone was saved.

As the sun came up on Monday morning, God's provision became clear to them. The island was in the middle of a natural harbor that was deep enough to admit ships twice the size of the *Mayflower!* When they explored the mainland, they found rich soil and a gentle slope just right for a settlement. Four spring-fed creeks gurgled nearby. The water was the best they had ever tasted. There was even a cleared area for planting crops.

Why was this ideal place so available, just waiting for them? Later they discovered that this area had belonged to the

Patuxet Indians, who were a hostile tribe that killed most white men who stepped ashore. Four years earlier, a mysterious illness had swept through the tribe, killing every member. The neighboring Indians believed that this devastation was the work of a supernatural spirit, so they wouldn't enter the area.

God had sent storms that blew the *Mayflower* two hundred miles off course, bringing them to the coast of Massachusetts. Then, through this latest storm, God provided a safe harbor for this little band of devout settlers who lived by the power of prayer. And in the process, a perfect site for their settlement was discovered.

What excitement and prayers of thanksgiving rang from the ship when the explorers returned with the news of their find. They decided to call their new settlement Plymouth because Plymouth was the last town they had left in the native country, and they had received many kindnesses from Christians there.

They anchored in the harbor on December 21, 1620, and on the twenty-third, they went ashore. At last they were in the New World. The Pilgrims had begun their long journey by kneeling in prayer and asking God's blessing. They ended it on the sands of Cape Cod, once again kneeling to thank God for a safe landing.

They began building the settlement by laying out the main street. Their only tools were axes, and the cold weather slowed their progress. Realizing that they couldn't raise enough homes to provide shelter for everyone, they asked Captain Jones to keep the *Mayflower* at Plymouth as long as possible. Long before this, Captain Jones had become an admirer of these humble Pilgrims, so he agreed to keep the ship in the harbor until spring.

As the winter progressed, one by one the Pilgrims began to sicken and die. They had been exposed to the cold and damp and were weak from the journey, and their bodies began to give out. Bradford described this sad time:

> That which was most sad and lamentable was that in two or three months time half of their company died, especially in January and February, being the depth of winter, and wanting houses and other comforts; being infected with scurvy and other diseases, which this long voyage and their unaccommodate condition had brought upon them. They died, sometimes two or three on a day. . . and of the times of most distress six or seven sound persons.[3]

The Massachusetts winter of 1620–21 was harsh. Six died in December and eight in January. By February the death rate more than doubled to seventeen. March brought about thirteen deaths. Altogether, forty-seven died. But this did not make the Pilgrims forget God or become bitter. As the physical conditions deteriorated, they prayed more fervently. Unlike the Jamestown Colony, there was no complaining or fighting. Instead, they drew closer to each other. They continued to meet every Sunday to hear William Brewster preach. Inspired by the Pilgrims' faith, the sailors joined them for worship.

A HELPER SENT BY GOD

When everything looked hopeless, God sent his second provision. It was a man he had been preparing for many years to help the Pilgrims learn how to survive in this rugged new country. In the spring, the Pilgrims' prayers were answered in an unusual way. Bradford wrote:

> About the 16th of March [1621], a certain Indian came boldly amongst them and spoke to them in broken English. . . . His name was Samoset. He told them also of another Indian

whose name was Squanto, a native of this place, who had been in England and could speak better English than himself. . . . About four or five days after, came . . . the aforesaid Squanto. . . . [He] continued with them and was their interpreter and was a special instrument sent of God for their good beyond their expectation.[4]

Squanto's story is fascinating. Fifteen years earlier, Squanto had been taken captive by sea captain George Weymouth. He and four other Indians were shipped back to England and taught English. He spent the next nine years in England; then he was brought back to the New World as an interpreter by Captain Thomas Dermer. But once back near his homeland, Squanto jumped ship and arrived in Plymouth just six months ahead of the Pilgrims. What a shock and great disappointment it must have been for him to arrive at the Patuxet land to find the bones of his tribesmen and their dilapidated homes. He was the only person left from his tribe! After many days of wandering, he came upon the Wampanoag Indian camp. After hearing his story, they took pity on him and allowed him to stay.

Massassoit, chief of the Wampanoag tribe, was also a godsend for the Pilgrims. He was a peace-loving man who, with Squanto's help, signed an important peace treaty with the Pilgrims that lasted until 1675. It read as follows:

1. That neither he nor any of his, should injure or hurt any of their people.
2. That if any of his did hurt any of theirs, he should send the offender, that they might punish him.
3. That if anything were taken away from any of theirs, he should cause it to be restored; and they should do like to his.

4. If any did unjustly war against him, they would aid him, if any did war against them he should aid them.[5]

Compare this relationship with the treachery used by John Smith and the Jamestown colonists.

When Massasoit and his warriors left, Squanto stayed on. He showed the colonists how to catch eels for food by squashing them out of the mud with their feet. He also showed them how to stalk deer, plant pumpkins, collect maple syrup, and find good herbs for food and medicine. But he made three even greater contributions that ensured their survival.

First, he taught them how to plant corn and fertilize it with fish. The wheat and grains they brought from England were not suitable for this area. Corn would be their food staple for years to come.

Second, Squanto helped them start harvesting beaver pelts. Beaver were plentiful in the creeks and woods and were in high demand in Europe. Originally, the Pilgrims had planned on making money by fishing the coast, but pelts would provide a better income to pay debts and buy supplies.

Third, he served as an interpreter for the colonists in their dealings with other Indian tribes. No wonder the Pilgrims called Squanto "a special instrument sent by God."

After the first spring and summer, the Pilgrims reaped a bountiful harvest. They believed that God had provided for them far beyond their expectations. They were also grateful to Squanto, Massasoit, and the Wampanoag Indians, so in October, Plymouth governor William Bradford declared a holiday to celebrate the first harvest with prayer and feasting. The Pilgrims invited Massasoit to the feast. He arrived with ninety people! The Pilgrims hadn't planned on feeding that many hungry appetites! But the Indians brought five deer. They all played games together and participated in shooting contests, foot races, and wrestling matches. The celebration lasted for three days and was the inspiration for our annual Thanksgiving holiday.[6]

The Pilgrims practiced true thanksgiving. They thanked God for providing for all their needs, for keeping them safe, and for their friendship with the Indians. They also thanked him for taking some of their group home to be with him. What an example for us! In good circumstances and in tragedies, they believed God's sovereign will was the perfect plan for them.

MIRACLE OF RAIN

The third provision God gave in answer to prayer was rain. In the summer of 1623, a severe drought occurred, which lasted twelve weeks. About the same time, the *Fortune* arrived from England, dropping off sixty more colonists at Plymouth. But neither the original settlers nor the newcomers showed much Christian charity toward each other. Both sides refused to share their provisions. Governor Bradford was appalled. He ordered a public Day of Prayer that lasted for nine uninterrupted hours. Edward Winslow described the story in his journal:

> There scarce fell any rain, so that the stalk of that [planting which] was first set, began to send forth the ear before it came to half growth, and that which was later, not like to yield any at all, both blade and stalk hanging the head and changing the color in such a manner as we judged it utterly dead. Our beans also ran not up according to their wonted manner, but stood at a stay, many being parched away, as though they had been scorched before the fire. Now were our hopes overthrown, and we discouraged, our joy turned into mourning . . . be-

cause, God which hitherto had been our only shield and supporter, now seemed in His anger to arm Himself against us. And who can withstand the fierceness of His wrath?

These and the like considerations moved not only every good man privately to enter into examination with his own estate between God and his conscience, and so to humiliation before Him, but also to humble ourselves together before the Lord by fasting and prayer. To that end, a day was appointed by public authority, and set apart from all other employments.[7]

If you had been in Plymouth during that time, would you have reacted to this test with fasting and prayer? Often we do exactly the opposite when things begin to go wrong. We blame God or people around us. But these Pilgrims humbled themselves before God and set aside a day to examine their own lives. Everyone did this, not just a chosen few.

Edward Winslow continues with the rest of the drama:

O the mercy of our God, who was as ready to hear, as we were to ask! For though in the morning, when we assembled together, the heavens were as clear and the drought as like to continue as it ever was, yet (our exercise continuing some eight or nine hours) before our departure, the weather was overcast, the clouds gathered on all sides. On the next morning distilled such soft, sweet and moderate showers of rain, continuing some fourteen days and mixed with such seasonable weather, as it was hard to say whether our withered corn or drooping affections were most quickened or revived, such was the bounty and goodness of God![8]

Moderate rain showers continued for fourteen days, ending all signs of the drought. The result was an abundant harvest for the Pilgrims. The Indians, whose rain dances had failed them, were astonished by the greatness of the Pilgrims' God.

They must have marveled at the humble attitude of these Pilgrims as they entreated God. Edward Winslow spoke of these neighbors as they watched the Lord provide:

> All of them admired the goodness of our God towards us, that wrought so great a change in so short a time, showing the difference between their conjuration [rain dances] and our invocation on the name of God for rain, theirs being mixed with such storms and tempests, as sometimes, instead of doing them good, it layeth the corn flat on the ground, to their prejudice, but ours in so gentle and seasonable manner, as they never observed the like.[9]

And again, a day of thanksgiving was held to praise God.

So far, we have seen the Pilgrims remain steadfast in their faith through persecution in England, through harsh conditions and storms while on the *Mayflower,* and in sickness and death during that first winter.

ANOTHER IMPORTANT LESSON

Another lesson the Pilgrims learned was about communal property. The contract they had signed in England forced socialism on the colony. All property was owned by the company that financed the voyage. So initially the colonists held all things in common and contributed their goods and produce to a common storehouse to be rationed out as needed. Any extra produce went to the investors.

But the system failed in the spring of 1623, and after much prayer, Governor Bradford instituted a system of free enterprise, giving families their own land for a second planting and allowing them to keep, barter, or sell what they produced. An amazing thing happened. Let's take a walk with one family on the way to their garden plot. . . .

In the before-dawn darkness of the room, Sarah helped her two little daughters pull on their long brown stockings and dark petticoats. She then threw brush on the red coals in the fireplace to make the fire blaze higher. She laid out the table with a clean tablecloth, bowls, and spoons. When William came in with fresh, foamy goat's milk, they all sat at the heavy wooden table. William led them in prayer; then Sarah dished up heaps of pottage.

As soon as the sun began to spread its warmth over the spiked fences in the yard, the four left the house and walked down the crunchy gravel of the main road. They passed by the unpainted houses, which now had touches of orange light splashed on the gray roofs. The spring breezes wafted off the harbor, riffling the girls' skirts.

William stopped to talk to a neighbor who was chopping wood. "John, how are you this beautiful morning?"

"Just fine," John answered.

Sarah patiently listened to the men talk.

"Isn't it something? Bradford and the others giving us twice as much land to plant?"

"Yes, that is an answer to my prayers."

William stroked his long beard, then laughed. "I'm sure the corn will grow better on the private plots than on the communal land."

John's deep baritone rolled. "Yes, my good man. I think so, too."

Then William and Sarah and the girls went on to work in their now-sunny patch of garden just beyond the village. . . .[10]

The Pilgrims had learned a valuable lesson—private ownership creates prosperity. The women now joined the men in the fields, along with their little ones. No one had to be coerced to work. The colony soon had more food than they could use. They began trading their surplus with the Indians for beaver pelts!

These hardy Pilgrims gave us many good principles for the foundation of our country, such as establishing friendships across racial lines, working together to meet a common goal, and giving people private ownership to create prosperity. Most important, they showed us the incredible power of ceaseless prayer for developing good leadership. Throughout their long struggle to obtain freedom of worship, the center of their community was prayer! What an example for us!

For Discussion and Reflection

Adult Discussion
Bring four knotted rags. Have group members sit in a circle, and pass the four knotted rags to four members of the group. Explain that the rags they hold are "Thanksgiving Starters." The rags can be tossed to any person in the circle, and that person must tell one thing he or she is thankful for. Then he or she must toss the rag to someone else. When people begin having trouble thinking of things to be thankful for, stop the activity. Ask:

* How did it feel to give thanks to God?
* How was our thanksgiving similar to that of the Pilgrims?
* What did the Pilgrims have to be thankful for?

Read Psalm 100, and form groups of four to discuss the following questions:

★ Why should thanking God be an essential part of our every-
day lives?
★ What can we learn from the Pilgrims that will help us be
more thankful?
★ What will you do this week to exhibit more thankfulness to
God?

Have everyone read Psalm 100 again, this time aloud and in
unison as a prayer of thanksgiving to God.

Youth Discussion

On separate slips of paper, write each of the following words
and put them into a basket: *family, school, church, God, myself.* Make enough duplicate sets for each class member to
have at least one slip.

Have kids sit in a circle. Ask someone to read Psalm 100
aloud. Ask:

★ How did the Pilgrims apply these verses in their lives?
★ What things could have kept them from being thankful?

Have each person draw one slip of paper and name one
thing he or she is thankful for in that area. For example, if *family* is drawn, he or she could say, "I am thankful because my
mom works hard to give me the things I need." After all the
slips of paper have been drawn, discuss these questions:

★ What were you thinking when your turn to draw was coming up?
★ Why do you think it can be hard to think of things for which
we can thank God and others?
★ What does giving thanks do for a person's attitude?

★ What does giving thanks do for a person's relationship with God?

★ How can you make giving thanks a more important part of your day?

Have the kids read Psalm 100 aloud together as a prayer of thanksgiving for what God does for us.

NINE

The
Puritans Arrive

Do you remember the difference between the Pilgrims (Separatists) and the Puritans? They had different views of how to change the Church of England. The Pilgrims saw no hope of changing the church from within, so they separated from the church, but the Puritans pledged themselves to purify the church from within. They believed their Spirit-filled example would turn the church leadership back to the New Testament model.

Unfortunately, the harder the Puritans pushed for reform, the more the Anglican bishops dug in their heels. As the years passed, the Puritan movement gathered momentum among the people as thousands joined their ranks. Some of the most influential and educated people in England belonged to their group, yet they began to be ridiculed by their own countrymen.

James I instigated a movement to resist reform that made life unbearable for the Separatists. The Puritans, however, didn't feel the sting of persecution until Charles I came into power. He appointed William Laud as Bishop of London. Laud started a campaign to promote clergy who were not from the Puritan camp. He also began purging Puritan ministers from

England. Branding and life imprisonment became the punishment for criticizing church policies; therefore, Puritan sermons were outlawed.

Within a short while, life became hard for the Puritans. They faced a dilemma. The only solution to the persecution was to go underground and separate from the Church of England, but this way out was against their beliefs.

THE INCREDIBLE SOLUTION

Then an incredible solution surfaced. Why not reform the church from thousands of miles away in America? They could still be loyal to England and the church, but they'd be far enough away to purify it without interference! The Puritan leaders began praying for God to lead them.

And God showed his mighty hand in answering their prayers. In March 1629, a royal charter was granted to the Massachusetts Bay Company, in which the Puritans had been led to invest. The Puritans were more than ready to move to America. They felt that this was God's plan and that they would make a mark on history. Today we know that they were absolutely right because they would play an important part in establishing an American democracy based on biblical principles.

God would use many Puritan men and women to build his church in America. One man who exemplifies the kind of influence the Puritans had was John Winthrop.

IN SERVICE TO THE LORD

John Winthrop was probably the most well-known Puritan. He helped start the Puritan settlement in America and was the strength and leadership for this new colony for years.

John was born into a wealthy family at Groton, England. At

age fifteen, he went to Trinity College at Cambridge. When he turned seventeen, he married and held the position of justice of the peace. In the world's view, he should have been extremely happy. He was well educated, very intelligent, had a promising career, and was very wealthy. But Winthrop was miserable. He attended church every Sunday, studied theology, and was considered very devout, but the emptiness lingered.

That's when he began reading the work of William Perkins, a Puritan writer. Winthrop began to realize that even though he had done many good things, he really deserved damnation and that his destination was hell. He wrote, "I acknowledged my unfaithfulness and pride of heart, and turned again to my God, and watching my heart and ways. O my God forsake me not."[1] This was the kind of conversion to the faith that every Puritan regarded as essential to eternal life.

By the age of forty, Winthrop was one of the more respected Puritan leaders and was chosen to lead the first group to America. Winthrop battled this responsibility. Was it God's will for him to go? He prayed and debated his decision. He made a list of pros and cons. In the end, he decided it was God's will for him to serve the Lord in America. Winthrop and a few others consented to take control of the Massachusetts Bay Company and invest in it. The company agreed to the following terms:

1. Officers of the company would be selected from the immigrants to America.
2. The stockholders would sell all the stock to the settlers.
3. The colonists would take the king's charter on the voyage.

The future colonists also wrote this statement, which allowed them to be an independent commonwealth:

It is fully and faithfully agreed amongst us . . . that . . . we will be ready in our persons . . . to embark for the said plantation by the first of March . . . to pass the seas (under God's protection) to inhabit and continue New England. Provided always, that before the last September next, the whole government together with the patent for the said plantation be first by an order of the court legally transferred . . . [and will] remain with us . . . upon the said plantation."[2]

THE EXODUS BEGINS

A group of two hundred colonists was sent in advance to America to prepare for future ships by building a settlement called Salem. By February 1630, the *Arabella* and the other ships were ready to sail. Winthrop stated:

We are a company, . . . professing ourselves fellow members of Christ. . . . The end is to improve our lives and to more service to the Lord . . . that ourselves and our posterity may be better preserved from the common corruptions in this world. . . . We must love brotherly without dissimulation; we must love one another with pure heart fervently.[3]

John Cotton, one of the most well-known preachers in England, gave a sermon as a farewell to many members of his congregation. He warned the colonists that if they didn't follow God's will, America would be not a land of milk and honey but a desolate land that would cause them much agony.[4]

On March 23, 1630, one thousand Puritans traveled to New England in four well-stocked ships. Unlike the journey of the Pilgrims, this voyage was a calm, peaceful trip. God protected the seafarers on this trip and the 198 journeys made by other Puritans to New England. Great Atlantic storms often destroyed ships in the 1600s, but during the Puritans' exodus, only one ship was lost!

Seventy-two days after she left England, the *Arabella* floated into the harbor of Salem. When the people came ashore, they met the men of the Puritan congregation who had arrived two years earlier to build homes for later arrivals. Instead of a flourishing town, Winthrop saw huts and canvas shelters. The small group of people that came to meet him were thin, ragged, and dirty.

Why was everything so desolate? In a private meeting with John Endecott, the acting governor, Winthrop discovered that of the 266 men who had come over, only 85 remained. More than 80 had died, and the rest had gone back to England. Many of the remaining colonists planned to return to England also.

As Winthrop rode in the boat back to the *Arabella* to spend the night, his heart must have been heavy and troubled. This was not what he had expected. He must have felt that all their plans were grinding to a halt. He had spent months dreaming of this moment. Despair hung heavy in the air.

But Winthrop didn't wallow in feelings of hopelessness. He spent the night writing A Model of Christian Charity, a document that ranks in importance with the Mayflower Compact. These two important documents were both written in times of uncertainty and despair and were proof of their writers' confidence that God would not leave his people desolate. Prayer played a vital role in the birth of these documents. This is what John Winthrop wrote:

> This love among Christians is a real thing, not imaginary . . . as
> absolutely necessary to the [well] being of the Body of Christ,
> [as] the sinews and other ligaments of a natural body are to the

[well] being of that body. . . . We are a company, professing ourselves fellow members of Christ, [and thus] we ought to account ourselves knit together by this bond of love. . . .

Thus stands the cause between God and us: we are entered into covenant with Him for this work. We have taken out a Commission; the Lord hath given us leave to draw our own articles. . . . If the Lord shall please to hear us, and bring us in peace to the place we desire, then hath He ratified this Covenant and sealed our Commission [and] will expect a strict performance of the Articles contained in it. But if we shall neglect the observance of these Articles . . . the Lord will surely break out in wrath against us.

Now the only way to avoid this shipwreck and to provide for our posterity, is to follow the counsel of Micah, to do justly, to love mercy, to walk humbly with our God. For this end, we must be knit together in his work as one man. . . . We must hold a familiar commerce together in all meekness, gentleness, patience, and liberality. We must delight in each other, make one another's condition our own, rejoice together, mourn together, labor and suffer together, always having before our eyes our Commission and Community in this work, as members of the same body. So shall we keep the unity of the Spirit in the body of peace. . . .

We shall find that the God of Israel is among us, when ten of us shall be able to resist a thousand of our enemies, when He shall make us a praise and glory, that men of succeeding plantations shall say, "The Lord make it like that of New England." For we must consider that we shall be as a City Upon a Hill.[5]

HARD WORK AND FAITH

In the next days, Winthrop and the other new settlers revived the dying colony. He called upon everyone to work and help each other. This was a bit unusual because in those days gentlemen did not do manual labor (remember Jamestown Colony?). They had brought along their servants for this. But Winthrop, one of the wealthiest, led by example by rolling up his sleeves and plunging in.

A seventeenth-century report described the scene this way:

> (So soon) as Mr. Winthrop was landed, perceiving what misery was like to ensue through their idleness, he presently fell to work with his own hands, and thereby so encouraged the rest that there was not an idle person then to be found in the whole plantation. And whereas the Indians said they [the newcomers] would shortly return as fast as they came, now they admired to see in what short time they had housed themselves and planted corn sufficient for their subsistence.[6]

One of the reasons Winthrop was able to turn the tide of despair into courage in Salem was the Puritans' dependence on prayer. They prayed before bed and when they got up in the morning. They prayed to prepare for the Sabbath, then prayed between services. They called for congregational fasts and thanksgiving services on special days. In addition, many people set aside a day for personal fasting and prayer. At night they thanked God for his blessings, and during the day they repented of their sins. In the morning they thanked God for their life and their salvation.

Families spent time in prayer together, usually in the morning before the day's work began, before meals, and in the evening. Author Charles Hambrick-Stowe describes their prayers:

> The prayers reflected a cycle of death and rebirth, evening and morning. In the evening, families confessed their sins, praying "O let us feel the Power of Christ's Death killing sin in our mortal bodies." In the morning, they gave thanks for God's

grace that "renews all thy mercies upon us" and praised God because he had "elected, created, redeemed, called, justified, and sanctified" the saints.[7]

The Pilgrims also had neighborhood prayer meetings. Everyone was included, from the minister to the servants. Puritans privately wrote their hearts' cries to God in devout diaries.

One of the greatest contributions the Puritans made was a result of their emphasis on freely spoken prayers. The Puritans were not the first to use spontaneous prayer, but they were the first to use these prayers in the public worship of their entire colony. Later, entire denominations followed their example.

Still, that first year proved hard. Scurvy attacked many of the new settlers. In September, Winthrop realized that their supplies would not carry them through the winter, so he sent the *Lyon* back to England to buy supplies with his own money. This selfless pattern occurred over and over throughout the years. At times Winthrop supported the colony alone. Because of his generosity, he used up much of his wealth.

A DAY OF PRAYER

By February, everyone was aware of their desperate situation. The leaders declared February 6 a day of humiliation and fasting in which the people would search their hearts for sin and pray for a miracle.

And God provided a miracle. In the book of Isaiah, God promises, "I will answer them before they even call to me. While they are still talking to me about their needs, I will go ahead and answer their prayers!" (Isaiah 65:24, NLT). And that's what happened. On February 5, the day before the fast, the *Lyon* returned with supplies. Now the day of fasting turned to a day of thanksgiving:

Circumstances no longer being appropriate for a fast, the Governor and council ordered a day of Thanksgiving. . . . Such was the deliverance which made a profound impression on the minds of that distressed people. It was recognized as a signal providence of God. About their firesides its story was told by fathers to their children for many a day in praise of the goodness of God and His guardianship over the colony.[8]

God answered their prayers even before they were offered!
These Puritans were an example of Christian devotion, and Winthrop stands above the rest. He willingly gave everything he had to further the cause of Christ. One of the chroniclers of his own day says this of him:

His justice was impartial, his wisdom excellently tempered. . . . His courage made him dare to do right. . . . Accordingly, when the noble design of carrying a colony of Chosen People into an American wilderness was by some eminent persons undertaken, this eminent person was, by the consent of all, chosen for the Moses.[9]

THE MATHER FAMILY

Another Puritan family that stood out from the rest in influence was the Mathers. After losing his position as an Anglican minister, Richard Mather and his family came to Massachusetts. He greatly influenced the government of the New England church. Richard's son, Increase Mather, became one of the most well-known preachers in American history. Like many prayer warriors before him, Increase experienced a time of crisis when he was just thirty-one years old. His reaction was a typical illustration of the prayer life of the Puritans. . . .

Increase woke with a start and sat up in his bed. He could feel fine beads of sweat covering his face and neck. "Not again," he moaned quietly. "How many nights has it been?"

He slipped from under the sheet and quietly left the dark bedroom. In the kitchen, he sat at the table next to an open window. The cool autumn night air fanned his feverish face.

He stared out at the trees gently rustling in the breeze. "Another night of horrible dreams," he said wearily. He watched a sliver of moonlight quiver on his outstretched hand.

What was he afraid of? That his faith was just a delusion. "How can I, pastor of Old North Church, be unsure of my faith? I fear I am going mad."

He knew there was only one thing he could do—pray. He began to quietly cry out to God, tears streaming down his face. "I put my life in your hands," he prayed, as he had done so many times before.

He thought of the tears Old Testament king Hezekiah had shed as he prayed to be cured of a fatal disease. The king had cried out to God, and God had answered miraculously. How Increase loved those old stories.

Gradually a sweet peace began calming his mind. "Surely, the one who comes to God with incessant prayer and fasting and faith will glorify God's name. He would not deny me that mercy."

Finally, his prayers brought complete peace. He resolved once more to trust God no matter what happened. . . .[10]

Increase Mather did remain faithful to God and helped the colonists in many ways. In fact, in 1688 he was sent to England to renegotiate the colony's charter, and he influenced King William for the benefit of the Puritans.

Cotton Mather, grandson of Richard, was also a scholar

who became a preacher. Cotton prayed for many years that God would pour his Spirit out on his people in America.

A NEW KIND OF GOVERNMENT

From the first, the Puritan colony was an experiment. The colonists came with the goal of setting up a new kind of government—one that did nothing to offend God. To do this, they built meetinghouses in every town. Since they believed every person should be able to read the Bible, they had schools for boys and for girls. Within the first ten years, they also built a college. Today we know it as Harvard University.

The Puritans gave our country a good start by worshiping God and depending on prayer through their passionate spiritual life. They conquered the wilderness to establish thriving communities. But their trials weren't over yet. In the next chapter, we'll discover how they carried on their faith over the years and we'll see the prayer miracles they experienced.

For Discussion and Reflection

Adult Discussion

Bring tape, scissors, wrapping paper, and boxes that are similar in size. Form pairs or trios, and give each group these materials. Tell the groups that they'll be wrapping a box but that each person can use only one hand. The other hand must remain behind each participant's back. The trick is to work together to get the job done.

Give the signal to go, and let them wrap. When groups finish, ask:

★ What was difficult about wrapping with one hand?
★ What did you have to do to accomplish your task?
★ How is this like the way the Puritans interacted with each other?

Say, "Winthrop's A Model of Christian Charity said: 'This love among Christians is a real thing, not imaginary . . . as absolutely necessary to the [well] being of the Body of Christ, [as] the sinews and other ligaments of a natural body are to the [well] being of that body. . . . We are a company, professing ourselves fellow members of Christ, [and thus] we ought to account ourselves knit together by this bond of love.'"

Read Ephesians 4:16, and have the groups discuss the following questions:

★ How did the Puritans live out the message of this verse?
★ How can we in this group help each other as members of the body of Christ?
★ What part does prayer play in the growth of the body of Christ?
★ What will you do this week to help build someone else up in love?

Have the groups pray together, asking God to help them work together to serve him this week, building each other up in love.

Youth Discussion

Before class, make a list of five or six things that Americans have a passion for, such as sports, entertainment, or food.

Form groups of three or four. Give each group a large sheet of paper and a marker. Explain that each group is to choose someone to draw things that you will assign. The object is to be the first group to guess what their "artist" is drawing. Tell the artist in each group the first item on your list. Say, "Start," to start the drawing. Stop the action when the first group guesses correctly. Do the same with each item on your list.

When all the words have been drawn, ask:

> ★ How did it feel to be the first to correctly guess an item?
> ★ What did you do to try to help your team win?
> ★ What was your passion in this game?

Form pairs, and have partners discuss the following questions:

> ★ What was the Puritans' passion?
> ★ What do you think the words we guessed represent?
> ★ How do the passions of most Americans compare to the Puritans' passion?

Have pairs report on the previous three questions; then have partners share with each other their answers to the following question. Ask:

> ★ What are some things you personally have a passion for?

Read aloud Psalm 42:1. Ask:

> ★ What does this passage say about the psalmist's passion?
> ★ How can we show more passion for God and his will?

Have people think and pray silently as you say the following: "Take a moment now to reflect on areas in your life that are not being permeated by a passion for God. Talk to God through prayer and ask him to remove the passions in your life that are shutting him out and to help you seek him more fully in your life."

TEN

Trials
of Faith

The Puritans were truly people of prayer. While today most people think of them as joyless people who were obsessed with eradicating sin, this picture is distorted. They did try to lead lives without sin by examining themselves frequently, but they also enjoyed fun and warm times. They had remarkable wisdom and discernment.

The Puritans also had a deep commitment to each other. They welcomed the advice and counsel of their neighbors. You've probably heard the saying "It takes a village to raise a child." The Puritans practiced this years ago, but in a rather different way than what is being advocated today. The Puritans felt that they had answered God's call together, so they worked as a team to build their houses and clear their fields. They thought of their community as a large family and wanted families to be orderly. Authority started in the home, and well-ordered families produced a well-ordered society.

As time went on, the Puritans flourished in New England. Thousands of Puritans left England to settle in New England. God blessed them with good land, plenty of food, and beautiful homes. They lived at peace with the Indians.

ORDINARY PEOPLE, EXTRAORDINARY LIVES

What makes the story of the founding of America so amazing? The fact that the drama didn't play itself out in the courts of kings and the estates of the rich. Instead, God used ordinary people who lived lives of prayer and trusted him for the small and large things they did. Many became pacesetters in their generation.

One such man was John Eliot. Like many other colonists, Eliot was an outcast. Born in England and trained at Cambridge to be a minister, Eliot was converted under the teaching of that great Puritan leader Thomas Hooker. At that point, of course, Eliot's prospects for establishing a ministry with the Church of England vanished. What options did he have? Only one. He sailed to Massachusetts, where he could preach as his conscience directed.

He arrived when the colony was barely two years old. At first, he diligently built his little flock at Roxbury, a small settlement town. He married and settled into his life as a frontier minister. He was a man of many talents who put the Psalms into verse form in a book called *The Bay Psalm Book.* This hymnbook was the first book published in America.

For years, Eliot saw Indians come and go in his little frontier town, but it wasn't until he was forty years old that he began to see the need of evangelizing the native people. How did he receive this vision to reach these people? Eliot's life, like that of most Puritans, was bathed in prayer. Cotton Mather admired his deep devotional life so much that he used Eliot's example as a model for other ministers.[1]

From this change of focus, Eliot pioneered the work of missions in our country. He was far ahead of his time. While others argued over whether or not the Indians should learn English, Eliot pored over the unwritten Algonquin language.

With his Indian helper, Cochenoe, he learned the guttural sounds and voice inflections. Eliot lived by the spirit of which the apostle Paul wrote, "Devote yourselves to prayer with an alert mind and a thankful heart. Don't forget to pray for us, too, that God will give us many opportunities to preach about [Christ]" (Colossians 4:2-3).

Finally, after two years of study, he was ready to preach his first sermon. He found that the Algonquins were deep thinkers who searched for reasons and who listened to the gospel. Many responded to his message with tears of repentance and joy.

Eliot spent the rest of his life working with the Algonquins and became known as "the apostle to the Indians." Eliot's work was steeped in prayer. He wrote, "Prayers and pains through faith in Christ Jesus will do anything."[2] He drilled the children in catechism, preached sermons about God's love, and answered difficult questions. Cotton Mather described his sermons: "His way of *preaching* was very *plain,* so that the very *lambs* might wade into his discourses on those themes where *elephants* might swim."[3]

The converted Algonquins were called "praying Indians." Eliot helped them set up a new community called Natick, where they could own their own land. One of the most unique things he did was translate the entire Bible into the formerly unwritten Algonquin language. Cotton Mather describes Eliot's work:

> With [Cochenoe], and later his replacement, Eliot began the tedious task of analyzing this Indian language. The Algonquian had a habit of compressing complex ideas into extended single words. Eliot would surely have earned the esteem of the thousands of Wycliffe Translators today who are at work in similar linguistic mission around the world.[4]

As the number of praying Indians grew, Eliot trained Indian leaders to evangelize and minister to their own people. That, too, was an idea ahead of its time.

Tragically, the praying Indians suffered terribly during the later part of Eliot's life. When King Philip's War erupted in 1675, the praying Indians were loyal to the British and even helped them fight. Not only were they an answer to Eliot's prayers for their salvation, but they also played an essential part in the war, as we will see later.

But Eliot did not give up helping his Indian friends. He said, "I can do little, yet I am resolved through the grace of Christ, I will never give over the worke [sic], so long as I have legs to go."[5] Eliot was faithful during a time when many others left their faith.

THE BEGINNING OF RELIGIOUS LIBERTY

Two other men also made their mark on the colonies, especially in pioneering for religious liberty. One of them was Roger Williams. A Separatist, Williams had a rocky relationship with the Puritans. When he argued for religious liberty, the Puritan magistrates threatened to deport him. To escape, he wandered in the forests during the winter for fourteen weeks. Eventually he founded a colony in Rhode Island in which he established freedom of religion. The town of Providence became a haven for Anabaptists, Quakers, and others whose beliefs were opposed by the established religions of the day. Rhode Island became the first center for Baptist churches. Although relations were rocky at times, Williams maintained his friendship with the Puritans until the end of his life.

William Penn began his adventure when he received a sizable inheritance from his father. He was a Quaker who had a keen social conscience. The king gave him a huge tract of land in New England. The colony Penn established was a haven for persecuted European Quakers and many other religious refugees. Penn insisted that blacks also be educated and free in his colony.

THE DECLINE

One of the greatest tragedies of the human spirit is that we tend to lose our direction and passion over time. Christians who are on fire for God risk health and life to worship and serve him. But as time goes on, they become spiritually complacent or their children do not carry on the spiritual heritage. As a result, prayers lose their power and miracles decrease.

The Puritans were not immune to this malady. As new generations arose that had never faced persecution or deep trials, their commitment to God began to fade. They didn't understand the strong faith of their parents and grandparents. Complacency set in. Most of them still went to church, but their minds were on their work and possessions. They began to "play church."

The influx of new settlers also affected colonial spiritual life. They quickly became prosperous and just as quickly forgot God. A sense of spiritual malaise arose among the people. Many no longer prayed or attended church, and a Christian regard for neighbors was seen as foolhardy. Therefore, the Puritans no longer had that strong communal unity, and their children were not being converted into the faith. Deeply concerned, William Bradford wrote:

> No man now [1632] thought he could live, except he had cattle and great deal of ground to keep them; all [were] striving to increase their stocks. By which means they were scattered all over

the bay quickly, and the town in which they lived compactly till now was left very thin and in short time almost desolate. And if this had been all, it [would have] been less, though too much. But the church must also be divided, and those that had lived so long together in Christian comfort and fellowship must now part and suffer many divisions. . . . And this, I fear, will be the ruin of New England, at least of the churches of God there, and will provoke the Lord's displeasure against them.[6]

In the years that followed, the folly of spiritual apathy became apparent through a series of events. The land was overcome by floods, plagues of insects, and diseases. One example was a rain of caterpillars that swept through much of New England in 1646. Winthrop described the devastation:

Great harm was done in corn (especially wheat and barley) in this month by a caterpillar, like a black worm about an inch and a half long. They eat up first the blades of the stalk, then they eat up the tassels, whereupon the ear withered. It was believed by divers good observers that they fell in a great thunder shower, for divers yards and other bare places where not one of them was to be seen an hour before, were presently after the shower almost covered with them besides grass places where they were not so easily discerned. They did the most harm in the southern parts, as in Rhode Island, etc. and in the eastern parts in their Indian corn.[7]

These disasters soon united many Christians who were awakened to their need to rely upon God. They began to seek him through intense prayer. One colonist wrote in his diary about one miracle that happened as a result of prayer:

[They] poured out their fervent prayers unto the God of heaven for their deliverance; immediately hereupon flocks of

birds have arriv'd that have devoured the devourers, and pre-
serv'd those particular fields, when others have been horribly
wasted.[8]

Winthrop himself wrote, "In divers places the churches
kept a day of humiliation, and presently after, the caterpillars
vanished away."[9]

But unfortunately most people continued in their self-
sufficient ways. Spiritual malaise and moral decline continued
to grow and impact the colonies. Unusual hardships continued
to occur. In 1670, the government of Massachusetts conducted a special investigation to determine why the people
were being afflicted with sickness, poor crops, and shipping
losses.

KING PHILIP'S WAR

In 1675, the colonies were beset by Indian attacks. Up to this
time, the Indians had been involved in tribal rivalries but had
lived at peace with the Englishmen. They also had an awe for
the God of the Puritans because of all the prayer miracles they
had witnessed. Their leader was Massassoit, who had helped
the Pilgrims and who had the wisdom to live peaceably with
these new settlers. But in 1675 his son, Metacomet (the settlers had given him the Christian name Philip), assumed the
leadership. He was well known for his hatred of Christianity.

The relationship between the British and the Indians deteriorated under Philip. He was angered at the many warriors
who were being pulled away from tribal worship into the
Christian faith. This hatred was fueled by the medicine men
who felt threatened by this new religion. With their support,
Philip organized an attack on the settlers.

An Indian named John Sassamon, who was an educated

man, had once been an aide for Philip. Eventually he left Philip, became a model Christian convert, and was given the task of teaching other Indians about the Christian faith. He answered the call for an Indian preacher at Nemasket, an Indian village located close to Philip. Because of his conversion, he was considered by Philip and his conspirators to be the vilest turncoat.

John Sassamon caught wind of the uprising Philip was planning. Risking his life, he went to the governor of Plymouth and his council and warned them of the impending attack. They took his message very lightly until he turned up under the ice in the river, murdered. But someone had witnessed the crime from the top of the hill and was able to identify the three assailants. One was the chief lieutenant to Philip.

A trial was set in June with two juries, one comprised of settlers and the other of the wisest Indians in the colony. Both juries came up with the same verdict—guilty. The three defendants denied this charge all the way to their hangings. As the last one was hung, his rope broke, which frightened him so much that he confessed to the murders. He was then re-hanged.

After the trial, large groups of warriors on the warpath began roaming the countryside. Many settlers in outlying areas moved into the populated areas for safety. For three weeks nothing violent occurred. Then it happened. The settlement of Swansea was attacked, and everyone was slaughtered. The streets were strewn with dismembered corpses of men, women, and children.

Settlement after settlement was attacked. New England was unprepared for the hostilities. Local militia were formed, only to be destroyed by ambushes. The British soldiers were used to fighting not in the woods but in the open British style.

Only after every tribe had put on their war paint were the settlers ready to humble themselves and heed God's warning. Finally the churches filled with people who hadn't attended in years, as the colonists humbled themselves and confessed their individual sins. The colonists who united in prayer and repentance, recognizing their true helplessness apart from God, were often miraculously spared.

So far Concord had not been attacked by the Indians because they feared the power of the minister, Edward Bulkely. In fact, an Indian chronicle said, "We no prosper if we burn Concord. The Great Spirit love that people. He tell us not to go there. They have a great man there. He great pray."[10]

Brookfield was another town noted for its religious strength. When the Indians attacked Brookfield, God provided miraculous answers to prayer to save the town. First, the townspeople were all able to get safely into the blockhouse and hold off the Indians with muskets. Then one man was able to slip through the Indian warriors without being detected to go for help, despite the Indians' superb tracking skills. He made it to Marlborough, thirty miles away, where Major Samuel Willard billeted his troops. We pick up the story back in Brookfield. . . .

The situation was desperate. That's why Jeremy was sent out for more water. As he ran with his wooden bucket through the center of the blockade, his heart pounded. Although he was only ten years old, he knew what he had to do. He could see the men crouching behind the walls of the catwalk. How could the men fight when they had so few weapons?

He finally reached the small storehouse near the blockade wall and ducked inside the door. He smelled the pungent odor of smoked ham and dried fish.

It took a moment for his eyes to adjust to the dusky light. He scanned the heaps of stored food and rows of barrels. There they were—the water barrels. He lifted the lid on the nearest one and dipped out water into his water bucket. Although the sight of the clear liquid made him thirsty, he turned and ran with the bucket, carefully holding it ahead of himself so he wouldn't slosh the precious liquid.

When he got to the other side of the blockade, he saw something that made him stop in his tracks. Arrows flaming with streaks of fire whizzed high into the air. Some landed harmlessly in the dirt and spent their heat, but others hit their mark on the blockade roofs.

Jeremy ran again. He crashed through the door of the house where his mother and brothers were huddled with many others. They were still praying, and Jeremy could see the earnestness in their faces. "The roof's on fire!" he yelled.

Two men grabbed a ladder and climbed onto the rafters. "Hand me an ax!" one of them shouted down. Jeremy handed up an ax, handle first. The men began cutting holes in the roof. Jeremy handed up his bucket, and they threw the water onto the fire and smothered the flames.

Jeremy peeked out the door. All over the blockade, people were dousing fires. Someone ran up to him. "Jeremy, we need more water. You boys go, too," the man commanded, pointing at Jeremy's brothers. The three of them ran back to the storehouse. When they returned with buckets of water, someone directed them to the ladder leading up to the catwalk. Jeremy carried two buckets up along the north side of the wall.

When he stepped off the ladder onto the walkway, he handed off the buckets. Then he peeked over the wall. Shivers crawled up his spine. The Indians were setting afire a huge stack of hay they had piled against the corner of the blockade.

Immediately, men began pouring buckets of water onto the

crackling fire. More buckets were handed up and poured down. Soon a pall of black smoke hung over the haystack. The fire was dead!

Jeremy noticed that in the distance the Indians were building something. "What's that?" he asked a man standing next to him. The man's eyes followed Jeremy's pointed finger. Suddenly, the mysterious object blazed. The Indians began pushing it toward the blockade gate.

"It's a moving torch!" the man gasped. "They're going to ram it into our gate!"

Everyone on the walkway stared. There was nothing they could do. Many began praying. Without God's help, their blockade would be burned to the ground and they would be at the mercy of the warring Indians. Jeremy prayed, too, but he couldn't take his eyes off that blaze moving ever closer.

Then, without warning, the skies opened up and rain poured down, sheeting off the wooden walls and running down Jeremy's neck. Through the heavy deluge, Jeremy could see the rolling blaze flutter, then die. All that was left were a few red-hot embers, but then they too washed out.

Prayers of thanksgiving rose up all around Jeremy. He looked up to heaven, letting the cold rain wash his dusty face. . . .[11]

Days later, Major Willard and his troops rode in ready to fight. After a hot skirmish, the Indian warriors fled into the woods.

A TURN FOR THE BETTER
Spirit-filled preaching and miracles like the one at Brookfield caused the settlers to jam the churches. They listened to every word. People fell to their knees and confessed their sins. Soon

hardly a man or woman remained in New England who was not searching daily for unconfessed sin. The repentance was considered the major defense in the war effort.

About this time, the outcome of the war was miraculously changed. Who turned the tide of the war? The praying Indians. These Christians became scouts and taught the settlers how to fight in the woods and under cover with mobility. These tactics not only enabled the settlers to defeat the warring Indians but they would also prove invaluable a hundred years later in the fight for American independence.

The settlers began to defeat the Indians, who surrendered in small bands, then in masses. The war ended when Philip himself was defeated at the Wampanoag settlement of New Hope.

Tragically, even the Indian uprising didn't have a long-term impact on the spiritual apathy of most of the colonies. Most colonists still maintained a fierce independence from God. At the same time, the calamities continued. Fires ravaged Boston in 1676 and again in 1679, and by 1685 the New England colonies had lost their representative assemblies. They were brought under the complete domination of England.

THE NOTORIOUS SALEM WITCH TRIALS

As time went on, the spiritual decline in the New World continued its downward spiral. Soon entire towns became infected with occultism, witchcraft, and demonic activity. Now, instead of turning to God for help with the problems of their society, people commonly turned to white magic, black magic, hexes, and superstition.

As a result, witchcraft hysteria swept through the colonies. Europe had already executed thousands for this crime. The colonists followed suit. Countless trials were held to determine whether each accused person was guilty of witchcraft. Mary Eastey was one of them. She was accused of practicing witchcraft by a number of young girls. They claimed she was causing them to have fits and was at times striking them dumb. They also said she was forcing them to sign the devil's book.

When Mary was asked what she would answer to these charges, she said, "I can say before Christ I am free. . . . I will say it, if it was my last time, I am clear of this sin."[12] But the court decided that there was enough evidence to bring her to trial.

Mary was indicted by the grand jury, then tried by a special Court of Oyer and Terminer. The jury returned a guilty verdict, and she was sentenced to be hanged. While waiting for her hanging date in jail, she sent a petition to the court. It stated:

> [I] doth humbly beg of you to take it into your Judicious and Pious consideration, that your poor and humble petitioner, knowing my own innocency (blessed be the Lord for it) . . . I petition to your honors not for my own life, for I know I must die, and my appointed time is set; but the Lord He knows it is, if it be possible, that no more innocent blood be shed, which undoubtedly cannot be avoided in the way and course you go in. . . . The Lord in His infinite mercy direct you in this great work, if it be His blessed will, that innocent blood be not shed; I would humbly beg of you, that your honors would be pleased to examine some of those confessing witches.[13]

She was hanged on September 22, 1692, with seven others. But her words echoed the feelings of many of the colonists. They knew that this hysteria had to stop. Responsible clergymen objected to the witch-hunt and pointed out the erroneous testimony of the accusers. But this did not stop the trials, and in 1692, twenty executions occurred in Salem alone.

Finally, the clergy prevailed upon Massachusetts governor William Phips to stop this madness. Phips wrote to the earl of Nottingham for advice on these witchcraft cases:

> At my arrival here I found the Prisons full of people committed upon suspicion of witchcraft, and that continual complaints were made to me that many persons were grievously tormented by witches, and that they cried out upon several persons by name, as the cause of their torments. . . . When I inquired into the matter, I was informed by the judges that they began with this, but had human testimony against such as were condemned, and undoubted proof of their being witches, but at length I found that the Devil did take upon him the shape of Innocent persons, and some were accused of whose innocency I was well assured.[14]

When he received a reply from England many months later, he issued a proclamation freeing the accused in jail and granting amnesty to those who had fled to escape persecution. This officially ended the witchcraft hysteria.

Popular thinking today condemns the Puritan clergy for instigating and performing the Salem witch trials. This certainly was a tragic way for the once-devout Puritans to handle themselves. But many of the clergy were the ones who eventually put a stop to the insanity.

THE REJECTED MESSAGE

Did this bloody war and the hard lesson of the Salem witch trials remain with the settlers for a long time? After a few years, most of the people began to forget all the things they had learned and confessed during these times. The preachers tried again to revive them and wake them up to their worldliness, but few heeded. Soon these men of God died and left a generation of preachers who did not know the Lord. New settlers arrived each year, and many of these were not believers. The message was not being sounded; few even knew the message. The people of New England settled into their worldly lifestyle. Conditions looked bleak for the spiritual health of the colonies and for the new country that would emerge in a few short years.

For fifty years, America suffered through a malaise of spiritual darkness. But then a fresh wind blew over the land, and the First Great Awakening swept through the Pilgrim and Puritan colonies. In the next chapter, we will see how God visited his people once again to revive their prayers and prepare them for the difficult future.

But what have we learned from the lives of the colonists? Prayer was a daily activity that provided the strength of their communities. They seized every opportunity for prayer. Cotton Mather's words show just how much they depended on prayer for even the smallest details: "In passing along the Street, I have sett myself to bless thousands of persons, who never knew that I did it; with secret Wishes, after the manner sent unto Heaven for them."[15]

The Pilgrims and the Puritans did not compromise in their daily lives and certainly not in their prayer lives. They gave us a tradition of free public education, separation of church and state, respect for learning (including the founding of our first college), and a representative government that included provisions for privately owned property. While struggling to build their lives in a wild land, they assembled a printing press that turned out books, and they built meetinghouses in every town. Although they were a minority, their fervent faith and powerful prayers spread their influence across our land and across the centuries.

But they also lost their first love for God when they began to focus on gaining material wealth, possessions, and comfortable living. Their lukewarmness led to a tragedy—the Salem witch trials—for which the Puritans are known today.

For Discussion and Reflection

Adult Discussion

Set up obstacles in the room, such as tipped chairs and tables, a stack of books, a broom held waist high by two people, and rolled-up rugs. Form pairs, and have one partner lead the other through the course. The leader must tell the follower each move to make. The follower must not take his or her eyes off the leader's face, listening carefully for directions to step up, crawl under, and so on.

When each pair has had a chance to try the course, have partners switch roles and go through the course again. Then ask:

* What went through your mind as you watched your leader?
* How tempting was it to take your eyes off the leader and go through the course yourself? Explain.
* How is this activity like the way the Puritans kept their focus on God during their difficult early years in America?
* What happened when the Puritans took their focus off God?

Form groups of four, and have them read Jeremiah 8:5-6. Then have the groups discuss the following questions:

* How do these verses describe the Puritans after they had taken their eyes off God?

* How do these verses describe us today?
* What can we do to avoid the downfall the Puritans experienced?
* How can the church function as a "village" to encourage the faith of children?
* What effect can prayer have in keeping us close to God?

Have the small groups pray together, asking God to help them keep their focus on him.

Youth Discussion

Before class, make up dough based on the recipe below. Make one batch for every twenty people in your class. Mix:

1 cup cornstarch
1 cup baking soda
1 cup water

Divide each batch into four portions, and put them in small zipper bags. Form groups of five, and give each group one of the bags. Encourage kids to experiment with the dough while it's still in the bag. It will roll into a hard ball if you squeeze it together but will run into a drippy liquid if you hold it loosely. When each person has played with the dough, have people discuss the following questions in their groups. Ask:

* How is what happens to this dough when squeezed tightly similar to what happened to the Puritans when they stayed close to God?
* How is what happens to the dough when you hold it loosely similar to what happened to the Puritans when they turned away from God?
* What are some things that loosened the Puritans from God's grasp?

143

★ What draws us away from God today?

Have the groups report on their discussion. Then read Jeremiah 8:5-6. Ask:

★ What attitude is displayed in this passage?
★ How do you see this attitude in action today?
★ How can we avoid falling away from God like the Puritans did?
★ What part does prayer play in keeping close to God?

Have the kids form pairs and discuss ways they can help each other stay close to God. Then have partners pray for each other, asking God to keep them close to himself.

ELEVEN

Wake the Sleeping Giant

At the darkest point in the spiritual decline that swept through the American colonies, it looked as if the Puritans' vision of a people dedicated to God in the New World would never come to pass. After all, how could a people who had abandoned their missionary and moral spirit be reclaimed? Was it possible to turn townspeople, farmers, businessmen, shippers, and others to the Lord? What cataclysmic event could change the course of such a hopeless generation?

But God was at work through the prayers of his people. In the late 1730s, a prayer revival swept through the colonies that changed the face of the land. Now known as the First Great Awakening, it spread across all denominations and revived the waning spiritual life of the colonists. In its tremendous wake, the great Puritan giant awakened.

Benjamin Hart describes the significance of the First Great Awakening:

> It is difficult for today's readers to fully comprehend the power
> of the Great Awakening in eighteenth-century America, in part
> because religious passion is no longer so central a component
> of mainstream American life. If we could see television footage
> of the events that took place across the American countryside

during the Great Awakening, first sparked by Jonathan Edwards and carried on by other revivalist preachers, the combination of the civil rights movement, campus riots, and rock festivals of the 1960s would appear mild by comparison.[1]

Movements like this one do not happen by chance. A movement of prayer accompanied the revival that brought the power of God in flames of repentance. Let's go back and pick up the beginnings of this prayer effort.

THE BEGINNINGS OF THE REVIVAL

Jonathan Edwards, one of the greatest theologians and thinkers America has produced, was one of the key leaders in the Great Awakening.

Edwards graduated from Yale at age seventeen and, soon after that, stepped into his grandfather's shoes as minister of the Northampton church. Martin Marty describes the moral climate of Northampton during that time:

> The youths were addicted to night walking. They frequented the tavern and engaged in unspecified lewd practices. Their corrupting mirth and the jollity of their nocturnal frolics fell far short of the standards set by God and the Puritan preacher. Then suddenly in 1733, while Edwards went about his usual business preaching the terror and mercy of God, people unaccountably began to stir. For the next two years—though some saw signs of revival as late as 1737—people crowded the aisles and pews, converting in such numbers that ever since some observers have liked to speak of the Massachusetts Great Awakening as having "broken out" there and then.[2]

In 1734, Edwards preached a series of sermons on spiritual justification. People began to stream into his church. Northampton was changed—almost overnight. The town seemed to be filled with the presence of God, and everyone was talking about spiritual matters. During 1734 alone, more than three hundred people were converted. Jonathan Edwards describes one of the people affected by the spiritual awakening:

> Particularly I was surprised with the relation of a young woman, who had been one of the greatest company-keepers in the whole town. When she came to me, I had never heard that she was become in any ways serious [about religion], but by the conversation I then had with her, it appeared to me that what she gave an account of was a glorious work of God's infinite power and sovereign grace, and that God had given her a new heart, truly broken and sanctified. I could not then doubt of it, and have seen much in my acquaintance with her since to confirm it.[3]

To spread the news of the revival, Edwards wrote a book called *A Faithful Narrative of the Surprising Work of God.* Through its distribution, Edwards learned of a great prayer movement an ocean's distance away.

CONCERT OF PRAYER

In the early 1700s, a revival spread across Scotland. Prayer societies sprouted up everywhere. These societies were supervised and regulated by ministers.

Soon after it was written, Jonathan Edwards's book caught the attention of these Scottish ministers, and one of them wrote to him describing the role of prayer in the Scottish revival. Edwards was intrigued. This was the power he needed to promote the revival in New England! So he wrote a second book, in which he said:

I have often thought it would be a thing very desirable, and very likely to be followed with a great blessing, if there could be some contrivance that there should be an agreement of all God's people in America; that are well affected to this work, to keep a day of fasting and prayer to God, wherein we should all unite on the same day in humbling ourselves before God for our past continual lukewarmness and unprofitableness . . . and together with thanksgiving to God for so glorious and wonderful display of His power and grace in the late outpourings of His Spirit, to address the Father of mercies with prayers and supplications, and earnest cries, that He would guide and direct His own people, and that He would continue and still carry on His work, and more abundantly and extensively pour out His Spirit upon ministers; and that He would bow the heavens and come down (II Sam. 22:10, Ps. 18:9) and erect His glorious Kingdom through the earth.[4]

In 1744, a group of Scottish evangelical ministers established the "Concert of Prayer" to further the revival. What was the Concert of Prayer? The participants agreed to set aside time on Saturday and Sunday to pray together. The first Tuesday of each quarter of the year was reserved for solemn prayer and fasting.

The Concert of Prayer was not publicized but spread by word of mouth and through letter writing. In Scotland, the Concert of Prayer was originally planned to continue for two years, but then was extended to seven additional years. This extension was outlined in a paper called a "memorial."

Five hundred copies of this memorial were sent to Jonathan Edwards, who distributed them in America. He also published another book in support of the Concert of Prayer. Local prayer societies in America began using the Concert of Prayer idea.

While Edwards was promoting revival through prayer, God

raised up another man to bring in the harvest that prayer was preparing. That man was George Whitefield.

THE GREAT ORATOR

No two men could have been more different than Jonathan Edwards and George Whitefield. Edwards was an intellectual who gave closely reasoned sermons in a cool, studied style. During his lifetime, he wrote twelve hundred sermons and served as president of Princeton University.

Whitefield, on the other hand, had studied acting and poured emotion and a dramatic flair into his preaching. Edwards's preaching ignited the fires of revival; Whitefield's spread the flames all over the colonies. Edwards was a product of colonial life and left a legacy in the books he wrote; Whitefield was a product of the Methodist movement of John and Charles Wesley in England, bringing a fresh spirit to the colonies.

Who was George Whitefield? He was a poor boy who grew up in Gloucester, England, and managed to attend Oxford University. While a student, he was converted and was ordained a minister in the Church of England. He became great friends with Charles and John Wesley and began preaching outdoors like they did, a practice despised by most clergy.

At age twenty-four, George Whitefield began the first of seven preaching tours to America, which would cover the years 1738–70. He traveled the length of the colonies and became acquainted with many colonial leaders. One of the most unusual friendships he developed was with the religious skeptic Benjamin Franklin. They met when Franklin was thirty-three years old and Whitefield was twenty-five. This is how Benjamin Franklin describes the first sermon he heard Whitefield preach, one in which Whitefield gave a plea for funds to help support the orphanage he had founded in Georgia:

> I happened soon afterwards to attend one of his sermons, in the course of which I perceived he intended to finish with a collection, and I silently resolved he should get nothing from me. I had in my pocket a handful of copper money, three or four silver dollars, and five in gold. As he proceeded I began to soften and concluded to give the copper. Another stroke of his oratory made me ashamed of that and determined me to give the silver, and he finished so admirably that I emptied my pocket into the collection dish, gold and all.[5]

We can get a glimpse of the drama of Whitefield's sermons through a newspaper account of a scene in Boston. Note how Whitefield began and ended his oratory—with the power of prayer:

> After he finished his prayer, he knelt a long time in profound silence; and so powerfully had it affected the most heartless of his audience, that a stillness like that of the tomb pervaded the whole house. Before he commenced his sermon, long, darkening columns crowded the bright sunny sky of the morning, and swept their dull shadows over the building, in fearful augury of the storm that was approaching.
>
> "See that emblem of human life," said he, as he pointed to a flitting shadow. "It paused for a moment, and concealed the brightness of heaven from our view; but it is gone. And, where will you be, my hearers, when your lives have passed away like that dark cloud! Oh, dear friends, I see thousands sitting attentive with their eyes fixed on the poor unworthy preacher. In a few days we shall all meet at the judgment seat of Christ. We shall form part of that vast assembly which will gather before His throne. Every eye will behold the Judge. With a voice

whose call you must abide, and answer, He will inquire, whether on earth you strove to enter in at the strait gate; whether you were supremely devoted to God; whether your hearts were absorbed in Him. . . .

"O sinner! by all your hopes of happiness, I beseech you to repent. Let not the wrath of God be awakened! Let not the fires of eternity be kindled against you! See there!" said the impassioned preacher, pointing to a flash of lightning. "It is a glance from the angry eye of Jehovah! Hark!" continued he, raising a finger in listening attitude, as the thunder broke in a tremendous crash. "It was the voice of the Almighty as He passed by in His anger!"

As the sound died away Whitefield covered his face with his hands, and fell on his knees apparently lost in prayer. The storm passed rapidly by, and the sun, bursting forth, threw across the heavens the magnificent arch of peace. Rising and pointing to it the young preacher cried, "Look upon the rainbow, and praise Him who made it. Very beautiful it is in the brightness thereof. It compasseth the heavens about with glory and the hands of the Most High have bended it."[6]

Was the storm a coincidence, or did it show the mighty power of prayer in Whitefield's life? Surely, the hand of God was working in this preacher's life!

THE LAST SERMON

The spiritual life of the colonies began to stir under Whitefield's preaching. Thousands responded to his message as they listened in field meetings and town squares. People were so eager to hear him that they often came to town in stampedes, leaving great clouds of dust rising along the roadway.

The sleeping giant was awaking. Hard-line denominational walls began to come down. Entire towns came to Christ as a mood of genuine tolerance attracted new followers. Fresh excitement replaced cold formalism and sterile theology. Spiritual renewal and commitment to prayer overtook the colonists.

Blessed with an extraordinary speaking ability, Whitefield delivered some thirty thousand sermons in his lifetime. When Whitefield spoke at Harvard, the student population fell to its knees. Even Jonathan Edwards was moved to tears by his preaching. His preaching led the colonists to recognize the sanctity of individual rights—a cornerstone of what would become a political democracy.

George Whitefield kept traveling and preaching until his health was broken. In 1770, he made his final journey to New England during an ominous time in colonial history. On August 1, British troops fired on civilians in Boston, and several Americans died in an incident called the Boston Massacre. It was a harbinger of the Revolutionary War.

In September, right after that incident, Whitefield came to New Hampshire. The clergy in Exeter requested that he speak to their people. It would be Whitefield's last sermon. Let's visit that powerful scene. . . .

George Whitefield sat in a chair, his breathing labored and wheezing. A local minister and good friend, Jonathan Parsons, set a drink beside him. "Are you feeling better?" he asked.

Whitefield nodded, saving his breath. But he gratefully took a long drink from the heavy glass.

"You aren't going to speak today, are you?" Parsons asked. "You should be in bed."

Whitefield laughed weakly. "How true," he said. Then he looked toward heaven and prayed, "Lord, I am weary *in* Thy work, but not *of* it. If I have not finished my course, let me go and speak for Thee once more in the fields, and seal Thy truth, and come home and die!"[7]

Hearing this cry, Parsons felt a shiver of hopelessness and a trembling of elation spin through his stomach. Surely this was a divine moment.

Hours later, thousands of people gathered on the Exeter green. Babies cried, children laughed, and a buzz of adult conversation wound its way across the green. Then Whitefield was led through the crowd to the preaching platform set up just for him. The people near his pathway hushed as they saw his pale face and heard his raspy breathing.

With great effort, he climbed the steps and leaned over the railing to catch his breath. When he had prepared himself, he prayed silently. Then he moved behind the small pulpit. He looked down at the sea of faces all turned up toward him. Mothers with babies in their arms, old men, teenagers, local ministers, everyone. They were all here on a busy Saturday afternoon to hear what he had to say. He must point their gaze even farther upward, to the God of heaven.

Parsons inched his way next to the platform as Whitefield began to speak. The voice that once could be heard by thirty thousand people without a public-address system was now weak. His words rambled as if he couldn't think clearly.

Then Whitefield grew silent. Minutes passed as he stood stock-still, deep in prayer. The crowd held its breath, not sure what was happening.

Finally, Whitefield opened his eyes and announced, "I will wait for the gracious assistance of God. For he will, I am certain, assist me to speak in his name."[8]

Then he began preaching again. This time his voice was full and sure. He spoke as if he had an inner fire giving him power and strength. Parsons could see in his face a love for Christ.

When Whitefield looked upward, it was as if he could see into heaven.

An hour passed, and Whitefield seemed to gather more strength. Parsons wondered where he was getting that power. It could only be God. People were spellbound and silent.

He kept preaching for almost two hours. Then he cried, "I go! I go to rest prepared. My sun has arisen and by the aid of heaven has given light to many. It is now about to set. . . . *No!* It is about to rise to the zenith of immortal glory. . . . My body fails, my spirit expands. How willingly I would ever live to preach Christ! But I die to be *with* him!"[9]

After the sermon was over, Parsons took Whitefield home to rest. Parsons gave him the best bed in the house and brought him food and drink, but Whitefield didn't seem very interested. He drifted off to sleep, but kept waking, gasping for air. Parsons helped him arrange the pillows so he could sleep in a more upright position and ease the pain.

Whitefield woke early with a crushing pain in his chest. "Please relax, and I will bring you all you need," Parsons insisted.

Whitefield lay quietly, his broad face white and wan. The sky was beginning to lighten outside the window. Then he sat up on the side of the bed.

"Where are you going?" Parsons asked, alarmed.

Whitefield smiled. "To see the first light of dawn," he panted.

"Just lie back," Parsons urged. "Build up your strength."

But Whitefield slowly stood and walked in his stocking feet to the window. He bent over the sill, struggling to breathe.

The room was silent except for Whitefield's wheezing. Parsons went to his side. The view was spectacular. The first rays of the sun splashed onto the bay below, brushing the waves in brilliant gold. Whitefield's face was entranced.

Then he collapsed into Parsons's arms. The struggle to breathe ended, and a holy quiet swathed the room. Whitefield was gone. . . .[10]

But the power of Whitefield's preaching and prayers lived on in the lives of the colonists. The revival had quickened the spirit of the American churches. Thousands of new converts were added to all denominations. In fact, 15 percent of the population was added to the membership of New England churches. People began to have an increased vision for missions. Schools for Indians were established—one of which eventually became Dartmouth College. Four other colleges were also founded: the University of Pennsylvania, and Princeton, Rutgers, and Brown universities.

As a result of this First Great Awakening, people began to more freely forgive and accept one another, the very foundation of religious tolerance. This Great Awakening also caused churches to work together and lessened the differences between denominations. That tolerance would later result in our constitutional guarantee of religious liberty.

ANOTHER MIRACLE OF PRAYER

But the power of prayer was evident not only in the churches and revival meetings. As prayer became a part of colonial life again, miracles began to happen. This is clearly illustrated in the attack by the French fleet on the British colonies. As the colonies grew in number and prosperity, so did competition among the great powers of Europe to rule over them. The British captured the French outpost of Louisbourg in Nova Scotia in 1744. In retaliation, the French sent half their navy under the command of Duc d'Anville to destroy the entire English colonial seacoast. In June 1746 the French Grand Fleet, consisting of seventy ships and eight thousand soldiers, eluded the British blockade and headed for the colonies, determined to destroy every British-American colony in the New World. Suddenly, 254 years of British settlements were in grave danger.

Realizing their danger, the colonists turned to corporate prayer, asking God to protect them from their enemies. Hearing their prayers, God set in motion the most unusual series of weather and plague disasters ever to inflict a naval fleet.

First, the French fleet was delayed by a prolonged calm. When the wind did come up, it developed into a fierce storm with lightning so severe that it disabled several ships. A plague broke out on the fleet, which killed thirteen hundred soldiers. Then the entire fleet was scattered by more storms. By August 26, only fifty-three ships remained. Once again, a violent storm erupted near the isle of Sable and stranded several more.

When Duc d'Anville finally reached Halifax, Nova Scotia, he expected to rendezvous with a large squadron of French ships coming from the West Indies. But the squadron had arrived weeks earlier, given up because of his delay, and returned to France.

Shortly after the duke arrived in Halifax, the horror of his situation shattered his confidence. The major part of his fleet was lost; many men were sick and dying. On September 1, he poisoned himself. More ships came in, but the men on these vessels were also ill, and food supplies were running out. The commander who replaced the duke fell on his sword, also committing suicide. The third commander tried to recruit French colonists and Indians to attack Annapolis, but before he and his men could go ashore, another thousand soldiers died of pestilence. Finally, the fleet set sail on October 13, still intending to attack the English colony.

Sighting the vessels off their coast, worried New Englanders planned to set aside October 16 as a day of fasting and prayer for deliverance from the anticipated attack. New England pastor Jonathan French described the scene:

> [The people were] filled with consternation. The streets filled with men, marching for the defense of the sea ports, and the distresses of women and children, trembling for the event made . . . deep impressions upon the minds of those who remember these scenes. But never did the religions, for which the country was settled, appear more important, nor prayer more prevalent, than on this occasion. A prayer-hearing God stretched forth the arm of His power and destroyed that mighty armament in a manner almost as extraordinary as the drowning of Pharaoh and his host in the Red Sea.[11]

On October 15, another violent storm hit the fleet, scattering and damaging the ships. On the following day—the very day the colonists had set aside for prayer and fasting—the weather improved. The French collected their scattered fleet and pressed forward to attack Annapolis. But that night, a catastrophic storm devastated the remnants of the French fleet. The remaining ships limped back to France, defeated, carrying the news that the British colonies in America were intact. The colonists knew that the awesome power of united prayer had saved them.

Second Chronicles 7:14 says, "If my people who are called by my name will humble themselves and pray and seek my face and turn from their wicked ways, I will hear from heaven and will forgive their sins and heal their land" (NLT). That's exactly what happened to the colonies. They were established with days of prayer and fasting. The revival brought them back to their prayer roots. And now God was blessing their future with his divine power and wisdom. As the colonists stood at the edge of independence, their faith and prayers would prove the difference between failure and unparalleled success. The colonists did not know it, but as these events took place, leaders were being prepared whose deep spiritual values and commitment to prayer would construct the foundation for a great nation.

For Discussion and Reflection

Adult Discussion

Form groups of three or four. Give each group a large piece of paper and markers. Ask the groups to imagine that the Great Awakening turned your city or town upside down. Have them make a banner with an exciting headline that might describe what was happening during the revival.

Give the groups a few minutes to complete their banners. Then gather as a large group and have group members show their banners and explain them.

Say, "Think about a time when a minister's message really made you think. How did you feel about that message?" Let volunteers answer. Then form groups of five or six to discuss the following questions:

★ How do you think people felt as Jonathan Edwards and George Whitefield preached?
★ What effect did their preaching have on the people?
★ What effect has preaching had in your life?
★ How did prayer affect the First Great Awakening?

Then bring the groups together to read Psalm 85:1-7 and discuss these questions:

★ In the First Great Awakening, God used two very different men, Jonathan Edwards and George Whitefield. How does knowing that God uses people of all kinds help you in your ministry?
★ In the verses we read, God promises to revive us when we rejoice in him. How does prayer fit into this promise?
★ How has prayer made an impact on your life?

Have people return to their groups to pray together for God's working in their lives and in your church.

Youth Discussion

Bring to class a small cup filled with vinegar, a large bowl, a teaspoon, and baking soda. Hold the cup of vinegar over the bowl, and put a teaspoon of baking soda into the cup. The mixture will foam up and out of the cup. Ask:

★ What went through your mind as I put the baking soda into the vinegar?
★ How is this like what happened in the First Great Awakening?
★ What changes took place in the Great Awakening?
★ What was the power behind those changes?

Have the kids form groups of four and read Psalm 85:1-7. Then have them discuss these questions in their groups:

★ Why would God send a revival as asked for in this psalm?
★ Why is prayer such an important part of a revival movement?

Have each group come up with a list of things that would probably change if our society had an awakening. After a few minutes, have the groups share their answers. Ask, "What can we do to increase the likelihood of a revival in our town?" Encourage kids to pray regularly for God's working in their homes, schools, and communities.

TWELVE

In God We Trust

The American Revolution was an unequal war. It pitted a group of farmers and preachers against the most formidable armed forces of that period—the British. Noah Webster, who wrote his *History of the United States* in 1832, just a few decades after the war ended, described the uneven battle strength like this:

> When the Americans determined to oppose their military strength to that of Great Britain, the disparity was such as might well appall the bravest heart. Great Britain possessed immense wealth and resources, her navy and merchantmen covered the ocean, her armies were considerable for numbers and discipline, her military and naval officers were of renowned skill and experience; great was her power, and still greater the pride of her sovereignty. The colonies, on the other hand, were destitute of all these advantages; they had no general government vested with powers to control the contending interests of thirteen distinct jurisdictions; the colonial governments were mostly dissolved: No skillful officers, no disciplined troops, no muskets proper for an army, no cannon, no ammunition, no camp equipage, no armed ships; nothing but consciousness of upright views, persuasion of the justice of their cause, dauntless courage, and confidence in the God of hosts, encouraged the Americans to hazard the unequal contest.[1]

Can you imagine what would happen today if America were threatened by a superpower greater than our own might? First, someone would take a poll. Experts would endlessly debate whether the country's leaders were making adequate decisions or not. Television cameras would be shoved under the chins of anyone who knew anything about the current situation. But few would suggest prayer or wonder if the action to be taken was right and moral under God's laws.

What would stir an unorganized, scattered bunch of colonists to form an army to oppose the military might of Britain? Harry Stout, professor at Yale University, writes:

> Eighteenth-century America was a deeply religious culture that lived self-consciously "under the cope of heaven." In Sunday worship, and weekday (or "occasional") sermons, ministers drew the populace into the rhetorical world that was more compelling and immediate than the physical settlements surrounding them. Sermons taught not only the way to personal salvation in Christ but also the way to temporal and national prosperity for God's chosen people.
>
> Events were perceived not from the mundane, human vantage point but from God's. . . . All events, no matter how mundane or seemingly random, were part of a larger pattern of meaning, part of God's providential design. The outlines of this pattern were contained in Scripture and interpreted by discerning pastors. Colonial congregations saw themselves as the "New Israel," endowed with a sacred mission that destined them as lead actors in the last triumphant chapter in redemption history.
>
> Thus the colonial audiences learned to perceive themselves not as a ragtag settlement of religious exiles and eccentrics but as God's special people, planted in the American wilderness to bring light to the Old World left behind. Europeans might ignore or revile them as "fanatics," but through the sermon,

they knew better. Better to absorb the barbs of English ridicule than to forget their glorious commission.[2]

The Reverend John Muhlenberg typifies the character of many American colonists. He was present at St. John's Church in Richmond when Patrick Henry, that outspoken lawyer, shouted, "Gentlemen may cry, 'Peace, peace,' but there is no peace. The war is actually begun. . . . Give me liberty or give me death!"[3]

As soon as Patrick Henry finished and the meeting was over, Muhlenberg looked for George Washington's head towering over the crowd, rushed up to him, and enlisted in the American army.

Before long, the day came when he would preach his last sermon before leaving for army duty. . . .

As John walked down the aisle to the elevated pulpit, his robe billowed around his arms. He took his position above his audience, laid his Bible gently on the pulpit as he usually did, then looked over the congregation. He saw all the familiar faces. How he would miss them! All his friends, all the workers in his mission field.

He launched into his sermon, gathering fire as he preached. The minutes flew by like messengers on winged feet. When he reached the end of his sermon, he opened his Bible to Ecclesiastes 3:1 and read: "To every thing there is a season, and a time to every purpose under the heaven" (KJV). Then he announced, "There is a time to preach and a time to pray, but there is also a time to fight, and that time has now come."

With those words still echoing in the room, he stepped from behind the pulpit where everyone could see him. He grandly pulled off his black robe. There he stood in front of his congregation, dressed in the full uniform of an American colonel. . . .[4]

What a statement! Almost the entire male audience—nearly three hundred men—enlisted on that day and followed him into battle for American freedom. They became the "German Regiment."[5]

THE BLACK-ROBED REGIMENT

In fact, many clergymen were the rallying force behind the war. They preached sermons and led prayer for the success of the fight for liberty. These black-robed men so greatly influenced the minds of the people that they were called the "Black-Robed Regiment."[6]

Of course, not everyone agreed with the prevailing view of waging a war for freedom. Some devout Christians sincerely believed that honoring the king was biblical and right. Many who opposed the war were unbelievers who had disrespect for the clergy and the churches. Yet the war was fought for high principles, and the majority of Americans looked to God as their protector and their guide.

To help us understand the miracles of prayer that occurred during the American Revolution, we need to take a quick overview of the events that happened during that time. The tensions between the British and the colonists began when Britain forced the Stamp Act onto the Americans in 1765. In 1770 the British fired on civilians, killing five. It was called the Boston Massacre. Relations between Great Britain and America deteriorated, leading to the formation of the First Continental Congress in 1774.

The year 1775 saw several strategic events: the Battles of Lexington and Concord occurred in April; the Second Continental Congress met in May; and the Congress created the Continental army and named George Washington as commander. The Battle of Bunker Hill was also fought that year.

In 1776 Thomas Jefferson wrote the Declaration of Independence and George Washington made his famous crossing of the Delaware. And in 1777 the Americans won the Battle of Saratoga and France joined the American effort. That winter, Washington's army suffered hardship at Valley Forge.

The Battle of Monmouth was waged in 1778, and British commander Cornwallis surrendered at Yorktown in 1781. Finally, in 1783, Britain recognized American independence. In 1787, the U.S. Continental Convention was held; the Bill of Rights came along in 1789. Within less than twenty years, thirteen separate colonies had defeated the mighty British army and formed a new nation.

The Americans approached this war effort through prayer. In this chapter, we will look at some of the official days of prayer proclaimed during the war years. In the next chapter, we will look at the deep prayer life of our first president, George Washington. We will see how God miraculously intervened for the American army during the war, largely due to Washington's faithful and fervent prayers. And finally, in the last chapter of this section, we will show how prayer impacted the great documents and governmental principles produced by the revolutionaries.

DAYS OF PRAYER AND FASTING

Most Americans today don't realize the perilous situation faced by the colonists. The danger wasn't just from physical harm. The colonists were being forced to give up the one thing they had risked their lives to gain—independence.

What was their response to their danger? Public days of fasting and prayer. The colonists humbled themselves and called upon God for help. They searched their hearts for sin. They implored God to help them in each decision and battle they fought. God heard their cries and guided them through many difficult situations.

Fasting is the practice of going without food for the purpose of having deeper fellowship with God. The Old Testament book of Esther gives a clear example of public fasting. Jesus fasted during the forty days he was tempted by Satan, and the Christians in the New Testament church also fasted (Acts 13:3). Many of the proclamations written by the colonists included a call to fast and pray. In doing so, the colonists were showing that they meant business in their relationship with God. They were also quick to call for public thanksgiving to God when he intervened on their behalf.

God's protection and timing can be seen in the first battle of the Revolutionary War. We have all heard about the "shot heard round the world," but most of us haven't heard about God's miraculous intervention in this encounter.

The first amazing fact about the Battle of Lexington occurred one month before the battle began. In March the governor of Connecticut, Jonathan Trumbull, set a day of public fasting and prayer to protect and preserve the colonies and to secure liberty. It was held on April 19, the very day that the Battle of Lexington occurred! So as their fellow patriots were fighting the first battle of the war, Connecticut citizens were entreating God's help in the fight for freedom. God answered that very day in the Battles of Lexington and Concord.[7]

CONNECTICUT'S DAY OF PRAYER AND FASTING

Governor Trumbull urged the Connecticut colonists to pray for all the colonies. He entreated them to search their hearts for sin. Since this was before the Declaration of Independence, he instructed them to pray for King George III and the rest of the rulers in the colony.[8]

The principles in the governor's prayer would be appropriate for us as a nation today. The first thing the colonists were exhorted to do was to search their hearts for sin that could be the root of the troubles in the colonies. Then when they discovered their sins, they were to mourn for them.

Think about our country today. What would happen if we lamented before God about the many problems we have? What if we searched our hearts to find the sin at the root of our country's troubles? How often do we mourn about the sins we have committed?

The great desire of this colony was to become a "mountain of holiness" and a "habitation of Righteousness forever."[9] The very day that these colonists prayed as a corporate body, the first battle of the war occurred at Lexington. Is it any coincidence that God's hand of mercy worked on behalf of the American army as his people in Connecticut spent the day in prayer?

General Thomas Gage was the British military governor of the rebellious colony of Massachusetts. On April 18, he sent out eighteen hundred soldiers to raid the colonists' ammunition store at Concord and to capture Samuel Adams and John Hancock, who were staying in Lexington.

Paul Revere, a Patriot spy, uncovered the British plan to attack. He made his famous ride to alert the minutemen in Concord and Lexington that General Gage and the British soldiers were coming. Revere had several close calls, but amazingly he suffered no harm. Adams and Hancock, who had been warned by Revere, escaped to a nearby village.

When the British army arrived at Lexington, the soldiers met the already-assembled small group of minutemen. The

British officers ordered the minutemen to disperse. As they started to leave, the British army opened fire, killing ten and wounding eight.

But even in this defeat, God seemed to be at work. All the Patriot leaders escaped capture, and the delay at Lexington allowed two hundred minutemen to prepare for the British attack on Concord at the Old North Bridge later the same morning. When they arrived, the British soldiers fired, killing several citizens. The militia returned fire, killing four British officers and many soldiers. The battle continued until the British retreated. They had lost 273 men. Because of the chaos, the British commander ordered a retreat to Boston. Panic-stricken, the British soldiers sprinted for safety, with the minutemen in pursuit.

While thousands of Christians were praying, a handful of Patriots decimated a British force of eighteen hundred at Concord. These were the best and most experienced soldiers in His Majesty's army. Never had the British suffered a more humiliating defeat.

MASSACHUSETTS DAY OF PRAYER AND FASTING, MAY 11, 1775

On April 15, 1775, four days before the Battle of Lexington, the Provincial Congress of Massachusetts declared May 11, 1775, a day of fasting and prayer for their colony. The order was signed by the president of the Congress, John Hancock. In the following excerpt from the proclamation, notice how important they considered God to be in the fight for freedom:

> In circumstances dark as these, it becomes us, as Men and Christians, to reflect that, while every prudent measure should be taken to ward off the impending judgements; . . . at the

same time, all confidence must be withheld from the means we use and reposed only on that God who rules in the armies of Heaven, and without whose blessing the best human counsels are but foolishness and all created power, vanity. It is the happiness of his Church that, when the powers of earth and hell combine against it, and those who should be nursing fathers become its persecutors then the Throne of Grace is of easiest access and its appeal thither is graciously invited by the Father of Mercies, who has assured it, that when his children ask bread he will not give them stone.[10]

The Day of Prayer and Fasting was only weeks before the clash of armies at Bunker Hill. During this battle, God intervened on behalf of the Americans.

THE BATTLE OF BUNKER HILL

Bunker Hill, overlooking the Boston harbor, was a strategic location because it was a lookout for monitoring the British movements in and out of the Boston harbor. This area was also the site of a major battle in the beginning of the war.

The Patriots heard about General Gage's plan to occupy this hill. The very first defense they made was a prayer service led by Rev. Samuel Langdon, president of Harvard College.[11] Then they proceeded to fortify the hill.

When General Gage heard of the buildup, he ordered an attack. Having suffered the Lexington and Concord humiliation, he wanted to solidly defeat the Patriot forces.

General William Howe led the attack for the British while General Gage remained aboard the British fleet in the Boston harbor. The plan was for the fleet to help by shelling the Patriots on Bunker Hill.

Knowing that they vastly outnumbered the Patriots, the

British regiments confidently ascended the hill with their front flank. They were a bit surprised when no shots were fired. But the Patriot leader, William Prescott, was a seasoned veteran of the French and Indian War. He had learned not to shoot until he could see "the whites of their eyes." When the British came close, he ordered his troops to fire. The British troops were mowed down, and those who survived made a mad retreat.

Howe regrouped his men and sent the second flank up the hill. Prescott allowed them to get even closer before he gave the order to fire. Again, the British troops were mowed down and the few to survive made a hasty retreat.

Howe sent for reinforcements. Meanwhile, the Patriots were almost out of gunpowder. As the British reinforcements mounted the hill for the third time, they were able to break the American lines because the Patriots didn't have enough ammunition. Prescott gave the order for retreat. Amos Farnwarth, a corporal in the Massachusetts army, described that scene:

> We within the entrenchment . . . having fired away all [our] ammunition and having no reinforcements . . . were overpowered by numbers and obliged to leave. . . . I did not leave the entrenchment until the enemy got in. I then retreated ten or fifteen rods. Then I received a wound in my right arm, the ball going through a little below my elbow, breaking the little shell-bone. Another ball struck my back, taking a piece of skin about as big as a penny. But I got to Cambridge that night. . . . Oh, the goodness of God in preserving my life, although they fell on my right hand and on my left! O may this act of deliverance of Thine, O God, lead me never to distrust Thee; but may I ever trust in Thee and put confidence in no arm of flesh![12]

The British had achieved their goal of taking the hill, but they had lost 1,150 men while the patriots lost only 400!

This battle inspired the people of New England and united them with patriotic pride. It showed them that they could defend themselves against British forces.

CONTINENTAL FAST DAY, JULY 20, 1775

On June 12, 1775, Britain declared the colonies under martial law because of the insurrection. The Continental Congress responded first by ordering a day of fasting and prayer to be observed by all the colonies. Their decree read, in part:

> This Congress, therefore, considering the present critical, alarming and calamitous State of these Colonies, do earnestly recommend that Thursday, the Twentieth Day of July next, be observed by the INHABITANTS of all the English Colonies on this Continent, as a DAY of public HUMILIATION, FASTING, and PRAYER, that we may with united Hearts and Voices unfeignedly Confess and deplore our many Sins.[13]

On July 20, the Congress led by example. They went as a group to church to hear a sermon on Psalm 80:14, "Come back, we beg you, O God Almighty. Look down from heaven and see our plight. Watch over and care for this vine" (NLT).[14]

That day sermons were preached all over the colonies. Prayers went up in hundreds of places, including the army. The following is an excerpt from a prayer that preceded a sermon preached at Yorktown to Captain Morgan's and Captain Price's companies of riflemen:

> O Most Mighty God, terrible in thy judgments, and wonderful in thy doings towards the children of men! We thy sinful servants here assembled before thee, confess and adore the mysterious strokes of thy supreme Providence.
>
> Long has the land rejoiced in the abundant emanation of thy

tender mercies. Not our merit but thy goodness, has turned the wilderness into fruitful fields. . . .

But alas with grief and shame we acknowledge that we have not always made a right use of thy continued favours. Not according to thy benefits have been our improvements, not according to thy bounty has been our gratitude. Our hearts smite us when we reflect on the many instances of our neglect of heavenly and our attachment to earthly things. . . .

In this severe distress whither shall we fly but to thy presence? As a religious society, prayer is our only weapon: O may it prove the prayer of the humble, may it pierce through the clouds, reach the footsteps of thy Almighty throne, and not turn away till thou, O most high, regardest it.[15]

This Day of Prayer was the first time that the thirteen colonies united in prayer. It was also the first action of the Continental Congress that affected every colony. What a legacy for us to look back on. The very first act of togetherness was prayer.

NATIONAL DAY OF PRAYER AND FASTING, MAY 17, 1776

After the Revolutionary War had been in progress for a year, the Continental Congress was frustrated because only one colony had voted for the Declaration of Independence. So the Continental Congress called for another National Day of Prayer and Fasting on May 17. The Congress again led by example, falling to their knees in prayer and listening to a sermon by Rev. John Witherspoon called "The Dominion of Providence over the Affairs of Men."[16]

God worked another miracle. Within two months, the Declaration of Independence was ratified!

NATIONAL DAY OF THANKSGIVING, DECEMBER 18, 1777

As the war dragged on, the Americans experienced many defeats. One of the most painful was at Brandywine in September 1777. Here the Continental army was almost destroyed as they tried to stop the British march to Philadelphia. This defeat opened a floodgate of discouragement for Washington's troops. He sensed a need for a breath of fresh air, so he began praying for a "signal stroke of providence."[17]

God signaled his providence in the defeat at Saratoga. First, the British orders got botched up. General Howe was supposed to march to Saratoga to join General Burgoyne. But back in London, England, Lord North was in a rush to leave for a holiday and forgot to sign the order.

Second, bad weather kept British reinforcements out on the seas. The reverse of either of these two factors would have changed the outcome of the battle.

Benedict Arnold led the troops for America. The British troops were trying to retake Fort Ticonderoga in New York. The Americans battled brilliantly on boats in the lake and used guerilla warfare in the forest as they repeatedly ambushed Burgoyne's army. On October 17, Burgoyne and seven thousand men surrendered.

The Continental Congress felt such gratitude to God that they proclaimed a Day of Thanksgiving and Praise. This is how the proclamation read:

> Forasmuch as it is the indispensable duty of all men to adore the superintending providences of Almighty God . . . and it having pleased Him in His abundant mercy . . . to crown our arms with most signal success . . . it is therefore recommended

. . . to set apart Thursday, the 18th day of December, for solemn thanksgiving and praise.[18]

NATIONAL DAY OF THANKSGIVING, MAY 7, 1778

When France agreed to become America's ally, the Continental Congress gave God the credit for this significant breakthrough. They declared a National Day of Thanksgiving on May 7, 1778. George Washington proclaimed:

> It having pleased the Almighty Ruler of the Universe propitiously to define the cause of the United American States, and finally by raising up a powerful friend among the Princes of the earth, to establish our Liberty and Independence upon a lasting foundation; it becomes us to set apart a day for gratefully acknowledging the Divine Goodness, and celebrating the event, which we owe to his benign interposition.[19]

A SPY INTERCEPTED

Another example of God's protection was the amazing interception of the British spy Major Andre, which led to the revelation of Benedict Arnold's treason. Washington wrote a letter to John Laurens of God's providence in this matter:

> In no instance since the commencement of the war has the interposition of Providence appeared more conspicuous than in the rescue of the Post and Garrison of West Point from Arnold's villainous perfidy. . . . A combination of extraordinary circumstances.[20]

These were the extraordinary circumstances. Three young Patriot militiamen posted themselves on the road closest to Tarrytown, New York, looking for cowboys stealing cattle for the British. A lone rider came down the road. It was Major Andre. They stopped him and found out he was on his way to New York. For some reason, Andre thought they were Loyalists and began to talk freely about things that made them suspicious. He eventually told them he was an officer in the British army. They searched him and found secret plans for the fortification of West Point, and in his shoes they discovered a pass signed by Benedict Arnold. They took him to North Castle, where the whole treasonous story came out. Arnold escaped, but the plan was foiled and West Point was saved. Washington wrote this message to the troops about Arnold's act of treason:

> Treason of the blackest dye was yesterday discovered! General Arnold who commanded at Westpoint, lost to every sentiment of honor, of public and private obligation, was about to deliver up that important post into the hands of the enemy. Such an event must have given the American cause a deadly wound if not a fatal stab. Happily the treason has been timely discovered to prevent the fatal misfortune. The Providential train of circumstances which led to it affords the most convincing proof that the liberties of America are the object of Divine Protection. [21]

Arnold spent the rest of his life in England, and his home in a plush part of London is pointed out to visitors taking city tours of London. His dying request was to be buried in his American uniform.

NATIONAL DAY OF PUBLIC THANKSGIVING AND PRAYER, DECEMBER 7, 1780

After the discovery of Benedict Arnold's treacherous plot, the United States Congress again called for a Day of Thanksgiving and Prayer. In their proclamation they spelled out the blessings they were thankful for:

> . . . More especially in the late remarkable interposition of his watchful providence in rescuing the person our commander-in-chief and the army from imminent danger at a moment when treason was ripened for execution; in prospering the labors of the husbandman, and causing the earth to yield its increase in plentiful harvests; and above all, in continuing to us the gospel of peace.

Their response? To "set apart Thursday, the 7th day of December, next, to be observed as a day of public thanksgiving and prayer; that all the people may assemble on that day to celebrate the praises of our Divine Benefactor, to confess our unworthiness of the least of his favors, and to offer our fervent supplications to the God of all grace."[22]

THANKSGIVING PROCLAMATION, OCTOBER 3, 1789

One of the first actions the newly assembled Congress took was to petition President George Washington to recommend to the people of the United States a day of public thanksgiving and prayer. One day after adopting the final language of the First Amendment, they adopted the following resolution for George Washington:

> Resolved, That a joint committee of both Houses to be directed to wait upon the President of the United States, to request that he would recommend to the people of the United States a day of public thanksgiving and prayer, to be observed by acknowledging, with grateful hearts, the many signal favors of Almighty God, especially affording them an opportunity

peaceably to establish a Constitution of government for safety and happiness.[23]

Washington acted on the recommendation of Congress by giving the First Thanksgiving Proclamation on October 3, 1789. This is a portion of his proclamation:

> Whereas it is the duty of all nations to acknowledge the providence of Almighty God, to obey His will, to be grateful for His benefits, and humbly implore His protection and favor . . .
>
> Now, therefore, I do recommend and assign Thursday, the 26th day of November next to be devoted by the people of these States to the service of that great and glorious Being Who is the beneficent Author of all the good that was or that will be . . . that we may then all unite in rendering unto Him our sincere and humble thanks for His kind care and protection of the people of this country previous to their becoming a nation. . . . And also that we may then unite in most humbly offering our prayers and supplications to the great Lord and Ruler of Nations, and beseech Him to pardon our national and other transgression . . . to render our National Government a blessing to all the people by constantly being a government of wise, just and constitutional laws, discreetly and faithfully executed and obeyed . . . [and] to promote the knowledge and practice of true religion and virtue and the increase of science among us.[24]

Can you imagine what would happen today if our governors, congressmen, and president set aside days of prayer this often? And these proclamations weren't just proclaimed and then filed in a cabinet in some government office. All over the colonies, in the halls of government, and in the armed forces, people fasted and prayed. They really did it!

The results were unbelievable! In our next chapter, we will

meet the one man who had the greatest influence on the outcome of the Revolutionary War—George Washington. His
deep prayer life set a standard that helped form our nation.

For Discussion and Reflection

Adult Discussion
Bring in a colorful and intricate picture or poster and place it at
the front of the room with the picture side to the wall. As class
starts, turn the picture so it shows, but don't call any attention
to it. Chat with the class for a few minutes; then turn the picture around so only the back side can be seen. Ask, "What did
you see in the picture?" Write the details they call out on a
chalkboard or sheet of paper. After all ideas are exhausted,
turn the picture around and have people look at it again. Then
have them call out details that were missed. Ask:

- ★ How did you feel when you realized how many things you
  missed in the picture?
- ★ What distracted you from concentrating on the picture ear-
  lier?
- ★ What distracts us from focusing on God more in prayer?
- ★ How does fasting help us concentrate on God?
- ★ What's the connection between prayer and fasting?

Form groups of three or four, and have the groups read Acts
14:23. Then have groups discuss the following questions:

- ★ Why did Paul and Barnabas pray and fast?
- ★ What things have you found to be effective in helping you
  focus on God in your quiet times?
- ★ When did the colonists call special days of fasting and
  prayer?

★ When might it be appropriate for us to spend time fasting?

Have the groups report on their discussion. Then ask people to consider whether God might have them fast for a time to help them focus on him in prayer.

Youth Discussion

Form groups of three or four. Give each group three paper cups, a sheet of paper, and enough water to fill one cup one-quarter full. Ask the kids to set the two empty cups about six inches apart and make a bridge between the cups with the piece of paper. Then have the groups try to balance the filled cup on the paper bridge. Provide paper towels for spills.

After a few failures, suggest that the groups fold their paper accordion style and balance the cup on the paper. Try adding more water to see how strong the bridge is. Ask:

★ How did you respond when your paper bridge failed?
★ Did you expect that anyone's bridge would work? Why or why not?

Say, "Just as it seemed impossible for the paper to hold the cup of water, it seemed impossible that the colonists could win in a war with the mighty British empire." Have kids form pairs to discuss the following questions:

★ What made the difference in the bridge's holding or not holding?
★ What made the difference in the war against the British?
★ Read Philippians 4:13. What difference can God make in your life?
★ What difference can God make in our country now?

* How can our prayers make a difference in situations that seem impossible?

Then have pairs spend a few minutes praying for America's future and for the "impossible" situations in their own lives.

Have the kids tear their bridges into pieces so that each person can take a piece home as a reminder that God can do what seems impossible.

THIRTEEN

A Man
of Prayer

We have all heard the legends about George Washington—his chopping down the cherry tree, crossing the Delaware, and wintering at Valley Forge. But most of us have not heard about his deep commitment to God. Above all, Washington was a man of prayer. That's one reason why God used him in many of the miraculous events of the Revolutionary War. He was God's instrument of prayer in those perilous times.

Washington was truly a person who looked out for the good of his country rather than his own welfare. Before he became America's first president, there was a strong movement in the colonies to make him king and later to bury him in our nation's capital (which he refused in favor of being buried at his Mt. Vernon home). After all, the colonists were used to looking toward a monarch to rule them, and Washington was revered and admired as deeply as a monarch by his fellow Americans. But he would have no part of such a movement. Instead, he unselfishly served his country for a total of forty-five years. William White, who knew Washington and wrote *Washington Writings,* said:

It seems proper to subjoin to this letter what was told to me by Mr. Robert Lewis, at Fredricksburg, in the year 1827. Being a nephew of Washington, and his private secretary during the first part of his presidency, Mr. Lewis lived with him on terms of intimacy, and had the best opportunity for observing his habits.

Mr. Lewis said that he had accidentally witnessed his private devotions in his library both morning and evening; that on those occasions he had seen him in a kneeling posture with a Bible open before him, and that he believed such to have been his daily practice.[1]

John Marshall, chief justice of the Supreme Court, had seen Washington in action when he served under him during the winter at Valley Forge. Marshall said, "Without making ostentatious professions of religion, he was a sincere believer in the Christian faith, and a truly devout man."[2]

Washington's part in the formation of our country was crucial. None of the colonists had ever taken part in the awesome task of forming a new nation, but many remembered the bloody revolution in France. The people looked to Washington to lead them toward the coming nineteenth century, give them a firm foundation in government, and help them achieve unity without the internal bloodshed experienced by France.

The underlying strength of Washington's character came from his prayer life. It's no coincidence that one of the most famous statues of this great man (located in front of the Treasury Building in New York City) is of him kneeling in the snow at Valley Forge. The same pose appears in stained glass as the central piece of the Congressional Prayer Room in our nation's Capitol. With faith he led his ragtag army to victory! What dependence on God he displayed throughout his public career! To understand him a little better, let's take a walk through some of the events in his life.

THE EARLY YEARS

Washington's father died when Washington was eleven years old. That left him with two people who deeply affected his life. The first was his mother, a devout Christian, and the other was his half brother, Lawrence. Lawrence was a regular in the British army and influenced Washington to choose a military career.

As a teenager, Washington worked as a surveyor, familiarizing himself with much of the American colonies. He also followed in his half brother's footsteps by joining the Virginia militia. Even at this early age, Washington seemed to sense the special purpose God had for his life. At that time, the militia was more of a political club than a regular army, but it allowed Washington to develop leadership abilities that would serve him the rest of his life.

By the time he was twenty, Washington had filled numerous pages of his diary with some of the most beautiful prayers ever written. The following is an example of Washington's tender heart toward God: "Let my heart therefore, gracious God, be so affected with the glory and majesty of it, that I may not do mine own works but wait on Thee, and discharge those weighty duties which Thou require of me."[3]

When the French and Indian War erupted between Britain and France, Governor Dinwiddie of Virginia asked Washington to deliver a message to the French, demanding that they leave the Ohio Valley. Before he left on this journey, his mother told him, "Remember that God is our only sure trust. My son, neglect not the duty of prayer."[4] Washington remembered and followed that advice throughout his long, successful career.

THE MIRACLE OF THE TWO COINS

In 1755, long before the American war for independence from British rule, Washington served as a British officer on General Braddock's staff. He was just twenty-three years old, but he already enjoyed the confidence of his superiors and was often picked to lead dangerous assignments.

One such assignment found him searching the frontier for John Fraser, a Scottish fur trapper who was loyal to the British. Fraser had promised to provide supplies and information to the advancing British army.

When Washington and two Indian scouts reached Fraser's cabin, they were amazed to see broken furniture scattered about, doors ajar, and the tracks of many horses—all signs of an enemy attack.

Knowing that Fraser had no doubt been killed or kidnapped by the French militia or their allies, Washington still felt drawn to this little cabin in the woods. He and his companions entered the building. Everything was in ruins.

The three men left the house, surveying the area around it. Suddenly Washington heard a faint sound. Following the sound, he saw a child's leg jutting out from a pile of firewood. Quickly, he cleared away the logs to find a ten-year-old boy.

Within moments, Washington and the scouts discovered a second child. Apparently Fraser had had just enough time to hide his sons in the woodpile. Both boys were nearly frozen from their night outdoors.

There was nothing to do but take them along. But as the little group hurried back toward their own lines, Washington knew that an army about to go on the attack was no place for two young boys.

When Washington and the group arrived at Braddock's camp, Washington asked permission to take the boys back to their nearest relative, their grandmother. General Braddock understood the need to send the boys back as quickly as possible, but he refused to send them without sufficient guards. Unfortunately, right at that moment his plan was to move his army farther into enemy territory. He could not spare even four or five men.

Washington respectfully pressed his case by volunteering to accompany the boys home. All he needed was one Indian scout. Washington persisted until Braddock agreed.

When Washington explained to the boys that he was going to take them to their grandmother's house, they were filled with fear. French soldiers or hostile Indians could be lying in ambush along the way. But Washington told them what his mother had told him: If they undertook their journey prayerfully, they would be just fine.

He dug into his pocket, produced two large coins, and gave one to each boy. He explained that the coins were tokens of his promise and reminders that God would keep them safe. The boys inspected the coins, then put them into their breast pockets as they were instructed.

During the colonial period, there were few roads, so often the best route was a straight line through the woods. It could also be the most dangerous one. Washington and the boys quietly followed the Indian scout through the woods.

After some time, the scout held up his hand to warn them to stop. Washington and the boys froze in their tracks. After a whispered consultation, Washington moved ahead cautiously.

Several Indians armed with French rifles were hidden in the brush. One aimed his rifle and shot at Washington once, then again. Taking a direct hit, Washington staggered backward. The loyal Indian scout aimed into the thicket and blindly fired his rifle.

Washington toppled to the ground, his eyes closed. He had taken two bullets in the chest. It seemed as if he were mortally wounded.

But then his eyes opened, and he started to pick himself up. He stood shakily, unhurt.

At that moment, something moved in the woods. The scout stepped in front of the boys to protect them from enemy fire. The little group of four watched in amazement as a hostile Indian chief gestured to his men and they all disappeared into the woods without harming anyone.

How had Washington escaped harm from the bullets? Smiling, he reached into his breast pocket and removed two large coins. Each one was dented by the impact of a bullet.

Soon after, Washington and the Indian scout delivered the boys safely to their grateful grandmother. But this was not the last time George Washington's life would be miraculously spared. Nor was it the last time he would be in the sights of that same Indian chief.[5]

MIRACULOUS BATTLE AT FORT DUQUESNE

During one particular battle, General Braddock needed someone who was familiar with the wilderness of Virginia to assist him in an attack on Fort Duquesne, located at the fork of the Ohio River. Washington was the natural choice.

Washington clearly saw that British warfare tactics were not appropriate for fighting the French and the Indians. The rows of red-clad military men were easy targets. Because of their heavy artillery, the British had to build roads, slowing their progress and wasting valuable time. Washington warned Braddock of these dangers, but the commander brushed him aside and continued his plans to invade.

On July 9, 1755, one thousand Indians ambushed Braddock's fifteen hundred regulars. After Braddock was shot, Washington took command and led the panicked British soldiers in an orderly retreat.

During the retreat, Washington had two different horses shot out from under him as enemy soldiers fired at him at near-point-blank range. Four bullets tore through his clothes and three through his hat. Yet he remained unharmed as he moved boldly through the shower of lead to help dozens of wounded soldiers.

In a letter to his brother, Washington wrote: "Death was leveling my companions on every side of me, but by the all-powerful dispensations of Providence, I have been protected."[6]

That battle ended in tragedy. Out of 1,459 men, 977 were either killed or wounded. It was an utter defeat. But Washington had gained respect, and his reputation spread throughout the colonies.

God continued to protect Washington during the rest of the war. As we look back, we can see that he was protected by God so that he could play a greater role in our nation's history. The men of Washington's day also noticed his miraculous protection and concluded the same thing. Samuel Davies, a famous clergyman of that day, wrote shortly after the above incident occurred: "To the public I point out that heroic youth . . . whom I cannot but hope providence has preserved in so signal a manner for some important service to our country."[7]

TREMENDOUS TESTIMONY

Even people who opposed the British recognized Washington's special role as a leader sent from God. An interesting event occurred in 1770, fifteen years after the devastating battle at Fort Duquesne. . . .

The forest was dark, entwining around the travelers like the vines in a fairy story. The two riders—the big one, six-foot-three inches tall, who rode easily on his big gray horse, and the smaller one, who leaned forward with fatigue—plunged their way through the undergrowth. "Does this area look familiar?" James Craik, an army physician, asked George Washington as he looked up into the tall man's face.

Washington looked around. "Yes, it does," he said. "This is the place where we fought so hard in the French and Indian War."

"Sure is," Craik said.

The two men rode without speaking, easy in each other's company. Finally they came to the Ohio River. Both men dismounted to give their horses a drink.

A band of Indians rode up. Both Washington and Craik were wary, but when they began talking to the Indians, they relaxed their guard. The conversation turned to the French and Indian War. The Indians were amazed when Washington told them his name.

"Come to our camp," one of the Indians suggested. "Our chief fought on the side of the French. He wants to talk to Washington."

Intrigued, the two men followed the Indians back to their village, where they were escorted to the central wigwam. Inside, they found an old Indian sitting on his blankets.

"I am chief and ruler over all my tribes," he said without an introduction. "My influence extends to the waters of the great lakes, and to the far blue mountains. I have traveled a long and weary path that I might see the young warrior of the great battle.

It was on the day when the white man's blood mixed with the streams of our forests that I first beheld this chief." He pointed to Washington. "I called to my young men and said, 'Mark yon tall and daring warrior? He is not of the redcoat tribe—he hath an Indian's wisdom, and his warriors fight as we do—himself alone is exposed. Quick, let your aim be certain, and he dies.'

"Our rifles were leveled, rifles which, but for him, knew not how to miss. I had seventeen fair fires at him and, after all, could not bring him to the ground. 'Twas all in vain; a power far mightier than we shielded him from harm. He cannot die in battle. . . . The Great Spirit protects that man and guides his destinies. He will become chief of nations, and a people yet unborn will hail him the founder of a mighty nation."[8]

Craik could only stand out of the way as the Indian chief paid honor to his tall companion. Craik took a closer look at Washington's calm bearing. He wondered what destiny had been prepared for this unusual man. . . .[9]

Amazing! Washington's reputation was so great that the Indian chief clearly remembered him after fifteen years. Truly God did have a great role for Washington.

Yet as the colonies began to boil under the heat and scrutiny of a tyrannical English ruler and British nation after the French and Indian War ended, Washington felt that his days of battle were finished. He had served for twenty years. Little did he know that an even greater war lay just over the horizon—just five short years after the old chief's prophecy was uttered!

A NEW COMMANDER

When Virginia held a Patriotic Convention in 1774, Washington attended and supported the American cause. He offered to "raise one thousand men, subsist them at my own expense, and march myself at their head for the relief of Boston."[10] The convention leaders didn't take him up on his offer, but they did send him as a delegate to the First Continental Congress. Here he met and influenced many other leaders of neighboring colonies.

When the Second Continental Congress gathered on May 10, 1775, to choose a general to lead the inexperienced American army, Washington was the leading candidate. The delegates remembered his heroic efforts in the French and Indian War and the great leadership he had displayed at the First Continental Congress. Since he was a citizen of Virginia, they hoped his involvement would help pull the southern colonies into the war.

When he was nominated as a candidate, he was reluctant to accept. But on June 15, he was unanimously chosen as commander in chief of the American army. He accepted the command on one condition—that Congress appoint and fund chaplains for his troops. This request came from his solid belief that prayer and the Bible were the most effective weapons for his soldiers.

Congress accepted his condition. In his usual humble attitude, Washington said, "With utmost sincerity, I do not think myself equal to the command I am honored with."[11]

A LIFE OF PRAYER

God had placed a man of prayer at the helm of the young American republic. Washington himself said, "It is impossible to govern rightly without God and the Bible."[12]

Today some people question Washington's belief in God and his prayer life. But to really know Washington is to read his diaries and writings. Through them, we can see his powerful attitudes toward God and prayer. We are fortunate to have copies of some of his private prayers. In his prayer diary, we discover that he prayed every morning and night. We also read about the things that he believed in and that he loved. The following are three prayers from that diary:

Monday Morning: O eternal and everlasting God, I presume to present myself this morning before Thy Divine Majesty, beseeching Thee to accept of my humble and hearty thanks. . . . Daily frame me more and more into the likeness of Thy Son, Jesus Christ, that living in Thy fear, and dying in Thy favor, I may in Thy appointed time attain the resurrection of the just unto eternal life. Bless my family, friends, and kindred, and unite us all in praising and glorifying Thee in all our works.

Monday Evening: Most Gracious Lord God, from whom proceedeth every good and perfect gift, I offer to Thy Divine Majesty my unfeigned praise and thanksgiving for all Thy mercies towards me. . . . I have sinned and done very wickedly, be merciful to me, O God, and pardon me for Jesus Christ's sake. . . . Bless O Lord the whole race of mankind, and let the world be filled with the knowledge of Thee and Thy Son, Jesus Christ. . . . I beseech Thee to defend me this night from all evil, and do more for me than I can think or ask, for Jesus Christ's sake, in whose most holy Name and Words, I continue to pray, Our Father, who art in Heaven, hallowed be Thy name.

Wednesday Morning: Almighty and eternal Lord God, the great Creator of heaven and earth, and the God and Father of our Lord Jesus Christ: look down from heaven, in pity and compassion upon me Thy servant, who humbly prostrate myself before Thee, sensible of Thy mercy and my own misery. . . . Help all in affliction or adversity—give them patience and a sanctified use of their affliction, and in Thy good time, deliverance from them; forgive my enemies, take me unto Thy protection this day, keep me in perfect peace, which I ask in the name and for the sake of Jesus. Amen.[13]

In these prayers, we see Washington's heart for God. He prayed daily for forgiveness of his sins. He also wanted others to share in this deep relationship with the almighty God. One of his first acts as commander in chief was to order his men to attend services and pray for safety and defense. This began a change in the undisciplined troops at Boston. When Washington took charge, these volunteers had no idea how to be soldiers. They had either come from haphazard hometown militias or were farmers who had just enlisted. Washington expected discipline and obedience. Rules were enforced under Washington's command. Order and regulation were instilled. That first summer the army spent endless days in marching, drilling, and learning how to obey orders.

Washington also ordered a day of fasting and prayer. To him, that was just as important as military training. The order reads:

The General orders this day [July 20, the first national fast day] to be religiously observed by the forces under his Command, exactly in manner directed by the Continental Congress. It is therefore strictly enjoined on all officers and soldiers to attend Divine service. And it is expected that all those who go to worship do take their arms, ammunition and accoutrements, and are prepared for immediate action, if called upon. [14]

What a way to start out his leadership! His very first act was a call to lead moral lives and to depend on the Lord to bestow his blessings and give them safety. Then he also asked his soldiers to observe the national Day of Prayer and Fasting. These were two very public witnesses to his reliance on prayer.

But this was only the beginning. Countless times on the battlefields, in camp, and in meetings, Washington would lead by example through his own prayers. An officer who served under him for eight years testified that on every occasion, Washington sought God's blessing and help. If there wasn't a chaplain available, he took the lead and called his staff officers together for prayer. No wonder so many miraculous events occurred under his leadership!

MIRACLE AT LONG ISLAND

Early in the war for American independence, God showed his protection of General Washington's troops on Long Island. Before that time, General Howe had inflicted heavy losses on the American army but had never captured or destroyed it. What a major blow to the Patriot morale if Howe could do just that.

During the summer of 1776, Washington had eight thousand men in Brooklyn Heights, half of them untrained. General Howe amassed thirty-two thousand men on Staten Island. On August 22, fifteen thousand British troops landed on the southeastern shore of Long Island, and five thousand more troops joined them three days later. They were gearing up to capture the colonial army.

General Howe's tactic was to use British regulars to surround the rebel army in a great semicircle. Quickly, the British troops surrounded the Americans on all three sides. Behind Washington's army was the mile-wide East River. Since the Patriots were greatly outnumbered, Washington realized that fighting would mean a defeat and would more than likely end the war.

Yet surrender was unthinkable. At this point, one of the most amazing episodes of divine intervention during the entire Revolutionary War occurred. General Howe suddenly stopped his advance and remained in his position for two days. No one knows why. He was a brilliant general with many strategic battles under his belt. On the second day, a northeast wind and rain blew in, making the East River unnavigable to the British ships. This prevented the British army from surrounding the Patriots.

Then Washington devised a plan. He decided to take the entire army off Brooklyn Heights by small boats so they could join twelve thousand American troops at Manhattan Island. All the other officers considered it a disastrous plan. They would be sitting ducks if the storm let up while they were on the water.

But Washington saw God's perfect timing in the fact that the last reinforcements to arrive were expert boatmen. These recruits were some of the best mariners in the world. Small boats were located, and the task began. All eight thousand men with their supplies, guns, carts, cattle, and horses had to be evacuated quietly during the night.

The evacuation was slow at first because of the strong wind. It made the sailboats useless. Only rowboats could make it across. At that rate, evacuation seemed impossible.

Then God intervened again. The wind that had howled for three days stopped at around eleven o'clock. Now all the boats could be used and loaded with extra weight. A full moon came out and guided the evacuation for the rest of the night. God also seemed to shut the eyes and ears of the British army because they never became aware of the Americans' activity. But as the sun began to rise, many troops still needed to be evacuated.

American major Benjamin Tallmadge recorded what happened next:

> As the dawn of the next day approached, those of us who remained in the trenches became very anxious for our own

safety, and when the dawn appeared, there were several regiments still on duty. At this time, a very dense fog began to rise [out of the ground and off the river], and it seemed to settle in a peculiar manner over both encampments. I recollect this peculiar providential occurrence perfectly well, and so very dense was the atmosphere that I could scarcely discern a man at six yards distance. . . . We tarried until the sun had risen, but the fog remained as dense as ever.[15]

The fog gave Washington and his troops extra time to get off the island. As the last boats left Long Island, the fog lifted. When the British troops learned of the evacuation, they sent soldiers to the river, but they found only one boat close enough to capture. It contained three vagabonds who had stayed behind to ransack the empty camp.

As a result of this incident, many people learned of Washington's faith in the midst of battle. The following note was published in the *Evening Post* on February 18, 1860:

To the Editors of the Evening Post:

MR. PRINTER:—In 1796, I heard the farmer referred to narrate the following incident. Said he, "When the British troops held possession of New York, and the American army lay in the neighborhood of West Point, one morning at sunrise I went forth to bring home the cows. On passing a clump of brushwood, I heard a moaning sound, like a person in distress. On nearing the spot, I heard the words of a man at prayer. I stood behind a tree. The man came forth: it was George Washington, the captain of the Lord's host in North America."

This farmer belonged to the Society of Friends, who, being opposed to war on any pretext, were lukewarm, and, in some cases, opposed to the cause of the country. However, having seen the general enter the camp, he returned to his own house. "Martha," said he to his wife, "we must not oppose this war any longer. This morning I heard the man George Washington send up a prayer to Heaven for his country, and I know it will be heard." . . .

From this incident we may infer that Washington rose with the sun to pray for his country, he fought for her at meridian, and watched for her in the silent hours of night.[16]

What a miraculous retreat! It could only be attributed to Washington's prayers and the hand of God.

MIRACLE NEAR PRINCETON

In January 1777, Washington faced the British on the Delaware River near Princeton. He crossed the river only to find the British already formed into battle lines and waiting for the American army.

Washington saw the mounting confusion and fear in the ranks of his men. In an attempt to steady the nerves of his wavering soldiers, Washington did a most amazing thing—he galloped out in front of his battle line. Mounted on his huge white horse, he was a conspicuous target for the British rifles. He stopped just thirty yards from the British lines and directed his men to take aim. Washington was between the two opposing forces as they began to fire fiercely at each other.

After the first volley, many men lay dead or dying, but Washington was still astride his horse, untouched by the shower of bullets. The old Indian's prophecy that Washington was protected by the Great Spirit and could not be killed in battle proved true once again. The Americans rallied and won the battle.[17]

VALLEY FORGE

One of the most difficult times Washington faced was the winter at Valley Forge, 1777–78. But the hardship had its purpose:

the winter encampment gave Washington time to prepare his men. During that time, Washington often prayed in the forest in a secluded glen. Isaac Potts, a farmer in the area, was walking quietly through the woods when he came upon Washington on his knees praying. As Isaac listened to Washington's prayer, he felt awed by its power and left unnoticed. When he returned home, he ran into the house to tell his wife:

> If there is any one on earth whom the Lord will hearken to, it is George Washington; and I feel a presentiment that under such a commander there can be no doubt of our eventually establishing our independence, and that God in his providence has willed it so.[18]

The winter of 1777–78 would prove to be a testing ground for the undisciplined solders of the American army. But God's hand and the incredible power of prayer can still be seen in one of the most-remembered examples of sacrifice for American freedom.

Washington chose Valley Forge, Pennsylvania, for his winter campsite because it was only fifteen miles from Philadelphia and it was easy to defend. But he wasn't prepared for the ferocious winter. His troops were already painfully short of shoes, clothing, blankets, and tents.

As the winter progressed, the situation only got worse. Food became so scarce that the soldiers went for days without anything to eat. When they did eat, it was likely to be less than a quarter cup of rice and a tablespoon of vinegar. During the months of January and February, more than four thousand soldiers were incapacitated due to exposure, disease, and starvation. One in every four died of exposure.

During these difficult times in the winter at Valley Forge,

George Washington prayed for God's protection. He was seen going daily to some secluded spot in the surrounding forest to kneel and pray.[19] An officer who was at Valley Forge said of Washington, "On every practicable occasion he sought God's blessing, and when no chaplain was present, he often called his staff officers around him and lifted his heart and voice in prayer."[20]

The chronic lack of food was the subject of many of his prayers. In mid-February, he wrote, "This Army must inevitably be reduced to one or the other of mere three things: starve, dissolve, or disperse, in order to obtain subsistence."[21]

One miraculous answer to Washington's prayer for food came from the Schuylkill River. Bruce Lancaster described the miracle:

> One foggy morning the soldiers noticed Schuylkill River seemed to be boiling. The disturbance was caused by thousands and thousands of shad which were making their way upstream in an unusually early migration. With pitchforks and shovels, the men plunged into the water, throwing the fish onto the banks. Lee's dragoons rode their horses into the stream to keep the shad from swimming on out of reach. Suddenly and wonderfully, there was plenty of food for the army.[22]

WASHINGTON'S FAITH

In the summer of 1779, Washington went on an exploration mission for his army. A sudden storm caused him to seek shelter at the cottage of an American farmer. The farmer was so impressed with Washington's language and manners that he listened at the bedroom door as the famous man prayed. This was the prayer he overheard:

Almighty Father, if it is Thy holy will that we shall obtain a place and name among the nations of the earth, grant that we may be enabled to show our gratitude for Thy goodness by our endeavors to fear and obey Thee. Bless us with Thy wisdom in our councels [sic], success in battle, and let all our victories be tempered with humanity. Endow, also, our enemies with enlightened minds, that they become sensible of their injustice, and willing to restore our liberty and peace. . . . Nevertheless, not my will, but Thine be done.[23]

Without a doubt, Washington possessed great faith in God. He believed that God directed every step this new nation was taking. He led the military in the same way he lived his life—with total reliance on God. God honored him for his faith with divine intervention.

THE SURRENDER OF CORNWALLIS

The war finally came to an end with the battle of Yorktown and the surrender of British general Cornwallis in October 1781. General Washington saw God at work again in this victory. In his congratulatory order to his army, he gave the credit to God and ordered a Thanksgiving service.[24] He also directed his troops to attend religious services!

Timothy Dwight, one of the most famous ministers of the day, preached a sermon from Isaiah 59:18-19. In the sermon, Dwight called upon his congregation to "remember with hymns of the most fervent praise how God judged [their] enemies, when [they] had no might against the great company that came against [them]." He concluded, "While we mark the Divine hand in the illustrious event we are now contemplating, can we fail to cry out, 'Praise the Lord, for He is good, for His mercy endureth forever'?"[25]

As the war came to an end, Washington met with his senior officers in Fraunces Tavern in Manhattan for a farewell luncheon. By this time he had endeared himself to his men and the whole nation. He was the most beloved man in the colonies.

At this final farewell, he said, "With a heart full of gratitude, I now take leave of you. I most devoutly wish that your latter days be as prosperous and happy as your former ones have been glorious and honorable."[26] Then each of his officers came and shook his hand and embraced him. Ben Tallmadge, a lieutenant colonel, wrote of this parting:

> Such a scene of sorrow and weeping, I had never witnessed, and hope I may never be called to again. . . . Not a word was uttered to break the solemn silence . . . or to interrupt the tenderness of the scene. The simple thought that we were then about to part from the man who had conducted us through a long and bloody war, and under whose conduct the glory and independence of our country had been achieved, and that we would see his face no more in this world, seemed to me to be utterly insupportable.[27]

After the war was over, Washington handed in an official resignation of his commission before Congress. As he did, he said: "I consider it an indispensable duty to close this last solemn act of my official life by commending the interests of our dearest country to the protection of Almighty God, and of those who have superintendence of them to His holy keeping."[28] His last words as commander in chief were centered on God. He knew that the success of our new country depended on the divine intervention of God with every decision and document signed.

THE END OF AN EXTRAORDINARY CAREER

With the war over, Washington wanted to retire to his beloved Mt. Vernon for a peaceful life away from the public eye. But God had other plans for him. He was to become our nation's first president. God knew that Washington's wisdom and strength would be invaluable during the formative years of our country.

Washington was elected unanimously. Everyone agreed he was the only man to lead the new nation. He was inaugurated on April 30, 1789. Placing his hand on the Bible he loved, he took an oath of office. He added the phrase, "I swear, so help me God," and leaned over and kissed the Bible. Every president since has said the same words. In his inaugural address, Washington stressed the role God's intervention had played in this young nation's birth:

> It would be peculiarly improper to omit, in this first official act, my fervent supplication to that Almighty Being, who rules over the universe, who presides in the councils of nations, and whose providential aids can supply every human defect, that His benediction may consecrate to the liberties and happiness of the people of the United States. . . . No people can be bound to acknowledge and adore the invisible hand which conducts the affairs of men more than the people of the United States. Every step by which they have advanced to the character of an independent nation seems to have been distinguished by some token of providential agency. . . . We ought to be no less persuaded that the propitious smiles of Heaven can never be expected on a nation that disregards the eternal rules of order and right, which Heaven itself has ordained."[29]

After giving this address, the president, the speaker, and the members of the House of Representatives went to St. Paul's Chapel to hear a sermon by a chaplain.

During the next eight years, Washington helped build a solid foundation for the young nation with the help of our other Founding Fathers. Many of their first official acts and proclamations glorified God. For example, the very first act of Congress was to elect chaplains to open each legislative session with prayer—which still occurs today.

In October 1789, as we saw in the last chapter, Washington proclaimed a Day of Thanksgiving to acknowledge God's providence in the forming of the nation. Congress authorized Washington to print the first American edition of the Bible in 1781. They wrote, "[We] recommend to the inhabitants of the United States, and hereby authorize him to publish this recommendation in the manner he shall think proper."[30]

A MEMORIAL TO A GREAT MAN

What a different Washington we see in the annals of history than what has been printed in our textbooks and in television dramas. Why haven't we been told of his deep prayer life and reliance on God? All Americans have missed out in the cover-up of the Father of America's personal life! This is a legacy we need to pass on and that Washington himself wanted to pass on to each generation.

The following is an article from *The Family Circle* published in 1847. It reminds us of how we should remember Washington—as a man of prayer!

> In this hour of darkness and of danger, when "foes were strong and friends were few," when every human prospect presented to the commander at Valley Forge was disheartening, he retired to a sequestered spot, and there laid the cause of his bleeding country AT THE THRONE OF GRACE. That country had appealed in vain to the justice of her acknowl-

edged sovereign; HE pleads her cause before the King of kings. He had before complained to Congress that there was deficiency in the chaplaincy of the army. But it was not the form he relied on. It was not a religious awe, as a matter of mere policy, with which he sought to imbue the minds of soldiery religiously educated. He sought to link our cause, by a sincere devotion, to the immutable throne of justice; to find wisdom to guide his own action; to place the country in the RIGHT, so that he might bring upon her prosperity, as the natural result of justice to the injured.

How full of interest is this scene! How instructive! How sublime! Let our children come up from their cradles through the remotest generations to contemplate this picture. Let parents open it to their admiring families. Let it be hung on the parlor walls, ornament the center tables, be pictured on the tapestry, be grouped with every cradle scene, recited in every nursery, that it may meet the early vision, and affect the young heart of every child who may breathe the free air of this land of freedom—WASHINGTON IS AT PRAYER. Well did he earn the title of "PATRIARCH"—The FATHER OF HIS COUNTRY. As we honor him, and teach our children to give him honor, may we also love and honor, and teach our children to acknowledge the God of our fathers, who, alone giveth the victory.

Because of the faith of George Washington and many others, and because the people fasted and prayed, the colonies saw many prayer miracles during the Revolutionary War. Once again, prayer changed the course of history.

God's work was evident in all the miraculous victories in the American Revolutionary War. His power can be seen in these incidents and many others. Our history books can't explain why a small colony was successful in breaking away from the strongest nation on the earth. But the answer seems clear.

It was because the Americans, as individuals, as separate colonies, and as a new nation, regularly humbled themselves and prayed.

In the next chapter, we'll see how prayer influenced the leaders of our new nation, those Founding Fathers who formed the first American documents. God would once again provide prayer miracles when events seemed at their darkest hour.

For Discussion and Reflection

Adult Discussion

On a chalkboard or large piece of paper, make a list of names of people who are famous for something in the past or present—people such as Judas, Babe Ruth, Marilyn Monroe, Mother Teresa, or Abraham Lincoln. Include George Washington as the final name. Go over your list of names, and have each person write one word that would describe that person. For example, someone might write *honest* for Abraham Lincoln.

When people finish writing, have them call out their answers, and write the words under each famous person's name. Then ask:

★ How does a person become known for something?
★ Why don't many people today know that George Washington was known as a man of prayer?

Have people form pairs to discuss the following questions:

★ What things characterized Washington as a man of prayer?
★ King David was also known for his prayers. Read Psalm 17;

204

Psalm 55:16-17; and Psalm 86, and discuss similarities between these prayers and Washington's prayers recorded in this chapter.

Have pairs share their findings. Then ask the group to reflect on these questions:

★ How do you think people would describe your prayer life?
★ How does that make you feel?
★ What could you do this week to begin making prayer a greater priority in your life?

Say, "One thing George Washington did was to write down some of his prayers in a prayer diary. That's something we might all consider doing as we begin taking prayer more seriously in our lives." Have partners pray together to end your session.

Youth Discussion

Write down a few familiar words from songs, movies, TV shows, or jingles for TV commercials. Also write down a few verses from well-known prayers in the Bible. Have a combination of at least ten phrases. When class begins, explain that you are going to play a game called Place That Phrase. Tell the kids that you'll begin reading a few words and that the first person to recognize which song, movie, TV show, TV commercial, or book of the Bible the words come from should stand up. When the game is finished, ask:

★ Which kinds of phrases were easiest to place? Why do you think that's so?
★ How did you respond when kids beat you on the Bible prayers?

★ How does this reflect on the importance of the Bible and prayer in our lives?

Form groups of four to discuss the following questions. Ask:

★ What gave Washington a reputation as a man of prayer?
★ Read Psalm 119:9-11. How can we keep our reputation pure?
★ From these verses, what part does prayer play in our staying pure?

Have the groups report their findings. Then have them take a few moments to reflect on these questions:

★ What traits characterize your life? How do you feel about that?
★ How could you make prayer a bigger part of your life?

Give the kids time to reflect on each question. Then have them each pray silently, committing to making prayer a bigger part of their lives.

FOURTEEN

Amazing Documents

Something happened between the spring and fall of 1787 that would prove to be miraculous. The Constitution of the United States was written. It was and is the most successful frame of government ever devised in history.

It was built upon the premise of the Declaration of Independence, which had been written during the Revolutionary War, eleven years previous. For this reason, a closer look at the Declaration of Independence will help us understand the intent of the men who signed the Constitution.

The Declaration of Independence spells out what most Americans believed at that time. They wanted to establish a new nation based on the laws of God and independent of the tyrannical rule of Britain. This is the beginning and ending of the Declaration of Independence:

> When in the Course of human events, it becomes necessary for one people to dissolve the political bands which have connected them with another, and to assume among the powers of the earth, the separate and equal station to which the Laws of Nature and of Nature's God entitle them, a decent respect

to the opinions of mankind requires that they should declare the causes which impel them to the separation.

We hold these truths to be self-evident, that all men are created equal, that they are endowed by their Creator with certain unalienable Rights, that among these are Life, Liberty and the pursuit of Happiness. That to secure these rights, Governments are instituted among Men, deriving their just powers from the consent of the governed. . . .

We, therefore, the Representatives of the United States of America, in General Congress, Assembled, appealing to the Supreme Judge of the world for the rectitude of our intentions, do, in the Name, and by the Authority of the good People of these Colonies, solemnly publish and declare, That these United Colonies are, and of Right ought to be Free and Independent States; that they are Absolved from all Allegiance to the British Crown, and that all political connection between them and the State of Great Britain, is and ought to be totally dissolved; and that as Free and Independent States, they have full Power to levy War, conclude Peace, contract Alliances, establish Commerce, and to do all other Acts and Things which Independent States may of right do. And for the support of this Declaration, with a firm reliance on the protection of Divine Providence, we mutually pledge to each other our Lives, our Fortunes and our sacred Honor.[1]

This document is unique in all the world. It declares that people "are endowed by their Creator with certain unalienable Rights." The first document of our country, therefore, begins with the rights God has endowed us with and ends with an appeal to that same Judge, acknowledging "a firm reliance on the protection of Divine Providence." To late-eighteenth-century Americans, it was self-evident that if there were no God, there would be no absolute rights.

TO SIGN OR NOT TO SIGN

Author Vincent Wilson Jr. explains why the Declaration of Independence is a landmark in history:

> This document stands as one of the truly great facts of human history: in one sudden thrust, man vaulted to an entirely new level of political life, and a kind of freedom that before had been only a matter of philosophical discussion was now a political goal to the achievement of which these founders of a new nation had most solemnly committed their "lives, fortunes and [their] sacred honor."[2]

The men who signed this Declaration were the leaders of the thirteen colonies. Twenty-five were lawyers or jurists, eleven were merchants, nine were farmers or large plantation owners, and others were doctors. But the signing of the Declaration of Independence was more than a momentous occasion to the men assembled. It was a threat to their lives.

A heated debate occurred right before the vote for approval. John Adams spoke very honestly when he warned them what it would mean for them to approve it. He said, "If you imagine that I expect this Declaration will ward off calamities . . . you are mistaken. A bloody conflict we are destined to endure."[3] When the debate and discussion were over, the delegates to the First Continental Congress voted to approve it. When the results of the approval were announced, a silence hung over the delegates as they thought of the gravity of this moment. Some wept; others bowed in prayer.

Samuel Adams rose to his feet. "We have this day restored the Sovereign to whom alone men ought to be obedient. He reigns in heaven and . . . from the rising to the setting sun, may His Kingdom come."[4]

These men understood the hardships they would face if

they signed. But they all rose and put their names on the document. William Ellery of Rhode Island watched closely as each man signed. "I was determined," he wrote, "to see how they all looked as they signed what might be their death warrant. I . . . eyed each closely. . . . Undaunted resolution was displayed on every countenance."[5]

A PRICE TO PAY

What a price these men paid! John Quincy Adams, the son of a Revolutionary, summed it up like this: "Posterity! You will never know how much it cost the present generation to preserve your freedom. I hope you will make good use of it."[6]

Look at the losses some of the signers suffered:

★ Francis Lewis: The British burned his home and held his wife in prison for two years in the worst conditions. She died shortly after her release.

★ Lewis Morris: His estate and home were burned; his family was driven off their land.

★ Richard Stockton: He rescued his family from approaching British troops but was captured and thrown into prison. There he was regularly beaten and starved. The British also destroyed his home. As a result of his prison treatment, he spent the rest of his life as an invalid.

★ John Hart: His home was burned, and he had to hide out in caves and forests. His wife died, and his thirteen children were scattered. He died of poor health three years after he signed.

★ Thomas McKean: He was "hunted like a fox" during the American Revolution and was "compelled to move [his] family five times in a few months."[7]

★ George Clymer: His home was overtaken by the British. He lost more than one hundred of his own ships during the war.

★ Philip Livingston: His 150,000-acre estate was seized by the

British, but he contributed much of what was left of his dwindling fortune to the war effort. Because of the strain of the war effort, he died two years after the signing.

★ George Walton: He was wounded and captured. After his release, he served as a governor of Georgia and as a U.S. Senator.

★ Carter Baxton: Every merchant ship he owned was sunk or captured by the British. He lost all his wealth and was forced to sell his land.

★ William Floyd: His estate in New York was overrun and ruined by the British. He could not return home for the seven years of the war.

What sacrifices were made to sign this national charter! John Adams wrote to his wife, Abigail, about the day the Declaration of Independence was signed:

> [This day] will be the most memorable . . . in the history of America. I am apt to believe it will be celebrated by succeeding generations as the great anniversary festival. It ought to be commemorated, as the Day of Deliverance, by solemn acts of devotion to God Almighty. It ought to be solemnized with pomp and parade, with shows, games, sports, guns, bells, bonfires and illuminations, from one end of this continent to the other, from this time forward forevermore.
>
> You will think me transported with enthusiasm, but I am not, I am well aware of the toil and blood and treasure that it will cost to maintain this Declaration, and support and defend these States. Yet through all the gloom I can see the rays of ravishing light and glory. I can see that end is worth more than all the means.[8]

Where did these ideas originate? Noah Webster, famous for *Webster's Dictionary,* looked back on the formation of the great documents of our nation and offered this explanation:

Almost all the civil liberty now enjoyed in the world owes its origin to the principles of the Christian religion. . . . Civil liberty has been gradually advancing and improving, as genuine Christianity has prevailed. . . . The religion which has introduced civil liberty, is the religion of Christ and his apostles, which enjoins humility, piety, and benevolence; which acknowledges in every person a brother, or a sister, and a citizen with equal rights. This is genuine Christianity, and to this we owe our free constitutions of government.[9]

MIRACLE AT THE CONVENTION

The Founding Fathers were very much aware of how God had preserved and blessed them. After the signing of the Declaration of Independence, they carried the national interests forward in spite of considerable personal peril. But they were sure of their success through prayer. In 1783, George Washington wrote:

I now make it my earnest prayer that God . . . would be pleased to dispose us all to do justice, to love mercy, and to demean ourselves with charity and humility, and a pacific temper of mind, which were characteristics of the Divine author of our blessed Religion, and without an humble imitation of Whose example in these things, we can never hope to be a happy nation.[10]

In 1787, Washington called a Constitutional Convention. At first, only seven of the thirteen states sent representatives. Eventually more arrived, until twelve of the thirteen states were represented. Rhode Island chose not to participate. The delegates to this historic gathering were all men of honor and great renown: Jefferson, Hamilton, Madison, Franklin, and, of course, George Washington.

After meeting for a short time, the men realized that they were not unified. Some delegates wanted a strong central government; others didn't trust a central government and argued for states' rights. Large states wanted proportional representation, and smaller states wanted an equal voice. Then there was the issue of slavery. Some states wanted it abolished; others defended the practice as necessary to their citizens' livelihood.

The concepts they proposed were sound, but the frailties of men soon got in the way. Washington, who presided over the meeting, was gravely disappointed. The petty bickering of the delegates soon drove him to despair. The situation looked hopeless. . . .

The arguing in the Philadelphia State House seemed to go on and on as voices clamored all over the room. The tension was thick and the air suffocatingly warm.

One delegate stood and began arguing against John Adams's ideas of how a government should be formed. "It's not fair," he shouted, "that the three biggest states, Virginia, Massachusetts, and Pennsylvania, combine to form a group. If they can, then the ten small states should do the same! I just can't agree to the Virginia plan for our government." He went on, his voice getting louder.

Another delegate across the room brought up the possibility that new states in the west would join in the future. "What will happen to them? Will they combine too, making it hard for the older states?"

Madison spoke up. "How could the three large states ever combine their interests? They have very little in common."

The argument had been going on for days. Most of the faces in the room were lined with tension and fatigue. George Washington, who sat on a dais to lead the group, looked as if he had lost control. A couple of the delegates got up, disgusted. "We've had enough arguing for one day. This meeting is not getting us anywhere," they announced, and they walked out.

The atmosphere was so charged with hostility that it looked as if the convention would break apart. No one wanted to give an inch.

Then Benjamin Franklin stood up. The room hushed in awe before this venerable old man. When he finally spoke, everyone listened. His words echoed through the room:

> In the beginning of the contest with Britain, when we were sensible of danger, we had daily prayers in this room for Divine protection. Our prayers, Sir, were heard, and they were graciously answered. All of us who were engaged in the struggle must have observed frequent instances of a super-intending Providence in our favor. . . . And have we now forgotten this powerful Friend? Or do we imagine we no longer need his assistance?
>
> I have lived, Sir, a long time, and the longer I live, the more convincing proofs I see of this truth: "That God governs in the affairs of man." And if a sparrow cannot fall to the ground without His notice, is it probable that an Empire can rise without His aid?
>
> We have been assured, Sir, in the Sacred Writings that except the Lord build the house, they labor in vain that build it. I firmly believe this. I also believe that without His concurring aid, we shall succeed in the political building no better than the builders of Babel; we shall be divided by your little, partial local interests; our projects will be confounded; and we ourselves shall become a reproach and a byword down to future ages. And what is worse, mankind may hereafter from this unfortunate instance, despair of establishing government by human wisdom and leave it to chance, war, or conquest.
>
> I therefore beg leave to move that, henceforth, prayers im-

ploring the assistance of Heaven and its blessing on our delib-
eration be held in this assembly every morning before we
proceed to business.[11]

When he sat down, a buzz of conversation passed quietly
among the delegates. . . .[12]

RENEWED VISION

Ben Franklin's remarks got the delegates' attention. They began to evaluate their priorities. Prayer was their first order of
business. They adjourned for three days, and many spent that
time praying and attending church.[13] Philadelphia pastors
preached and led the delegates in seeking God's will. Those
three days, beginning on June 28, 1787, marked a turning
point among the embittered convention delegates. New Jersey
delegate Jonathan Dayton remarked: "Every unfriendly feeling
had been expelled and a spirit of reconciliation had been cultivated."[14]

The reconciled delegates reassembled on July 2 with a new
vision. Soon after, the convention produced the Constitution
that has become the envy of freedom-loving people throughout the world. The Constitution could not have been written
in a selfish, dissentious atmosphere. These men needed
God's guidance and peace, and those three days of prayer and
listening to God's Word set them on the right track. Prayer
was the only answer for the melding of the many differences
of ideas.

One difference was resolved through the Connecticut Compromise, presented by Roger Sherman. It provided for two legislative bodies: equal representation for each state in the
Senate and representation on the basis of population in the
House of Representatives. This settled the differences of opin-

ion between large and small states. Because prayer had softened their hearts, most of the delegates were ready to accept this compromise.

For over a month, other differences were discussed and settled. Finally, on September 8, the rough draft was given to Governor Morris of Philadelphia for a final rewrite. He completed it in four days, adding many of the phrases we now treasure.

The American Constitution embodied an idea that had never been put into a constitution before. It gave the power granted from the Creator to the people, who would then grant rights to government. Up to this time, human rights had been based on the power of the state. The Constitution was the first written charter for self-government in modern history. It was the first prepared by the people and the first to recognize the people's right to self-government. Our Constitution has been used as a model by many nations for their own constitutions.

What a legacy these Founding Fathers left us! A legacy that was orchestrated by men who depended on God. The men who wrote this Constitution were overwhelmingly religious. Each of them professed and exhibited a deep faith in God. They believed God was the Creator and that he was active in human history. Although Franklin and Jefferson came to that conclusion late in life, they were students of the Bible and frequently quoted from it. All except Jefferson believed that Scripture was a revelation from God. They all worked to preserve the Constitution from anything that was contrary to the Bible.

While a few of the drafters of our Constitution are very famous, many are relatively unknown. Let's look at a few and their personal walks with God.

JAMES MADISON—FATHER OF THE CONSTITUTION

James Madison was born into a devout home in Port Conway, Virginia. His parents were plantation owners and members of the state church of Virginia. He was home schooled by his godly mother and grandmother. His schooling was supplemented by two tutors, one of which was a minister.

Madison was present when a great revival swept through Princeton. It is believed his life was touched by the religious flame because when he returned home, he conducted worship in his father's house. One historian wrote this about Madison's Bible study:

> After the manner of the Bereans he seems to have searched the Scriptures daily and diligently. . . . He explored the whole history and evidences of Christianity on every side, through clouds of witnesses and champions for and against, from the Fathers and schoolmen down to the infidel philosophers of the eighteenth century. No one not a professed theologian, and but few even of those, have ever gone through more laborious and extensive inquiries to arrive at the truth.[15]

Madison was a delegate to both the Continental Congress and the Constitutional Convention. He was a U.S. congressman, became a secretary of state under Thomas Jefferson, and engineered the Louisiana Purchase. He was our third president and served for two terms, including the War of 1812.

Madison wrote: "The belief in God All Powerful wise and good is so essential to the moral order of the World and to the happiness of man, that arguments which enforce it cannot be drawn from too many sources nor adapted with too much solicitude to the different characters and capacities to be impressed with it."[16]

ROGER SHERMAN

Roger Sherman was probably one of the most devout men at the convention. His pastor was Reverend Jonathan Edwards, and Sherman served as a deacon, clerk, and treasurer under his leadership. One of his common practices was to purchase a Bible when Congress started its session. He would study it daily, then give it to one of his children when he returned home. Here is part of his confession of faith:

> I believe that there is one only living and true God, existing in three persons, the Father, the Son, and the Holy Ghost, the same in substance, equal in power and glory. That the Scriptures of the Old and New Testaments are a revelation from God, and a complete rule to direct us how we may glorify and enjoy him. . . . That he made man at first perfectly holy, that the first man sinned, and as he was the public head of his posterity, they all became sinners in consequence of his first transgression, are wholly indisposed to that which is good and inclined to evil, and on account of sin are liable to all the miseries of this life, to death, and the pains of hell forever. I believe that God, having elected some of mankind to eternal life, did send his own Son to become man, die in the room and stead of sinners, and thus to lay foundation for the offer of pardon and salvation to all mankind, so as all may be saved who are willing to accept the gospel offer.[17]

Sherman was instrumental in the design of the Connecticut Compromise, which resolved the problem of representation at a time when that issue seemed to be tearing the Constitutional Convention apart. He also worked to have Thanksgiving Day established as a national holiday.

ABRAHAM BALDWIN

Baldwin was born into a deeply religious family and attended Yale Divinity School, studying to be a minister. Upon graduation, he joined the faculty of the college. During wartime, he served as a chaplain in the Continental army. He represented Georgia at the Constitutional Convention and was well respected.

JOHN LANGDON

At the time of the convention, John Langdon was the most popular man in New Hampshire. He supplied arms and money to the Continental army and served as a colonel in the militia. As the president of his state, he called for a Day of Fasting and Prayer and a Day of Thanksgiving a year before the convention. His proclamation gives us an idea of his deep Christian convictions.

> A Proclamation For a Day of Public FASTING AND PRAYER throughout this State. Vain is the acknowledgement of a Supreme Ruler of the Universe, unless such acknowledgements influence our practice, and call forth those expressions of homage and adoration that are due to this character and providential government, agreeably to the light of nature, enforced by revelation, and countenanced by the practice of civilized nations, in humble and fervent application to the throne for needed mercies, and gratitude for favors received . . . that he would rain down righteousness upon the earth, revive religion, and spread abroad the knowledge of the true GOD, the Saviour of man, throughout the world.[18]

He was one of the founders of the New Hampshire Bible Society and its first president. The society's goal was to place the Bible within the reach of every New Hampshire home. It is still in existence today.

CHARLES COTESWORTH PINCKNEY

Pinckney was a deeply spiritual man with an abiding faith. He was born into a wealthy, aristocratic family and schooled at Westminster School at Oxford under the godly legal genius of Sir William Blackstone, whose legal writings formed the basis of the American judicial system.

Pinckney was an active and vocal patriot during the war, which caused him to be imprisoned by the British for two years. Upon his release, he returned to the military service and reached the rank of brigadier general.

Only twenty-nine years old when he attended the convention, he commanded respect. He thought so highly of the Constitution that he pledged publicly to fight for its approval in South Carolina, which he did until his state ratified it in 1788.

His commitment to Jesus Christ was deep. Upon his death, a resolution was read by the Charleston Bible Society, which he had established. The following excerpt from that resolution gives you an idea of what he was like:

> The Board of Managers of the Charleston Bible Society . . .
> give devout thanks to Almighty God for the invaluable services
> which the life, influence and example of their late revered
> president, have rendered to the cause of religion, virtue, and
> good order, to his country and to mankind; and that they sub-
> mit themselves to this painful dispensation of providence, with
> a sorrow mitigated by the grateful remembrance of his virtue,
> and by a pious trust in Divine mercy.[19]

MEN OF ACTION

The reason these men saw miracles of God was that they put their prayers into action. They weren't content to write documents, then wait to see what happened. They put their faith into action in many ways. One of these was to plant Sunday schools, a new concept at that time. Author Robert Flood writes:

> Perhaps no movement in early America undergirded its evangelism with the spirit of patriotism as did the American Sunday School Union. The Sunday school movement had originated in England with Robert Raikes. It was transplanted to America by another Englishman, Robert May. It took root with special vigor around Philadelphia, and out of that city in 1824 came a national movement called the American Sunday School Union.
>
> Then in the next century and a half it planted thousands of Sunday schools across America, following the migration west from the Appalachian cabins to the frontier towns and the isolated hovels of the western Indian. Churches eventually sprang up from the majority of these Sunday schools—more than three thousand of them in this century alone.[20]

The American Sunday School Union was begun by our Founding Fathers. Notice the names associated with its early history:

* ★ Dr. Benjamin Rush: He signed the Declaration of Independence and was one of the most highly regarded doctors of his day.
* ★ Bushrod Washington: He was George Washington's nephew and wrote the most-circulated American Sunday School Union book on the life of his uncle.
* ★ John Marshall: He was one of the greatest chief justices of the U.S. Supreme Court.
* ★ John Pollock: He was governor of Pennsylvania and headed the mint in Philadelphia.
* ★ Francis Scott Key: He was the man who penned our national

anthem, "The Star-Spangled Banner," while he was a prisoner aboard a British ship near Fort McHenry.

Many of our Founding Fathers also started Bible societies to distribute Bibles throughout the new nation. Their concern began when British trade was cut off during the American Revolution, which also cut off the supply of new Bibles. Immediately, a printing press was set up to print Bibles.

Another demonstration of the faith of the Founding Fathers was that the first official act of the U.S. Congress was to select a chaplain who would begin the sessions with prayer. This was an acknowledgment that the representatives needed divine guidance, wisdom, and strength to lead a ship of state. Today the U.S. Congress still follows this tradition, with the more recent addition of the Congressional Prayer Room open only to congressmen for their private meditations.

A NATIONAL DAY OF PRAYER

After the Constitution was ratified, the Bill of Rights was added on December 15, 1791. The First Amendment, creating the separation between church and state, was debated in the House of Representatives for the entire summer of 1789 and was approved on September 24.

What did the framers intend by approving this amendment? That religion have no part in government? Certainly not. At that time, several states had established "state churches." In fact, a citizen of Connecticut could be fined fifty shillings for missing church. The congressmen wanted to ensure religious liberty, not to isolate religion from government.

How do we know this? On September 25, *one day* after they ratified the First Amendment, Congress passed a resolution calling for a National Day of Prayer and Thanksgiving:

We acknowledge with grateful hearts the many signal favors of Almighty God, especially by affording them an opportunity peacefully to establish a constitutional government for their safety and happiness.[21]

Then the congressmen called on President Washington to proclaim a day for prayer and thanksgiving. This is what President Washington said:

It is the duty of all nations to acknowledge the providence of Almighty God, to obey His will, to be grateful for His benefits and humbly to implore His protection and favor . . . that great and glorious Being who is the beneficent author of all the good that was, that is, or that ever will be, that we may then unite in rendering unto Him our sincere and humble thanks for His kind care and protection of the people.[22]

President George Bush, who proclaimed a National Day of Prayer in 1989, said this of our Founding Fathers:

The great faith that led our Nation's Founding Fathers to pursue this bold experiment in self-government has sustained us in uncertain and perilous times; it has given us strength and inspiration to this very day. Like them, we do very well to recall our "firm reliance on the protection of Divine Providence," to give thanks for the freedom and prosperity this Nation enjoys, and to pray for continued help and guidance from our wise and loving Creator.[23]

These men were not extraordinarily brilliant, wealthy, or experienced in government. They just had a strong faith in God, ideas that sprang from God's Word, and a belief in the incredible power of prayer.

For Discussion and Reflection

Adult Discussion

Bring to class paper plates, paper cups, straws, glue, and tape. Form groups of five, and tell the groups they each have five minutes to make the strongest bridge possible. Let them choose from the supplies you brought. After five minutes, test each bridge by piling books on it.

After testing all bridges, ask:

★ What was your response when your bridge collapsed?
★ How is this similar to what happens when young nations collapse?
★ What was most important in building a strong bridge?
★ What is most important in building a strong country?

Say, "America has been a strong nation for two hundred years, at least partly because of its strong foundation. Let's talk about that foundation." In their groups, have people discuss the following questions:

★ What were some of the biblical foundations our country was built on?
★ What does 1 Corinthians 3:10-13 say about our foundation?
★ What does that mean in relation to a government? in relation to our personal lives?
★ In what ways did our nation's founders build on that foundation?
★ What's happening to that foundation today?
★ What can we do to help make that foundation strong again?

Have people pray together in their groups, asking God to turn people back to him and strengthen our nation's spiritual foundation.

Youth Discussion

Bring in children's wooden building blocks. Form groups of four, and give each group the same number of blocks. Explain to each group that they will have two minutes to build the tallest structure possible.

When the time is up, compare the structures and then toss one of the blocks at the structures to knock them over. Then give the groups three minutes to build the strongest structure possible. When the groups are finished, try to knock the structures over by tossing another block. Ask:

★ How did it feel to see your first structure fall?
★ What was better about your second structure?

Say, "In many areas of life, the foundation is the most important part in creating something strong." In their groups, have kids discuss the following questions:

★ What were some of the biblical foundations our country was built on?
★ What does 1 Corinthians 3:10-13 say about our foundation?
★ What things do people sometimes build their lives on?

After the groups have come up with several ideas for the last question, have them report on their discussion. Then say, "Now make a list of things you can do to keep your foundation firm." After the groups have made their new lists, have each person select one thing from the list to work on this week and share it with his or her group. Then pray together, asking God to help the kids keep their lives built on Christ.

THE REVIVALISTS

★ ★ ★

FIFTEEN

Miraculous Intervention by God

After winning its independence, this new nation's trials were just beginning. The American Revolution had disrupted the work of the churches. Ministers had become soldiers; laymen had gone off to fight. Other influences also began to tear down the religious fabric so carefully woven during the colonial years.

By the end of the eighteenth century, in the wake of the American Revolution, a movement of pessimistic humanism known as Deism had gained a foothold in New England. This movement asserted that God created the world but was no longer active in it. Deists denied God's revelation, refused to accept miracles, and scoffed at the reality and significance of the resurrection of Jesus Christ.

As a result, the newly formed United States of America began spinning headlong into a moral slump under Deist philosophy. Drunkenness was epidemic. Of a population of five million people, three hundred thousand were confirmed drunkards. Fifteen thousand died of alcoholism every year. Bank robberies were a daily occurrence, profanity was rampant, and women were afraid to go out at night for fear of being assaulted. Sensual gratification and the desire for wealth had captured the American scene.

The churches of the day seemed unable to do anything about the moral decay. All major denominations were losing members. Reverend Samuel Shepard of Lennox, Massachusetts, described the condition of many American churches when he pointed out that he had not taken one young person into church membership.[1]

In the late 1700s, colleges like Harvard and Yale, which were founded as seminaries, were also caught up in humanism. In his video, *The Role of Prayer in Spiritual Awakening*, Dr. J. Edwin Orr, college professor and prayer historian, describes the climate in these schools:

> They took a poll at Harvard, and they discovered not one believer in the whole student body. They took a poll at Princeton—a much more evangelical place—[and] discovered only two believers in the student body and only five that didn't belong to the filthy speech movement of that day. Students rioted; they had a mock communion at Williams College; they had anti-Christian plays at Dartmouth; they burned down Nassau Hall at Princeton; they forced the resignation of the president of Harvard; they took a Bible out of a Presbyterian church in New Jersey and burned it in a public bonfire. Christians were so few on campus, they met in secret like a communist cell and kept the minutes in code so that no one would know what they were doing to persecute them.[2]

Spiritual enthusiasm all over the new nation was on the decline. Church membership was dropping, and baptisms and confirmations were few. Dr. Orr describes the prevalent feeling of doom:

> The chief justice of the United States, John Marshall, wrote to the bishop of Virginia, Bishop Madison, and he said the church

is too far gone ever to be redeemed. Voltaire said Christianity will be forgotten in thirty years' time, and Tom Paine preached this cheerfully all over America. In case you think it was the hysteria of the moment, Kenneth Latourette, the great Christian historian, said, "It seemed as if Christianity were about to be ushered out of the affairs of men." The churches had their backs to the wall. It seemed as if they were about to be wiped out.[3]

At the same time, the western frontier opened all the way to what is now eastern Ohio. By the year 1800, nearly one million people had picked up what they owned and moved west, where the soil had not yet been cultivated and land was cheap. The wilderness contained no churches, schools, or ministers. Immigrants who didn't have a deep faith in God poured in from across the Atlantic. To counteract some of the secular influences, preachers cried from the pulpit about the lack of morals and the indifference to God. Jeremiah Hallock, who pastored a church in Canton, Connecticut, wrote:

> The religion of Jesus gradually declined among us. The doctrine of Christ grew more and more unpopular; family prayer and all the duties of the gospels were less regarded; ungodliness prevailed, and particularly modern infidelity had made and was making alarming progress among us. Indeed it seemed to any eye of sense, that the Sabbath would be lost, and every appearance of religion vanish—yea, that our Zion must die, without an helper, and that infidels would laugh at her dying groans.[4]

But another prayer intervention on a national scale was just over the horizon. Years earlier, Jonathan Edwards had written a book with the imposing title *A Humble Attempt to Promote Explicit Agreement and Visible Union of God's People in Ex-*

231

traordinary Prayer for the Revival of Religion and Christ's Kingdom on Earth. An American by the name of Isaac Bacchus read the book and took its plea for extraordinary prayer to the ministers of every denomination in the United States. Those who still worshiped and served the true God began praying. Reverend Shepard wrote:

> In the month of April 1799, several members of the church manifested great anxiety about the state of religion among us, and expressed a desire that meetings might be appointed for religious conference and special prayer for the outpouring of the Holy Spirit. This request was afterwards made known to the church as a body. They unanimously approved of it, and a conference meeting was accordingly appointed.[5]

These people were pleading for another revival like the Great Awakening. Prayer meetings among young people and within the congregations of churches began to spread. Ministers who wanted renewal for their people met together for prayer. They believed that revival could come only as a result of fervent prayer.

Some churches set aside whole days for prayer for revival. Throughout New England, "Aaron and Hur" societies of four or five people met for an hour before Sunday morning services to pray. Then, as the ministers preached, they held them up in prayer as Aaron and Hur had held up the hands of Moses during a crucial battle.

In 1794, a group of twenty-three ministers in New England agreed to promote the Concert of Prayer once again. They signed a circular letter that was sent to every Christian denomination. A year later, this prayer effort became widespread and influential. Would all these prayer efforts have any effect on the tide of humanism?

THE FIRE BEGINS

Amazingly, the 1795 Concert of Prayer came just two years before the beginning of the Second Great Awakening. Was this a coincidence? By 1797, revival was spreading rapidly. In fact, many towns were inundated with church renewals. Edward Dorr Griffith, who was present during these revivals, gave this description of the proliferation of revivals going on at once: "In 1799, I could stand at my door in New Hartford, Litchfield County, and number fifty or sixty contiguous congregations laid down in one field of divine wonders, and as many more in different parts of New England."[6]

A grandson of Jonathan Edwards, Timothy Dwight, played an important role in the New England revival. In 1795, he was elected president of Yale College. His greatest concern was for the spiritual life of the students. In 1802, an awakening came to Yale. As the young collegians went home for spring vacation, they ignited revivals in their home churches. Eventually, half of these students were converted, and one-third of the class was called into the ministry.

THE FIRE IN THE WEST

The awakening also spread to the frontier. But the revival in the West broke out in red-hot flames. At the time, Kentucky was the raw frontier: lawless, irreligious. James McGready, a frontier evangelist, began to see God work, beginning with a service in Gaspar River in 1799. Author Robert Flood writes:

> As McGready preached the realities of Heaven and Hell, many fell to the ground and lay "powerless, groaning, praying and crying for mercy." Women screamed and tough men sobbed like children. Later during a meeting at Red River as Methodist preacher John McGee "shouted and exhorted with all possible

energy," numbers professed conversion. It was here that the great western revival began, which came to be known as the Logan County, or Cumberland, revival.[7]

Kentuckians flocked to the camp meetings by the thousands. In 1801, Barton Stone, a Presbyterian who worked in Bourbon County, attended a camp meeting, then went back to his area and began his own camp meetings. On Friday, August 6, 1801, at Cane Ridge, the most famous gathering of the Second Great Awakening was held. People attended from as far away as Ohio and Tennessee. It is estimated that between ten thousand and twenty-five thousand came, and reports of this revival meeting spread throughout the country.

THE CIRCUIT RIDERS

One of the greatest new strategies that developed as a result of the Second Great Awakening was the circuit-riding preacher. These men spent hour after hour on horses, carrying their Bibles, preaching to people deep within the wilderness. Their efforts produced huge growth in the Baptist and Methodist denominations. John Wigger, assistant professor at St. Olaf College in Northfield, Minnesota, writes of the Methodist expansion:

Between 1770 and 1820, American Methodists achieved a virtual miracle of growth, rising from fewer than 1,000 members to more than 250,000. In 1775, fewer than one out of every 800 Americans was a Methodist; by 1812, Methodists numbered one out of every 36 Americans. At mid-century, American Methodism was almost ten times the size of the Congregationalists, America's largest denomination in 1776.[8]

234

Francis Asbury was the most influential force in establishing the Methodist circuits. He was born in England but was challenged by John Wesley to help the American churches. In October 1777, he arrived in Philadelphia and began preaching. He had a gift for organization, so after the Revolutionary War ended, he began setting up districts of churches to be served by circuit riders.

In 1795 Asbury adopted the extraordinary prayer plea. Soon every church was holding prayer meetings. Asbury spread Methodist camp-meeting Christianity from Georgia to Maine and inland to the frontier areas. He preached strict values and moral issues; he also took a stance against slaveholding. This brought many blacks into the Methodist church.

Asbury never married, and he didn't own a home. He carried all he owned in the two saddlebags on his horse. He preached well over 16,000 sermons, ordained more than 4,000 preachers, traveled on horseback or by carriage more than 270,000 miles, and wore out three faithful horses. Before his death, Asbury had become one of the best-known preachers in America.

Circuit riders like Asbury changed the way people lived and worshiped. They helped frontier families build their lives on prayer. They helped communities start neighborhood prayer meetings. A. Gregory Schneider, professor at Pacific Union College in Angwin, California, gives this picture of the prayer ministry of the circuit rider:

> Circuit preachers would visit the various households to their memberships and use family prayer to attend especially to the "rising generation," as the Methodist Discipline told them to do. William Fee remembered George Washington Maley, an early Ohio circuit rider, as a particularly impressive children's

pastor. "The whole family where he visited would often be bathed in tears. He appeared to understand the character and the peculiarities of every child. He prayed for all, and we thought he prayed for everything."

Family prayer yielded a harvest of Christian converts. David Sullins, a Tennessee preacher, recalled that the first convert from his parents' "family altar" was his father.[9]

A HEART FOR THE WORLD

One of the most far-reaching results of the Second Great Awakening was the rise of mission societies. Once again, prayer was the foundation that produced a new zeal to reach the lost for Christ.

American mission societies were patterned after British mission groups, which began in the heart of William Carey, the founder of modern missions. Carey spent his life serving in India. Because of Carey's vision for the world, prayer meetings were established in 1784. John Sutcliff organized a Call to Prayer, in which ministers committed themselves to set aside the first Monday of the month for prayer.[10]

Consequently, the New York Missionary Society was organized in 1796. It crossed denominational lines and had as its purpose to evangelize the Indians. Other home mission bodies were also formed.

In 1798, Samuel J. Mills Jr. was converted in a Connecticut revival. That summer, he and four friends took a walk through the countryside. A drenching thunderstorm came up, and they ran for cover under a haystack. While waiting for the storm to clear, they began talking about the spiritual darkness of Asia. One of the young men suggested praying. They prayed and talked and prayed some more. Suddenly, they all realized that they wanted to be the ones to take the gospel to Asia. The group called themselves "The Brethren," and they became the driving force behind a new foreign-mission movement.[11]

The Concerts of Prayer also incited interest in missions. Concerts of Prayer adopted a goal of praying for worldwide revival. It was just another step to begin praying for worldwide missions and then to establish mission societies to help accomplish that goal.

Although this prayer movement eventually ended, devout Christians of the twentieth century once again revived the Concert of Prayer gatherings in North America in 1981. Today Concerts of Prayer International, headquartered in Wheaton, Illinois, recruits, equips, and mobilizes people for leadership in prayer movements and conducts Concerts of Prayer events around the world.

As colonialism and imperialism became more prevalent worldwide, they opened a way for missionaries to reach lands that had previously been inaccessible. William Carey was the first to strike out into India. Adoniram and Nancy Judson, the first American foreign missionaries, joined him in 1812. Hiram Bingham and his wife, Sybil, began work in Hawaii.

Revivals, camp meetings, circuit riders, and mission societies—all part of the Second Great Awakening. What an exciting time to be one of God's people! Lives were changed; denominations grew; religion became a part of the family's day-to-day activities. The Second Great Awakening energized not only the antislavery movement but also prison reform and the temperance movement. Christians began using printed material to further their cause, and Bible societies were formed. Circuit riders brought along thousands of pamphlets to leave with those they met. Dr. Orr explains:

Out of that Second Great Awakening . . . came the whole missionary movement—all the missionary societies. Out of it came the abolition of slavery; out of it came popular education. I could mention so many social benefits as well as evangelistic drive. More than six hundred colleges in the Middle West were founded by revivalists.[12]

Of course there were excesses. Many people fell away after emotional experiences at camp meetings. Some revival meetings were uncontrolled and chaotic. But American life was turned in a new direction. The devout now believed that prayer was the key to revival and that prayer belonged at the center of the family, not just in the church.

THE SECOND GENERATION

Many of the Christian leaders who took part in the Second Great Awakening looked back to the First Great Awakening and saw how quickly its effects had faded. To guard against that happening again, they began grooming the next generation of spiritual leaders. For example, Timothy Dwight left his work in the capable hands of several godly Yale graduates. Dwight personally trained one pupil, Lyman Beecher. Among Beecher's legacies were the temperance societies he founded in response to the severe alcoholic problems proliferating during this time.

Beecher's enthusiasm spread through his congregation and into the community. It wasn't long until his church pews were full. The revival spread until seventy converts at a time were joining at each Communion service.[13]

These revivals continued for years, truly changing New England society. Denominations established orphanages, homes for the elderly, hospitals, and other benevolent societies. Asylums for the deaf and dumb and for the mentally ill were built. Prison reform began at Newgate Prison in East Granby, Connecticut. The American Tract Society and the American Bible Society were formed. In fact, the duration of the Second Great Awakening was remarkable, lasting forty years. One man was very influential in extending the revival—a young lawyer named Charles Finney.

CHARLES FINNEY

In 1825, Charles Finney made a commitment of faith to Christ. Within twenty-four hours, he met with twenty-four others, all of whom became Christians. This was the kind of faith and enthusiasm that characterized Charles Finney. Finney gave up his law practice and committed himself to telling others about his faith.

One of Finney's main spiritual strengths was his life of prayer, which led to his teaching on prayer. He was discipled by his pastor, Reverend George Gale. It was in Gale's church in Adams, New York, that Finney first began attending prayer meetings—even before his conversion. At first he found the meetings confusing, but after his conversion, Finney dedicated his time to prayer and fasting. He spent days alone in the woods, praying to God.

Finney advocated "prevailing in prayer," which meant beseeching God until the answer came through. He also believed that prayer was a necessary prerequisite to revival. Years later, looking back at his prayer ministry, he said:

> Unless I had the spirit of prayer, I could do nothing. If even for
> a day or an hour I lost the spirit of grace and supplication, I
> found myself unable to preach with power and efficiency, or to
> win souls by personal conversation.[14]

Finney had several friends who helped him in his revivals by praying. One was Father Nash, a minister who kept a prayer list of unbelievers and prayed for them daily. Wherever Finney preached, Father Nash remained seated behind him and prayed during the entire service. Some of Finney's worst critics were converted through Father Nash's prayers. Abel Clary was a minister who was so burdened for souls that he spent most of his time in prayer. At times, he and others agonized in prayer day and night.

Finney believed that "a prayer meeting is an index to the state of religion in the church."[15] He made significant contributions to the role of prayer in revival. He allowed women to pray in meetings, encouraged specific prayer, emphasized the importance of the Holy Spirit in prayer, and developed a conversational type of prayer meeting.

What impact did Finney have on American society? Wherever he chose to conduct his evangelistic campaigns, thousands responded. In Boston, fifty thousand made faith commitments in just one week. One estimate says that he was responsible for half a million conversions during his lifetime.[16] In fact, Finney propelled the Second Great Awakening onto center stage in America and extended it another fifteen years.

Although he campaigned for social reform, Finney's main burden was for the lost sinner. His prayer life revolved around praying for people. Because of this prayer power, he saw tremendous success. The following incident shows just how powerfully God was at work through this man of prayer. . . .

The sewing factory buzzed with whispers. Up and down the rows of machines, the hushed voices announced, "Finney's coming! Finney's here!"

Everyone had heard about his preaching and the tales of

240

people kneeling and confessing their sins. It seemed like such a strange world to these hardworking, unchurched men and women.

But when Finney passed into the high-ceilinged room, conversation stopped dead. Every pair of eyes watched him move through the aisles of machines while their fingers flew through their work.

As Finney walked by the chair of a young woman with dull red hair, she leaned to her neighbor and made a rude remark about him under her breath. Her neighbor laughed loudly.

Finney stopped, then turned toward the young woman. Feeling uncomfortable, she stopped working, but when she did, her thread broke. Nervous, she picked up the heavy piece of thread and tried to stuff the end through the needle. But the end just bent. The more she tried, the more the thread missed the eye.

Finally she stood, tossed the material onto her chair, and looked out the window. She was so nervous, she couldn't even see the trees in the distance. Although he didn't say a word, she knew he was still there behind her back. Her eyes filled with tears. With a sigh, she turned back to her machine, impatiently tossed aside the material, and dropped into her chair.

Finney began talking to her softly, but all she could hear was the record of her sins pounding in her ears. Feeling as if her heart would break, she began pleading with God for forgiveness.

Without a word of preaching, the entire room came under a deep awareness of sin. The young woman's neighbor fell to her knees and began crying out to God. One by one, everyone stopped working. Within a short time, the entire factory came to a standstill. An unusual hush stilled the whirring machines, revealing the prayers and sobs.

When the short, bombastic owner saw the machines idle, he stomped into the large workroom. "Get back to work! Get back to work!" he commanded. But no one responded.

He surveyed the roomful of people who were crying and praying. It was Finney! He had done this. The owner determined to throw Finney out. But then he, too, began to see his sins. They were displayed in his mind like cuts of meat rotting in a butcher's case. "Come here!" he commanded the workroom manager.

The manager came up to him slowly, wondering what the boss would say about all the time being wasted on religion.

"All work's stopped!" the owner shouted.

The manager cringed, sure of what was coming next—a tongue lashing.

But then the owner amazed the manager. "The work's stopped," the owner said in a softer tone. "It's more important that these people get converted than that we get more production out at a time like this. Let's get a prayer meeting going."

The manager was shocked, but he flew to obey. Somehow this little workaday world had been turned upside down—for the better. . . .[17]

Later Finney wrote about this incident in one of his books: In a few days, the owner and nearly all the three thousand employees were fully converted. The Lord's rebuke of this woman's comment through Mr. Finney's reverent, yet compassionate, reaction brought her under conviction. Seeing this undoubtedly inspired the massive revival.[18]

A FLOOD OF CONVERTS

Spiritual awakenings truly are a miraculous work of God begun through the prayers of his people. Because of the Second Great Awakening and the prayers of God's people, society in the United States changed dramatically. Converts flooded into the churches. Author Keith Hardman summarizes the impact of the Second Great Awakening:

> The approximate number of converts during the forty years of the Second Great Awakening in America can be determined by examining the membership records of many Protestant churches. In 1855 Robert Baird reported the number of evangelical Protestants as 4,176,431. While some of this increase was through other means, a gain of almost 3 million within fifty years must be due in part to intensive evangelism. The one hundred thousand new converts reported for the revival year 1831 alone indicates how intensive the evangelism was. Based on available statistics, it would seem that the Second Great Awakening converted, by conservative estimate, at least one million people from 1795 to 1835.[19]

No ordinary human effort could have accomplished such a change. Only the miraculous intervention of God—who has the power to change not only hearts but also nations—could have orchestrated the Second Great Awakening.

One of the issues that boiled to the surface of American life because of Christian benevolence and social consciousness was the evil of slavery. Most abolitionists were devout Christians. For forty years, their organizations had grown and united to reform social evils and spread the gospel in the United States and to the world. Many times, however, it seemed as if their voices were lost in the wind.

Could the power of prayer accomplish a greater movement

than this awakening? God had still greater plans in store for the nation, which was not yet one hundred years old. A Third Great Awakening, coming on the heels of the Second Great Awakening, would once again be built on the incredible power of prayer and would prepare the American people for the greatest tragedy of our national history—the Civil War.

For Discussion and Reflection

Adult Discussion

Choose a song that everyone knows. Gather in a circle and have two people start the song and go around the circle, adding voices until the whole circle is involved. When finished, sing the entire song in unison. Then ask:

- ★ How much different was the power of our song after all the voices were added?
- ★ How did that feel?
- ★ How might that be similar to the power of the concerts of prayer described in this chapter? How is it different?
- ★ How might God feel about concerts of prayer?

Form pairs, and have them discuss the following questions:

- ★ What was the best thing about a powerful concert you've heard?
- ★ Who was the audience?
- ★ How might this have been like the concerts of prayer?
- ★ Who was the audience for those?

Have partners separately look up Matthew 18:19-20 and report to their partner what the passage says about prayer. Then have all the partners report to the group on what they discovered. Ask:

> ★ What positive effects can come from group prayer?
> ★ How might we incorporate it into our lives more?

Spend several minutes in group prayer, allowing those who feel comfortable doing so to pray aloud. Suggest possible topics for prayer, such as spiritual renewal in your church or community or special needs within your congregation.

Youth Discussion

Select a cheer that would be familiar to the kids, or have one of the kids select it for you and write it down. Begin class by reading it aloud. Then ask two people to do the cheer, then four people, and finally the whole group. Ask:

> ★ What was the cheer like when I read it?
> ★ How was it different when everyone cheered?
> ★ How might our cheer be similar to the concerts of prayer described in this chapter?
> ★ How are prayers more powerful when people pray together?

Form two groups. If you have more than fifteen kids, form multiple groups of no more than eight. Assign each group one of the following passages and have them create an advertisement to tell the rest of the class about the benefits of group prayer. Each person in the group must be involved in the advertisement. Assign Matthew 18:19-20 and Acts 12:1-12, and allow about five minutes for the kids to prepare their advertisements.

After the advertisements have been presented to the class,

ask, "How might we encourage group prayer in our youth group? in our church?"

Have the kids pray together, allowing anyone who feels comfortable doing so to pray aloud. If the kids are willing, consider setting up a special time for them to gather for group prayer.

SIXTEEN

The
Prayer Revival

Times were good. Railroads were snaking their way across the continent at an astounding pace. The government had such a surplus of revenue that President Buchanan considered paying off the national debt. Bank credit and mortgages were easy to get. Gold, which was discovered in California in 1848, poured into the rest of the country.

Immigration was at an all-time high, and the population of the United States more than doubled between 1825 and 1850. New states and territories were added: Texas in 1845, California in 1848, and the Gadsden Purchase (part of Arizona and New Mexico) in 1853. The Industrial Revolution opened thousands of new jobs in factories, mills, and mines. Samuel Morse invented the telegraph in 1837, and telegraph poles were erected everywhere.

Can you imagine what it was like to live during the middle of the nineteenth century? It must have seemed as if opportunities were unlimited.

But the religious picture wasn't nearly as bright. The church wasn't a part of the expansion; it was on the decline. Churches within denominations bickered with each other. The slavery issue was causing turmoil within most major denominations. In fact, many churches split along the Mason-Dixon line.

How did the issue of slavery become so heated? Many of our Founding Fathers believed that involuntary slavery was an evil institution. Jefferson wanted to condemn slavery outright in the Declaration of Independence, but others thought such a stance would be too divisive. During the Constitutional Convention, however, a Christian statesman by the name of George Mason did address the issue:

> Every master of slaves is born a petty tyrant. They bring the judgment of heaven upon a country. As nations cannot be rewarded or punished in the next world, they must be in this one. By an inevitable chain of causes and effects, Providence punishes national sins by national calamities.[1]

At the convention, southern states agreed to abolish slave trade both nationally and between states by 1808. Slavery itself, however, continued.

America failed to resolve the issue of slavery, and the next generation arose with fewer convictions and more greed. Slave owning became more entrenched as slave owners profited; and people once again turned their backs on God.

But Mason was right. God was allowing a chain of causes and effects to bring the evil boil to the surface. By 1834, many clergymen had entered the antislavery movement, speaking out against this great national sin.

Slavery and abolition soon became a flash point throughout the nation. Harriet Beecher Stowe's *Uncle Tom's Cabin,* the Dred Scott decision, and the Fugitive Slave Law brought abolition to national attention. The Underground Railroad added more heat to the already bubbling pot.

A CALL TO PRAYER

In the midst of these undercurrents, God's Spirit was working quietly and powerfully. Voices began once again calling for a revival. In 1856 William Arthur published a book, *The Tongue of Fire,* which emphasized the work of the Holy Spirit in the church. Arthur called for earnest, united, persevering prayer that would bring an outpouring of the Holy Spirit. This was the final prayer in the book:

> And now, adorable Spirit, preceding from the Father and the Son, descend upon all the churches, renew the Pentecost in this our age, and baptize thy people generally—O baptize them yet again with tongues of fire! Crown the nineteenth century with a revival of "pure and undefiled religion" greater than that of the last century, greater than that of the first, greater than any "demonstration of the Spirit" ever yet vouch-safed to men![2]

The prayer baton that had been passed from Jonathan Edwards to Charles Finney from the First to the Second Great Awakening was now handed to those who responded by taking up the prayer call.

Then a financial crisis hit in 1857. Although it was short-lived, more than five thousand businesses went bankrupt that year. People lost their jobs, and interest rates soared. Warren A. Chandler, a Methodist bishop, described what happened:

> And now that the wheels of industry stood still and the noisy cries of greed were hushed, men stopped to hear the voice of the Spirit calling them to repentance. And they heeded the heavenly call. Another renewal of national extent began.[3]

The country was once again on the brink of a miraculous answer to prayer—the Third Great Awakening!

THE REVIVAL BEGINS

The Third Great Awakening was unique for several reasons. First, it had no foremost figure such as an Edwards, Dwight, or Finney to spur on the movement. Second, it was a layperson's revival. Third, it was born out of prayer and spread through prayer. And fourth, it received tremendous coverage in the secular newspapers.

The first spark was ignited in Hamilton, Ontario. Dr. Walter Palmer and his wife, Phoebe, both laypersons in the Methodist church, spent half of each year speaking at local revivals and camp meetings. They were waiting to catch a train to New York when Samuel Rice, a Wesleyan pastor, invited them to stay and speak at the McNab Street Wesleyan Methodist Church.

They stayed for several weeks and saw six hundred people converted. Around the same time, the New York Sunday School Union sent its members to visit homes to urge people to attend church. Prayer meetings arose out of these visits. Most of these prayer meetings were interdenominational.

Conventions were also being held. The Presbyterians gathered in Pittsburgh for a three-day meeting. Three hundred ministers and one thousand elders spent much time praying for revival. A pastoral letter calling for a day of fasting and prayer on the first Thursday of January 1858 was drafted and mailed to churches.

God was ready to send another awakening. Then an electrifying event occurred. . . .

Jeremiah Lanphier sat alone in an upper room of the North Dutch Church in a decaying area of New York City. He wasn't young, but he had a pleasant face and a kind manner. He was praying and thinking.

He thought about all the years he had been a businessman. One moment of those years stood out like a bolt of lightning. He remembered that day clearly even though it had occurred nearly fifteen years ago. He had gone to hear Charles Finney preach in his Broadway Tabernacle. Why had he gone? He couldn't even recall now.

It wasn't Finney's piercing eyes or his preaching that had unnerved Jeremiah that night. It was something else: the deep sense of the many wasted years, the futility of piling up money, and the sins he had committed. That night he had gone to the altar broken and repentant—and had been converted. *That holy moment changed my life forever,* he thought.

Now here he was, years later, an urban missionary in the North Dutch Church. Jeremiah pictured the dismal Sunday morning services in the burnished old sanctuary. Every Sunday, the congregation seemed to shrink. The businessmen and their families were all moving out of old downtown to newer areas north of the city.

Jeremiah had been hired to revive the congregation. It looked like a task far beyond his feeble talents. *How can I build up a dying church?* he asked himself. *Only the Lord can change the outward tide.*

In his hand he held one of the handbills he had tacked up all over the area. The headline jumped off the page: "How Often Shall I Pray?"

Will it attract many people? he wondered. He read over a few of the paragraphs on the handbill:

A day Prayer Meeting is held every Wednesday, from 12 to 1 o'clock in the Consistory building, in the rear of the North Dutch Church, corner of Fulton and William Streets (entrance from Fulton and Ann streets).

This meeting is intended to give merchants, mechanics, clerks, strangers, and business-men generally, an opportunity to stop and call upon God amid the perplexities incident to their respective avocations. It will continue one hour; but it is also designed for those who may find it inconvenient to remain more than 5 or 10 minutes, as well as for those who can spare the whole hour. The necessary interruption will be slight, because anticipated; and those who are in haste can often expedite their business engagements by halting to lift up their voices to the Throne of Grace in humble, grateful prayer.

All are cordially invited to attend.[4]

Here it was noon, and he was waiting in the Consistory, but no one had come. The seconds ticked away, minute after minute. Still he heard no footsteps on the stairway.

Finally one man toiled up the steps at twelve-thirty. Jeremiah welcomed him warmly, and they sat down to wait for others. A few more people slipped into the room until six chairs were filled. But many chairs remained empty. Out of one million New Yorkers, only six people showed up—even though the meeting had been widely advertised.

Undeterred, Jeremiah began the meeting, and they went to prayer. After the group left, Jeremiah sat looking at the chairs. *Is this any way to build a church? Yes, God can use such a humble beginning.*

The next Wednesday, Jeremiah once again waited in the Consistory for his prayer meeting to begin. Would his little group come again? But this time he didn't have to wait as long. The six original businessmen arrived, and so did fourteen more! As they all knelt in prayer, the murmur of voices thrilled Jeremiah's heart. . . .[5]

This little prayer meeting would become a prayer miracle. Two days after this prayer meeting, the Bank of Philadelphia failed. The financial crisis had begun. But soon Lanphier's attendance grew so rapidly that he was able to schedule a prayer meeting every day of the week. The rooms overflowed. Lanphier moved the meetings to John Street Methodist Church. And still the crowds grew.

On March 17, 1858, the prayer meeting was moved to Burton's theater. As the prayer meetings grew in number, they were called union prayer meetings. Union prayer meetings began to spread across the nation—from Albany, New York, to Omaha and St. Louis, and throughout the South. Charles Finney wrote of these prayer meetings in his *Memoirs:*

> I recollect in one of our prayer meetings in Boston that winter a gentleman arose and said: "I am from Omaha the capital of Nebraska. On my journey east I have found a continuous prayer meeting all the way. We call it," said he, "about two thousand miles from Omaha to Boston; and here was a prayer meeting about two thousand miles in extent."[6]

These were simple meetings. A layperson would lead the prayer and keep order. Many of the prayer requests were for unbelieving friends or loved ones. Because of the prayer effort, *The Presbyterian* magazine estimated that there were fifty thousand converts in New York by May of that year.

Chicago also experienced an extended renewal. Within a few short years, the city had grown to a population of one hundred thousand. Amazingly, twelve hundred men gathered daily for prayer. The secular press covered the movement, and the attendance jumped to two thousand per day.

One young man played an important part in the Chicago revival—D. L. Moody. He began his long career as an evangelist during the Third Great Awakening. In fact, one little group he led at that time became the seed for Moody Memorial Church. The group kept growing under his teaching until the average attendance reached six hundred in 1859. Then it expanded to one thousand and even to fifteen hundred.

The Third Great Awakening was a very public event. The telegraph flashed the news of the revival. Secular newspapers competed to see which could carry the best news coverage.

THE EXTENT OF THE REVIVAL

One miraculous result of the Prayer Revival was the incredible number of people who responded to the gospel. The movement spread across America as thousands came together to pray, often on a daily basis. In one year, more than one million people made faith commitments during these Christ-centered prayer meetings. The effect was felt for more than forty years. Dr. Edwin Orr, in his video, *The Role of Prayer in Spiritual Awakening,* says:

> People began to be converted—ten thousand a week in New York City. The movement spread throughout New England. Church bells would bring people to prayer at eight in the morning, twelve noon, six in the evening. The revival went up the Hudson and down the Mohawk. For example, the Baptists had so many people to baptize, they couldn't get them into their churches. They went down to the river, cut a big square hole in the ice, baptized them in the cold water. And when Baptists do that, they really are on fire![7]

A Boston newspaper recorded that in some small New England towns, there wasn't one unconverted person. In the South, church membership rocketed. The Young Men's Christian Association (YMCA) played an important role in the revival by organizing and promoting prayer meetings. The prayer movement spread to the West, and there were prayer meetings in San Francisco and Texas. What were the most prevalent characteristics of the Prayer Revival, as it has been called? It began through the prayers of laypersons and continued through the union prayer meetings. No one evangelist or preacher dominated the scene. This revival was truly a grass-roots prayer movement.

The revival united evangelical Christians across denominational boundaries and turned the focus to the salvation of unbelievers. During the year the Third Great Awakening was at its height, one million faith conversions to Christianity were recorded, out of an American population of 30 million!

It was a revival that was spread by businessmen to all areas of our country. Dr. Orr says it was the most wholesome revival in our national history.

The Third Great Awakening prepared our country for the most horrendous trial in our national history—the Civil War—which would begin in a few short years. As the South and the North became more hostile and armed themselves for battle, the revival was still being felt. It was this undercurrent of religious fervor that would make the greatest difference in the spiritual climate of the war.

But the war would test the mettle of the American people as nothing had done before. How would the church respond? How would the prayers of the reawakened populace be answered? How would God's hand move in answer to the pleas of his people? That's one of the greatest stories of prayer miracles in American history!

For Discussion and Reflection

Adult Discussion

To take the following survey, set up a continuum in your classroom. Designate one side of the room as "the pastor's responsibility" and the other side of the room as "the people's responsibility." In response to each task named in the survey, have people position themselves between the two sides of the room, indicating their opinion on whose responsibility the task is. Read off the following tasks:

> Telling others about Jesus
> Praying
> Leading others in prayer meetings
> Preaching to crowds
> Organizing prayer services

After you read each task, have a few volunteers share why they decided to stand where they did. After you've gone through all the tasks, have people sit down and discuss the following questions. Ask:

★ How did you respond when people disagreed with you?
★ What was a big difference between the first two Great Awakenings and the third one?
★ What tasks did ordinary people take on during the Third Great Awakening?
★ How did ordinary people make a difference in the Third Great Awakening?

Form groups of six. Have the groups read aloud Nehemiah 1:1-11 and discuss the following questions:

★ What was Nehemiah's job?
★ What were his credentials for leading a group of Israelites?
★ What were his spiritual qualifications?
★ How were the businessmen who led the Third Great Awakening similar to Nehemiah?
★ How are we in this group similar to Nehemiah? How are we different?
★ What part did prayer play in Nehemiah's situation? in the Third Great Awakening?
★ How could we make a difference in our generation the way Nehemiah did? the way Jeremiah Lanphier did? the way D. L. Moody did?

Have the groups report their discussion to the rest of the class, and then encourage people to commit to doing whatever God might want them to do to make a difference in our world for him.

Youth Discussion

As you begin your class, say, "I'm going to assign each of you a role for this activity. As I make the assignments, think about the spiritual importance of the role you've been assigned."

Assign each person one of the following roles:

president of your denomination
Billy Graham
the Pope
the best preacher in the state
a successful businessman
a shoe salesman
a newspaper reporter

Make sure the roles are assigned to equal numbers of kids. Ask:

> ★ How did you respond to the role you were assigned? Why?
> ★ How was your response similar to the way we often evaluate the importance of leaders in the church today?
> ★ Is this different from the way leaders were raised up in the Third Great Awakening?

Now have the kids form groups, making sure they have one of each role in each group. Have them read Nehemiah 1:1-11 and discuss the following questions:

> ★ How was Nehemiah's role similar to that of some of the businessmen who led the Third Great Awakening?
> ★ How are we different from those businessmen? from Nehemiah?
> ★ How are we similar to those businessmen and Nehemiah?
> ★ What part did prayer play in Nehemiah's situation? in the businessmen's situations?
> ★ What might God want us to do to encourage change in our situations?

Have the groups divide into pairs and share with each other one thing they will commit to do to make a difference for the Lord. Have partners pray for each other in following through on what they've committed to do.

SEVENTEEN

The Blue
and the Gray

If you read most histories of the Civil War today, it is likely that you won't see any mention of religion. Perhaps you're wondering: *Did the Third Great Awakening die out so completely that it had no effect on the most costly war in our country's history?* Definitely not! All the forces of revival that preceded the Civil War were still evident during the Civil War, weaving a story that shows the power of prayer.

As we mentioned in chapter 15, Lyman Beecher was a great preacher who took the reins of revival leadership from Timothy Dwight during the early part of the Second Great Awakening. Beecher's impact was still being felt through his children. Beecher's daughter, Harriet Beecher Stowe, wrote *Uncle Tom's Cabin,* a novel that brought the cause of abolition to the forefront of American social consciousness. One million copies of her book sold before the war began. Beecher's son, Henry Ward Beecher, used his pulpit in Brooklyn to stir up antislavery sentiment.

There were many other well-known abolitionists, and they were hated for their stand. In the South they had a price on their heads. In the North they were mobbed, pelted with vegetables, and shouted down whenever they spoke.

The majority of abolitionists were devout Christians, and many had been converted during the revivals. In fact, Charles Finney was one of the foremost abolitionists. Some blacks also became prominent in the abolitionist cause. Harriet Tubman and Sojourner Truth, two escaped slaves, helped other slaves find their way north and also spread the abolitionist message. In the 1830s, there were hundreds of abolitionists; by the 1840s there were thousands. And the movement kept growing.

Because the abolitionists couldn't go into the South to preach their message, they sent literature instead. Theodore Dwight Weld, who was converted under Finney's ministry, wrote many of the most effective pamphlets and was a great speaker for the cause. This new strategy of prolific literature distribution later made an important impact on the spiritual life of the armies during the Civil War.

Abolitionists believed that if the churches—both Northern and Southern—would repent and reject slavery, they would force an end to the practice. But that repentance didn't happen. Instead, most major denominations split over the issue as new denominations were formed in the South that advocated slavery. The church refused to take up the cause for the most defenseless of our people.

Early in the abolitionist fight, Finney came to realize that the cause was an explosive issue. In 1836 he wrote: "[Brother] Weld, is it not true, at least do you not fear it is, that we are in our present course going fast into a civil war? Will not our present movements in abolition result in that? . . . How can we save our country and affect the speedy abolition of slavery?"[1]

As Finney was beginning to realize, the slavery-conflict train had been sent down the mountain without brakes. It would only gather speed, leaving destruction in its wake until it spent itself in the Civil War. But would prayer change the outcome of the war? Yes, in a way no one could have imagined.

THE WHEELS OF CHANGE

If you had been a young man enlisting for service and traveling to join the troops in 1861, you would have been excited. It was probably your first time away from home. Here was your chance to escape boring church services and your parents' stifling rules. After all, everyone thought this would be a short war, and when you returned home, you could resume your moral lifestyle. But until then, you could live as you pleased.

That was the sentiment of many soldiers—both Union and Confederate. During the first year of the war, army camps were full of profanity, gambling, illicit sex, and many other kinds of evil. Since the end of the Revolutionary War, few chaplains had served in the army. So when war broke out in 1861, the army was unprepared to handle the spiritual life of its troops. Four influences changed this dismal picture. First, many men enlisted as chaplains. As we will see later, some of the highest-ranking officials in both the Union and the Confederate armies actively supported the work of chaplains. Second, colporteurs (itinerant hawkers of religious tracts and books) from the tract and Bible societies and the YMCA began serving the troops. These workers distributed millions of tracts, testaments, pocket Bibles, and other religious books. Scholar Terry Bilhartz writes: "At the height of their work, not less than one million pages of gospel tracts were circulated each week among the Confederate veterans."[2] Third, many nonmilitary ministers served as missionaries to the troops. These ministers called on their churches to send more people to help in the tremendous spiritual harvest, and the churches responded.

Fourth, as in the Revolutionary War, many ministers enlisted as soldiers. They had a great influence for good on the spiritual temperature of the brigades.

Dr. Gardiner H. Shattuck Jr., professor at Episcopal Diocese of Rhode Island, writes about the type of scene that began to be repeated within both the Union and the Confederate armies:

> Early in 1862, chaplain James Marks pondered how to help the soldiers of the 63rd Pennsylvania Regiment. Bitterness after the defeat at Bull Run gripped the army. Homesickness and boredom were rife, and cold, wet weather depressed generals and privates alike. Marks made up his mind to lift the soldiers out of their unhappiness and bring their thoughts to a higher, religious plane. Purchasing a tent to hold worshipers, he began a revival season that lasted until the spring. Hundreds of men soon were "born again."[3]

William Bennet, who wrote soon after the Civil War ended, described conditions in the South:

> Up to January 1865, it was estimated that nearly *one hundred and fifty thousand* soldiers had been converted during the progress of the war, and *it was believed that fully one-third of all the soldiers in the field were praying men,* and members of some branch of the Christian Church. A large proportion of the higher offices were men of faith and prayer, and many others, though not professedly religious, were moral and respectful to all the religious services, and confessed the value of the revival in promoting the efficiency of the army. [Bennet's italics][4]

As the big battles of Gettysburg, Vicksburg, and Chattanooga were fought in 1863, revivals became a regular occurrence in the Union army. Several high-ranking officers helped the efforts of the spiritual renewal. One was Oliver O. Howard (called "Old Prayer Book"), an abolitionist who lost an arm at the Battle of Seven Pines and frequently spoke during chapel services.

Estimates set the number of conversions in the Union army at between one hundred thousand and two hundred thousand soldiers! When you consider that many of the Union soldiers probably were already Christians, the number of conversions is staggering.

The Confederate army also experienced a major revival, which many histories written around that time refer to as the Great Revival. When considering all Civil War troops on both sides, it is estimated that 10 percent or more of the total became new Christians.[5] These were America's future leaders! The prayers of Americans were reaping miraculous dividends—although they may not have been the expected results.

The Confederate army also had devout leaders. In fact, several high-ranking officials were converted during the war and actively participated in the spiritual life of the army. Let's look at two of the most well-known spiritual leaders.

STONEWALL JACKSON

Thomas Jonathan "Stonewall" Jackson was a man of prayer. He graduated from West Point and fought in the Mexican-American War. After the war, he was converted and baptized. In 1861, he prayed with his wife and left to serve as a commander in the Confederate army. He was consistent in his devotional life on the battlefield. Historian John W. Schildt says: "[One day] his men saw [Jackson] stumbling and falling over trees and rocks. They almost thought he had too much to drink. That was not the problem. He was praying with his eyes closed while he walked."[6]

Jackson always displayed extraordinary calm and fearlessness in battle. He once said: "My religious belief teaches me to feel safe. God has fixed the time for my death. I do not concern myself about that, but to be always ready."[7] While he led Confederate troops under his command, they never lost a battle.

Stonewall Jackson was known as an extraordinary military leader and a dedicated Christian. He was considered a spiritual leader by his troops. His soldiers often heard his booming voice praying for his men and for others who were in his presence. After every victory, he ordered his chaplains to hold a thanksgiving service, and he participated in the chapel services in camp. He also formulated a plan for a chaplaincy system that helped further the revival in the army.

He died on May 10, 1863, after his own troops accidentally shot him. A month before he died, he wrote a letter to his pastor in which he said:

> When in the Valley there was much religious interest among my troops, and I trust that it has not died out. It appears to me that we should look for a great work of grace among our troops, officers, and privates, for our army has been made the subject of prayer by all denominations of Christians in the Confederacy. . . . I am very grateful for your prayers and the prayers of other Christian friends. Continue to pray for me. I wish I could be with you in the church and lecture room, whenever our people meet to worship God. . . . Let us work and pray that our people may be the nation whose God is the Lord.[8]

After General Jackson's death, his memory spurred on the revival as much as his life had. Chaplains all over the Confederate army used his life and his death as examples of godliness. His prayers for more conversions were answered even after he could no longer offer them. Even in his tragic death, Jackson believed that God was fulfilling his purposes and was causing all things to work together for good to those who love God.

GENERAL ROBERT E. LEE

Robert E. Lee was known in both the North and the South as a gentleman and a spiritual giant. As he rode through the troops on his big gray horse, his men adored him. Even after the tragic battle of Gettysburg, where Lee was defeated and four thousand Confederate soldiers died, his men still had confidence in him and loved him.

Lee practiced daily prayer and Bible reading. At times he conducted services for fallen soldiers. On days of fasting and prayer proclaimed by Confederate president Jefferson Davis, Lee issued proclamations suspending all but the most necessary military duties. He also attended every preaching service in camp that he could.

Lee had a treasured prayer book, which he had used during the Mexican-American War and kept with him during the Civil War. While he was in Richmond, he traded in his old book to a bookseller and got a dozen new ones in return. He gave them to a chaplain to distribute to his men. That shows the importance Lee placed on prayer.

On April 8, 1864, General Lee issued orders for his troops to observe a day of fasting and prayer. He proclaimed:

> Soldiers! Let us humble ourselves before the Lord our God, asking through Christ, the forgiveness of our sins, beseeching the aid of the God of our forefathers in the defense of our homes and our liberties, thanking Him for his past blessings, and imploring their continuance upon our cause and our people.[9]

General Lee also wrote:

> Knowing that intercessory prayer is our mightiest weapon and the supreme call for all Christians today, I pleadingly urge our people everywhere to pray. Believing that prayer is the greatest contribution that our people can make in this critical hour, I humbly urge that we take time to pray—to really pray.
>
> Let there be prayer at sunup, at noonday, at sundown, at midnight—all through the day. Let us pray for our children, our youth, our aged, our pastors, our homes. Let us pray for our churches.
>
> Let us pray for ourselves, that we may not lose the word "concern" out of our Christian vocabulary. Let us pray for our nation. Let us pray for those who have never known Jesus Christ and redeeming love, for moral forces everywhere, for our national leaders. Let prayer be our passion. Let prayer be our practice.[10]

God did not answer Lee's prayers for Confederate victory because that was not God's will for our nation. However, God did answer Lee's prayers for the spiritual welfare of his men. Lee's spiritual leadership was one of the most vital elements of revival within the Confederate army.

THE GREAT REVIVAL

The first extensive revival broke out following the bloodbath at Antietam. On September 17, 1862, during the Battle of Antietam, 22,719 soldiers were killed, wounded, or declared missing in action. Bodies were piled seven or eight deep. To this day, that remains the bloodiest day in our national history.

Lee's army retreated across the Potomac River and camped in the lower valley of Virginia at Bunker Hill. Pleasant weather and rest made for a peaceful October, and the carnage and destruction the men had just been through led many to consider the issues of life, death, and eternity. The religious excitement that broke out at Antietam spread from camp to camp.

Once cold weather set in, soldiers built log chapels at each place they camped for an extended period of time. One of these chapels was so large that it could hold one thousand men. As the revival intensified, the crowds overflowed the chapels. If the army was stationed near a city, the soldiers met in churches. For example, in Fredericksburg twelve hundred people packed into St. George's Episcopal Church, the largest building in town.

Sometimes up to five hundred men were converted at once when a revival swept through a brigade. One chaplain of the Twenty-sixth Alabama Regiment wrote that his unit saw one hundred converts a week.[11]

Family prayer clubs were formed and met for regimental prayer meetings, usually conducted by one of the Christian soldiers. Sometimes praying and preaching continued twenty-four hours a day.

FUTURE SPIRITUAL LEADERS

Many of the converted soldiers, both Union and Confederate, went into full-time Christian ministry after the war. Two participants in the revival deserve to be mentioned here.

E. M. Bounds, who wrote several classic works on the power of prayer that are still in print today, learned how to pray in the trenches of the Civil War. He was the pastor of a congregation in Missouri when the war broke out. Union troops arrested him in 1861 and charged him as a Confederate sympathizer. He was in a federal prison in St. Louis for one and a half years before he was released in a prisoner exchange. He then enlisted as a Confederate chaplain. He prayed with the troops who served under General John Bell Hood. Bounds was once again captured by the Union army near the end of the war. When he was released, he resumed his pastoral duties—this time in Fredericksburg, near where he had been held as a prisoner.

Bounds, probably America's most prolific thinker and writer on prayer, prayed three hours daily and left us with profound wisdom regarding the power of prayer. He wrote:

> God's great movements in this world have been conditioned on, continued, and fashioned by prayer. God has put Himself in these great movements just as men have prayed. Persistent, prevailing, conspicuous, and mastering prayer has always brought God to be present.
>
> How vast are the possibilities of prayer! It lays its hand on Almighty God and moves Him to do what He would not do if prayer was not offered. Prayer is a wonderful power placed by Almighty God in the hands of His saints, which may be used to accomplish great purposes and to achieve unusual results.[12]

D. L. Moody, the future evangelist, ministered among the Union troops. He worked with the YMCA Devotional Committee to pitch a big tent for evening prayer services at Camp Douglas, south of Chicago. He eventually financed the building of a chapel on the site. Moody went from barracks to barracks day and night, praying and talking with the men about spiritual matters.

Under the Christian Commission, he made ten trips to the war front, where he preached, visited the wounded, and worked among the soldiers. When Richmond fell, Moody was one of the first to enter the city. He ministered to all soldiers, no matter which uniform they wore.

THE PRAYERS OF THE OPPRESSED

One more group deserves equal mention with the Confederate and Union armies—the slaves. Their prayers surely had a great effect on the outcome of the war.

Do you remember when slavery began in our country? Back in the 1600s the Jamestown settlers bought several slaves from a ship that appeared out of nowhere on the East Coast. Although the Jamestown colonists recognized that slavery was wrong, they went ahead anyway. Not too long after that, tobacco was introduced as a crop, and slavery became an economic part of the colony of Virginia.

In 1833 Britain abolished slavery without national bloodshed, but America held on to this institution despite our Constitution, which said that all men were created equal. Eventually, the United States abolished all slave trade from outside the country, but slavery was still permitted within the Southern states. Our country compromised on the issue by trying to establish a balance of power between slave and free states as new states in the West joined the Union.

When the slaves first arrived on our shores, they were not Christians, but most accepted the Christian faith in time. Many slaves risked their lives to worship God. When masters allowed slaves to congregate for services, the meetings were often just vehicles to teach the slaves to obey their superiors. And many plantation owners did not allow slaves to have religious services. Consequently, secret gatherings cropped up everywhere. What were these meetings like?

Hettie slipped out of the shack in the darkest part of the night. She carefully slid past the plantation outbuildings until she could duck under the cover of the huge trees growing along the edge of the fields. As soon as she was hidden by underbrush, she began running down the faint path. Her too-large shoes made running over the tree roots and fallen branches difficult, but she was still agile on her feet.

It took her a good thirty minutes to find the "hush harbor." When she got close, she could see the tabernacle the men had built under a large cypress. As she came into the tiny clearing, she touched the wet blankets that formed the walls of the tabernacle. It was true. The wetness deadened the sound. She couldn't hear a sound coming from inside the tabernacle.

Hettie ducked inside. She saw many dark heads huddled in a circle and heard voices pouring out their heartfelt sorrows and joys. One woman fervently cried, "O Lord, listen to the prayers of your people. We are aching for freedom from our heavy burdens. We ask, 'Let your people go.'"

Then someone began singing a spiritual, and the hushed voices all joined in. The preacher spoke next. He had news about the war going on so far from Georgia. Hettie strained her ears to hear every word.

When the preacher finished, Brother Wilson spoke. "The master is getting suspicious of our meetings. We have to stop for a while. We must find a new place to hold our meetings."

The others all murmured their agreement. Hettie knew what it meant to be caught at a secret meeting—a public flogging. They would have to find a new hush harbor in which to erect their tabernacle.

As the meeting ended, everyone went around the circle, bidding each other farewell until the next meeting. Before they left, they sang a song of praise and prayed.

As Hettie ran back to her shack, her heart was light. Surely God would answer their prayers for freedom. Until then, they would all meet to hear the preacher preach and to pray and to sing together. . . .[13]

Slave preachers were often illiterate, but they had wonderful gifts of oratory. Some were allowed to travel from place to place holding prayer meetings. Although the slave preacher had to be the mouthpiece of the white owners in public, during the secret meetings he spread news of the Civil War and led prayer for the success of the Union army.

The slaves believed that they were like the children of Israel in bondage to Egypt. Exodus 1:14 describes the hard life of slavery in Egypt: "[The Egyptians] were ruthless with the Israelites, forcing them to make bricks and mortar and to work long hours in the fields." Doesn't that sound like the plight of the American slaves?

In Exodus 2:23-25, we read about the cries of God's people:

> Years passed, and the king of Egypt died. But the Israelites still groaned beneath their burden of slavery. They cried out for help, and their pleas for deliverance rose up to God. God heard their cries and remembered his covenant promise to Abraham, Isaac, and Jacob. He looked down on the Israelites and felt deep concern for their welfare.

The slaves also cried out to God because of their burden and pain. They asked him to send someone like Moses to lead them out of slavery to the Promised Land. You can hear that cry in many of the Negro spirituals that came out of the torment of that time. Just as God had miraculously helped his people thousands of years ago, the slaves believed that he would do so now.

The one clear result of the Civil War was that, while racism and prejudice continued, slavery was abolished. Did God answer the prayers of the slaves? Yes. God is concerned with the cries of the helpless and the needy. Psalm 10:17-18 says: "Lord, you know the hopes of the helpless. Surely you will listen to their cries and comfort them. You will bring justice to the orphans and the oppressed, so people can no longer terrify them."

God did send a Moses to lead the slaves out of their oppression. That man was Abraham Lincoln. In the next chapter, we will discover the mission Abraham Lincoln set for himself and how prayer helped him accomplish that goal.

For Discussion and Reflection

Adult Discussion

Bring to class a flashlight; something with a white surface, such as a large sheet of white paper (or use a white wall); a red sheet of paper; and a blue circular cutout about three inches in diameter. Place the red sheet of paper over the white surface. Put the blue cutout in the middle of the red sheet. Darken the room and, with people facing the display, shine the light on the blue design. Have the class members stare at the design for three minutes. Remove the red sheet and blue cutout, revealing only the white surface. The students will see a yellow dot on a green background. Ask:

- ★ What did you see?
- ★ Are you sure about what you saw?
- ★ Was there really a yellow dot on a green background?
- ★ How might this illusion be similar to those Christians who thought slavery was appropriate?
- ★ How is this like the way we sometimes develop blind spots to sin in our lives?

Have everyone read 2 Chronicles 25:1-4. Ask:

- ★ What did Amaziah do right?
- ★ What did Amaziah do wrong?

★ How is this similar to many Christians today?

Form groups of four, and have them discuss the following questions:

★ What issues face us today on which Christians are divided?
★ What blind spots may exist in relation to those issues?
★ What can be done to help erase those blind spots?
★ What part can prayer play in all of this?

Have groups report on their discussions; then ask people to reflect on the following questions:

★ What blind spots may you have in your outlook on today's issues?
★ What are you going to do to make sure you're seeing things the way God sees them?

As you wrap up in prayer, encourage people to seriously consider their opinions and attitudes to see if they're in tune with what the Bible tells us God wants for our lives.

Youth Discussion

Bring to class a flashlight; something with a white surface, such as a large sheet of white paper (or use a white wall); a red sheet of paper; and a blue circular cutout about three inches in diameter. Place the red sheet of paper over the white surface. Put the blue cutout in the middle of the red sheet. Darken the room and, with people facing the display, shine the light on the blue design. Have the students stare at the design for three minutes. Remove the red sheet and blue cutout, revealing only the white surface. The kids will see a yellow dot on a green background. Ask:

* What did you see?
* Why do you think you saw that?
* Was what you saw real? Explain.
* How was the illusion you saw similar to the illusion some people had that slavery was OK with God?
* What illusions do you think people have today about what's OK with God?

Form pairs, and have them read 2 Chronicles 25:1-4. Then have them discuss the following questions:

* Where did Amaziah go wrong?
* Where did people who wanted to keep slaves go wrong?
* Where do teenagers go wrong today?

Ask the kids to think silently about the following question: "What kinds of things might be 'illusions' to you today, making you think something is OK that's not?"

In their pairs, have the kids pray together, asking God to help them see areas in their lives in which they may be experiencing illusions as to what God wants. Encourage the kids to dig into God's Word to discover what it tells us clearly about what God expects of us.

EIGHTEEN

Let My People Go

The little cabin with the split-log chimney was nestled near the trees. A weathered gray rail fence protected the only door and small window. As the sun hung low in the west, the shadows from the trees fell over the roof.

Inside the one-room cabin was a dirt floor and furniture made of split logs. In one corner, on a bed of dried leaves, lay a woman. Her husband sat beside her, nervously twisting his hands.

"Nancy, are the pains just as bad?" he asked her.

"Yes, Thomas," she answered weakly. "Please, you must get the doctor. There's something wrong. The baby is just not coming." Her words were cut short as another pain made her grasp the blanket around her.

Thomas immediately turned to go. "Will you be all right?" he asked as he looked back at her. His forehead was creased in worry.

"Just go," she insisted.

After he shut the door quietly behind himself, silence settled on the plain cabin. Nancy tossed on her bed, the pain making her bite hard to keep from crying out. A low fire glowed from the fireplace, but it didn't spread much warmth.

It seemed like an eternity before Thomas's huge frame darkened the doorway once more as he lumbered back in. "Nancy?" he asked.

"Yes, Thomas, I'm still here."

"Is the pain any better? Is the baby coming?"

"No."

"Our neighbor is riding to summon the doctor. Help should be here soon."

Thomas sat beside her and cooled her face with a wet rag he dipped into a basin of water. He tried to soothe her by talking softly about things he knew she liked. But Nancy wasn't listening. The pains had increased until they left her breathless. Thomas could see that she was getting weaker.

Hours passed. Thomas added more logs to the fire to take the chill from the room. As he straightened up from stoking the fire, he heard a loud rap on the door. *Finally, the doctor,* he thought.

When Thomas opened the door, he saw his neighbor with hat in hand. "Where's the doctor?" Thomas asked desperately.

"I'm sorry. He's on a call fifty miles away. He won't be coming. The missus says to get that midwife in Lexington. Miss Richards is her name. I can go for her."

"But that will take hours." Thomas glanced back at the bed now covered in shadows. "Yes, go. And please hurry. If I lose Nancy and the baby, I lose everything."

Thomas shut the door as the neighbor left. He went to Nancy's side and explained the situation to her. Then he took her hand and began praying. His thin voice pleaded with God to let his wife and first child live. Nancy prayed, too, in the few moments when the pain was not so great.

As night wore on, Nancy spoke less and less. Thomas felt so

helpless and alone. *Oh, God,* he agonized, *I can't do this alone. I will lose them both unless you help me.*

In the wee hours of the night, a loud pounding jarred him from his prayers. The door. It was too soon for the neighbor and the midwife. Who could it be? He ran to open the door. Outside stood a young woman carrying a large leather bag.

"You . . . Are you Miss Richards?" he asked.

"No, sir. My name is Sarah Parsons, and I'm a midwife. I understand you need help to deliver a baby." Without another word, she brushed past Thomas and rushed over to the bed. She pulled her equipment out of her bag. Thomas brought her a bucket of hot water he had dipped from the black kettle bubbling on the fire.

As Sarah worked calmly and quickly, Thomas felt a sense of hope warm him for the first time that night.

"The baby's turned in the womb," Sarah announced. The delivery was difficult. Sarah helped Nancy the best she could while Thomas waited patiently at the table. Then it came—the weak cry of the baby. As Sarah wrapped it in a clean blanket, the baby's cries gained strength. "It's a boy!" Sarah said.

Nancy turned and smiled at Thomas.

After Sarah had made Nancy and the baby comfortable and cleaned up the small room, she packed her bag.

"I must pay you," Thomas insisted, opening a small bag of coins.

"Oh no!" Sarah insisted. "I have no need of money. But you can do something for me. Name the baby Abraham."

"Oh yes, we will," Thomas assured her.

Sarah bundled up in her coat and scarf and picked up her bag. "I must go now."

With many thank-yous, Thomas opened the door for her. As

soon as she was gone, Thomas went back to Nancy's side. "Where's Sarah?" Nancy asked.

"She had to go."

"What's the matter with you, Thomas? You can't let her walk to town alone. I'm fine now. Go catch up to her!"

Thomas jumped up and flew out the door to catch the midwife. He ran out of the yard and down the road. She couldn't have gone far. But she had vanished. He couldn't find her anywhere. . . .[1]

THE RAIL SPLITTER

That baby was Abraham Lincoln. Thomas never found out where Sarah had come from or gone. Her disappearance led many to believe she was an angel. Abraham Lincoln, future president of the United States, was brought safely into this world on the miraculous wings of prayer. Throughout the remainder of his life, the great leader often fell to his knees in humility and supplication.

Like most of us, Lincoln spent his formative years being taught and nurtured by his mother. She had only one book to read to him, and that was the Bible. She read from it every day and taught him to base his life on its principles. When her son was ten years old, Nancy died, but she left behind a young boy who knew much of the Bible by heart. After he had grown into manhood, Lincoln said, "All that I am or hope to be, I owe to my angel mother! Blessings on her memory!"[2]

As Lincoln matured, he pursued knowledge. Because he didn't have access to higher education, he read books. The first book he read, besides the Bible, was Weems's *Life of Washington.* Little did he know that one day he would be immortalized with Washington as one of America's most well-loved presidents.

Lincoln worked very hard. Once he split four hundred railroad rails to buy each yard of material needed to make a pair of jeans. His work later earned him the nickname "rail splitter" by his political foes.

He also had a reputation for honesty. One example was during the time he managed a mill at New Salem, Illinois. Discovering he had overcharged a customer six and one-quarter cents, he walked several miles that night to return the money. Another customer bought a half pound of tea. Later Lincoln discovered he had mistakenly used a four-ounce weight on the scale. Again he walked a long distance to correct his mistake.

Hard work and honesty are two characteristics we would expect in a great leader. But would you expect a great leader to be a failure? Between 1831 and 1860, this young man experienced defeat after defeat. He failed in business twice, suffered a nervous breakdown, and lost his bid for public office eight times! He was defeated in elections for legislator, speaker, elector, congressman, senator, and vice president. But in 1860, he was elected as our nation's first Republican president.

The most important weapon Lincoln had during his hard and lonely days of leadership was a deep devotion to God through Bible reading and prayer. He said, "I have been driven many times upon my knees by the overwhelming conviction that I had nowhere else to go. My own wisdom, and that of all about me, seemed insufficient for that day."[3]

Upon Lincoln's election as president, South Carolina seceded from the Union and America was thrust into a great Civil War. Because of his stance against slavery, Lincoln received hundreds of petitions from clergy and other groups thanking him for his position and urging him to banish slavery completely. Lincoln made it clear that as president he would do everything in his power to stop the spread of slavery into new states and territories, and he undertook policies that would make slavery less profitable to the South. However, the Supreme Court decision upholding the rights of slave owners prevented him from going further.

Meanwhile, other Southern states, determined to pursue their own destiny in banking, shipping, trade, and lifestyle—which included slavery—began following South Carolina's lead. They felt certain they could win independence quickly, especially with such noble Christian leaders as Robert E. Lee and Thomas "Stonewall" Jackson commanding their troops.

But Lincoln was also a man of God. During his presidency, people often reported seeing him pick up the well-worn Bible from the stand near the sofa, especially during his darkest hours. He would get absorbed in its pages, finding refuge and answers from God. His favorite visitors were ministers. He welcomed them with open arms. He commented, "There is nothing as great under heaven as to be an ambassador of Christ."[4] At one particular party, a man named Mr. Jay missed the president and started to search for him. He found him in a quiet corner, alone with God, reading his well-worn Testament.[5]

It was probably during his quiet times with God and his ten-year relationship in Springfield with the black Marich Vance family that Lincoln began to have a passion to free the slaves. Marich was Mrs. Lincoln's maid, who came to work each day until he was elected president. Lincoln protected the Vance family when they had legal problems and financial needs and often sought Marich's wisdom as a strong Baptist believer. Lincoln took up the cause of blacks as early as 1857, when he opposed the Dred Scott Supreme Court decision that declared blacks to be mere property rather than persons. At the beginning of the war, he was willing to compromise on this issue, but as the battles progressed, Lincoln became more and more convinced that slavery was a horrible sin. Undoubtedly, he weighed the severe consequences the war would exact on our country; yet in the first great speech of his political career, he said, "The battle of freedom is to be fought out on principle. Slavery is a violation of the eternal right. We have temporized with it from the necessities of our condition; but as sure as God reigns and school children read, that black foul lie can never be consecrated into God's hallowed truth!"[6]

God was beginning to answer the prayers of the slaves.

After he was elected president in 1860, Lincoln gave a farewell speech to his friends and supporters in Springfield, Illinois. He knew the gravity of his situation, and he also knew that his success depended on God's help. He asked his fellow citizens for prayer support:

> Today I leave you. I go to assume a task more difficult than that which devolved upon General Washington. Unless the great God who assisted him shall be with me and aid me, I must fail; but if the same omniscient Mind and Almighty Arm that directed and protected him shall guide and support me, I shall not fail—I shall succeed. Let us all pray that the God of our fathers may not forsake us now. To Him I commend you all. Permit me to ask that with equal sincerity and faith you will invoke His wisdom and guidance for me.[7]

As Lincoln assumed leadership of this great nation during a very troubled time, some of his first acts involved proclaiming days of prayer for the people to call upon God and turn away

281

from their sin. As tensions built between the North and the South, Lincoln did what his mentor George Washington had done: He called the nation to pray and fast. Here is an excerpt from that proclamation:

> Whereas when our beloved country—once, by the blessing of God, united, prosperous, and happy—is now afflicted with faction and civil war, it is peculiarly fit for us to recognize the hand of God in this visitation, and, in sorrowful remembrance of our own faults and crimes as a nation and as individuals, to humble ourselves before him, and to pray for his mercy,—to pray that we may be spared further punishment, though justly deserved, that our arms may be blessed and made effectual for the re-establishment of law, order, and peace throughout our country, and that the inestimable boon of civil and religious liberty, earned, under his guidance and blessing, by the labors and sufferings of forefathers, may be restored in all its original excellence.[8]

THE GREAT BURDEN OF WAR

Once the Civil War began, newly elected president Lincoln came under extreme pressure. Thousands of young American men were dying on the battlefields. He read the long lists of casualties and brooded over them. Meanwhile, a great many Americans despised him. Newspapers ridiculed him and ran critical political cartoons.

How did he manage to lead effectively through this morass?

Through the power of prayer.

Lincoln and his wife, Mary Todd Lincoln, attended the New York Avenue Presbyterian Church. Often, he took time to attend the midweek prayer meeting. Before long, various politicians learned that he would be at the church every week, and they began standing at the door to speak to him. To avoid them, Lincoln would slip in and out of a small passageway into a room adjoining the prayer meeting, where the pastor would leave the door slightly ajar for him. Lincoln sat in the dark, listened to the prayers, and silently prayed along.[9]

One woman who was a member of the church told writer William Gladstone that "her husband, then a boy, attended the prayer meetings. He often saw Lincoln's shadow or silhouette on the window, resting his elbow on the arm of the chair, and his head on his hand. He said it was the saddest picture he ever saw."[10]

Although Lincoln was maligned by many, he also had a dedicated body of supporters. The most helpful were those who were his prayer supporters. On Sunday morning, October 26, 1862, a woman, Eliza Gurney, and three of her friends asked President Lincoln for a fifteen-minute interview. The woman was the widow of Joseph John Gurney, an English banker and Quaker minister. She felt deeply wounded by the horrors of the war and was sympathetic to Lincoln, with his awesome responsibility in leading the nation.

Eliza and her friends did not come to ask the president for anything, they just wanted to give him spiritual support. The president responded warmly. The four visitors stayed much longer than their allotted fifteen minutes as they prayed with the famous man. The president was so comforted by the prayer support that he asked Eliza to write to him.[11]

FREEING THE SLAVES

As the Civil War went on, Confederate victories became more numerous. The South rejoiced and attributed its success to God. Religious fervor mounted, and Southerners felt sure of God's continued favor. Yet the Confederate success didn't lead to victory quite as they expected. Instead, heavy Union losses brought a great deal of soul-searching and humility to the leaders in the North.

Lincoln himself began to question why the South was so successful in every battle. He turned to God for the answer and decided that God wouldn't honor the North because it had not rejected slavery or humbled itself before him. Lincoln's first solution to the problem was the Emancipation Proclamation, which he issued under his Emergency War Power authority on September 22, 1862. As a matter of law, it freed all slaves, even the ones in the states that were in rebellion against the Union.

When a gentleman called on Lincoln to congratulate him on this proclamation, Lincoln said:

> It is a great satisfaction to me to feel that I have the support of the people in the great struggle to save the nation's life. I never believed in slavery, but I felt I was elected President of both the North and the South. When Sumter was fired upon, and I called for seventy-five thousand men, my determined purpose was to save this country and slavery, and I called for over half a million men with the same determination. But, on many a defeated field there was a voice louder than the thundering of cannon. It was the voice of God crying, "Let My people go." We were all very slow in realizing it was God's voice, but after many humiliating defeats the nation came to believe it as a great and solemn command. Great multitudes begged and prayed that I might answer God's voice by signing the Emancipation Proclamation, and I did it, believing we never should be successful in the great struggle unless the "God of Battles" has been on our side.[12]

Just as Moses had done for the children of Israel so many years before, Lincoln had freed his people from slavery.

284

Then Lincoln addressed the second part of the nation's problem—pride. On April 20, 1863, he called for a National Day of Humiliation, Fasting, and Prayer throughout the North to be held on April 30. He had concluded that the entire nation was guilty of the sins of slavery and pride. Here is part of the proclamation:

> It is the duty of nations as well as of men to own their dependence upon the overruling power of God; to confess their sins and transgressions in humble sorrow, yet with assured hope that genuine repentance will lead to mercy and pardon; and to recognize the sublime truth, announced in the Holy Scriptures and proven by all history, that those nations only are blessed whose God is the Lord. . . .
>
> Intoxicated with unbroken success, we have become too self-sufficient to feel the necessity of redeeming and preserving grace, too proud to pray to the God that made us!
>
> It behooves us then to humble ourselves before the offended Power, to confess our national sins and to pray for clemency and forgiveness.[13]

When Lincoln realized what the national sin was, personally dealt with it, and publicly turned the nation back to God through prayer, the tide of the Civil War changed.

PRESIDENTIAL PRAYER

Within two days of the observance of this Day of Prayer, General Stonewall Jackson, one of the best generals in the Confederate army, was fatally shot, accidentally, by his own men. Jackson's death opened the door for Union victory at the battle that would turn the war around—Gettysburg. Was this part of the answer to Lincoln's prayers?

In July 1863, 163,000 soldiers came together at Gettysburg,

Pennsylvania, engaging in a three-day battle. Not even Lincoln could have imagined how powerfully the manifestations of the answers to his prayer would come through this conflict. One event deserves mention. . . .

Colonel Joshua Chamberlain slowly got to his feet. The esteemed members of the War Department waited eagerly for his report.

"Gentlemen," Chamberlain began, every eye riveted to him. "During the fiercest part of the fighting, our lines began to break before the overwhelming number of rebel soldiers. Our guns let loose, but the enemy kept coming. We had to defend that hill. To lose Little Roundtop would have been to lose everything. The shouts and noise of the battle became a roar. Then a terrible thing happened. We ran out of ammunition.

"I thought we would have to fall back, when out of nowhere rode a tall figure on a shining white horse. I know this is incredible, but the rider was dressed as a Revolutionary general. And the face, I will swear, was the face of George Washington. He raised his arm high and gave the signal to advance. My men began to shout and cheer. The rebels saw it too, and they began to shoot at it. The figure rode back and forth, and the Confederate guns followed it. He should have been killed a thousand times over. No human being could have survived that fire.

"The rider urged our men on and, raising their bayonets, they charged down the hill on top of the rebels. The bayonet charge must have taken them by surprise, for they turned and fled. We almost lost Little Roundtop, and if we had, we could have lost Gettysburg."[14]

Did General Washington ride his white charger into the forefront of the battle, inspiring the troops just as he had his own troops a hundred years earlier? Was it the intervention of a protecting angel? Or was the rider a figment of Colonel Chamberlain's imagination? We'll probably never know, but the event can clearly be seen as an answer to prayer.

In the final analysis, the Battle of Gettysburg proved to be a decisive turning point in the war, leading to an eventual victory for the Union. But the cost was astronomical. The Battle of Gettysburg left 51,000 men either dead or wounded.

How did Lincoln feel about this victory? Soon after the battle, Lincoln visited General Sickles, who had been severely injured, in the hospital. Sickles asked Lincoln if he had been worried about the outcome of this important battle. Lincoln firmly replied, "No, I was not; some of my Cabinet and many others in Washington were, but I had no fears."

General Sickles probed, "How were you able to achieve such calm?"

Lincoln hesitated but finally replied:

> Well, I will tell you how it was. In the pinch of your campaign up there, when everybody seemed panic-stricken, and nobody could tell what was going to happen, oppressed by the gravity of our affairs, I went to my room one day, and I locked the door, and got down on my knees before Almighty God, and prayed to him mightily for victory at Gettysburg. I told Him that this was His war, and our cause His cause, but we couldn't stand another Fredericksburg or Chancellorsville. And I then and there made a solemn vow to Almighty God, that if He would stand by you boys at Gettysburg, I would stand by Him. And after that (I don't know how it was, and I can't explain it), soon a sweet comfort crept into my soul that God Almighty had taken the whole business into His own hands and that things would go alright at Gettysburg. And that is why I had no fears about you.[15]

Only the power of prayer could have given Lincoln that peace of mind.

In the days following the bloody Battle of Gettysburg, the task of burying the dead was so overwhelming that many soldiers were interred near Gettysburg. Months later, Lincoln traveled by train to give a speech at the dedication of the new national cemetery set aside in honor of the dead. His talk was the shortest that any president would ever give; it lasted only two minutes. But his Gettysburg Address is the most well-remembered speech in our history. These are its immortal words, delivered on November 19, 1863:

> Four score and seven years ago our fathers brought forth on this continent a new nation, conceived in Liberty, and dedicated to the proposition that all men are created equal.
>
> Now we are engaged in a great civil war, testing whether that nation, or any nation so conceived and so dedicated, can long endure. We are met on a great battlefield of that war. We have come to dedicate a portion of that field, as a final resting place for those who here gave their lives that the nation might live. It is altogether fitting and proper that we should do this.
>
> But, in a larger sense, we cannot dedicate—we cannot consecrate—we cannot hallow—this ground. The brave men, living and dead, who struggled here have consecrated it, far above our poor power to add or detract. The world will little note, nor long remember, what we say here, but it can never forget what they did here. It is for us the living, rather, to be dedicated here to the unfinished work which they who fought here have thus far so nobly advanced. It is rather for us to be here dedicated to the great task remaining before us—that from these honored dead we take increased devotion to that cause for which they gave the last full measure of devotion—that we here highly resolve that these dead shall not have died in vain—that this nation, under God, shall have a

new birth of freedom and that government of the people, by the people, for the people, shall not perish from the earth.[16]

We often think that only educated and refined orators can touch the hearts of men. But God took an ordinary man like Lincoln and made him extraordinary because his heart was turned toward God.

UNPOPULAR PRESIDENT

Although Lincoln was unpopular in many sectors of the North, he was reelected for a second term. The main point in his second inaugural speech was that on both sides of the Civil War, great Christians had taken a stand. He later talked about this speech:

> Both read the same Bible and pray to the same God, and each invokes His aid against the other. It may seem strange that any men should dare to ask a just God's assistance in wringing their bread from the sweat of other men's faces, but let us judge not that we be not judged. The prayer of both could not be answered. That of neither has been answered fully. The almighty has His own purposes. Woe unto the world because of offenses, for it must needs be that offenses come, but woe to that man by whom the offense cometh. If we shall suppose that American slavery is one of those offenses which, in the providence of God, must need come, but which having continued through His appointed time, He now wills to remove, and that He gives to both North and South this terrible war as the woe due to those by whom the offense came, shall we discern there any departure from those divine attributes which the believers in a living God always ascribe to Him? Fondly do we hope, fervently do we pray, that this mighty scourge of war may speedily pass away. Yet if God wills that it continue until

all the wealth piled by the bondsman's two hundred and fifty years of unrequited toil shall be sunk, and until every drop of blood drawn with the lash shall be paid by another drawn with the sword, as was said three thousand years ago, so still it must be said, that the judgments of the Lord are true and righteous altogether.[17]

The Reverend Father Charles Chiniquy visited Mr. Lincoln in the White House several times to warn him of assassination plots. On his last visit Lincoln replied, "You are not the first to warn me against the dangers of assassination. . . . But I see no other safeguard against these murderers, but to be always ready to die, as Christ advises it. As we must all die sooner or later, it makes very little difference to me whether I die from a dagger plunged through the heart or from an inflammation of the lungs. Let me tell you that I have, lately, read a message in the Old Testament which has made a profound, and I hope a salutary impression on me."

He then took out his Bible and read these verses from Deuteronomy 3:22-27:

Ye shall not fear them: for the Lord your God he shall fight for you. And I besought the Lord at that time, saying, O Lord God, thou hast begun to shew thy servant thy greatness, and thy mighty hand: for what God is there in heaven or in earth, that can do according to thy works, and according to thy might? I pray thee, let me go over, and see the good land that is beyond Jordan, that goodly mountain, and Lebanon. But the Lord was wroth with me for your sakes, and would not hear me: and the Lord said unto me, Let it suffice thee; speak no more unto me of this matter. Get thee up into the top of Pisgah, and lift up thine eyes westward, and northward, and southward, and eastward, and behold it with thine eyes: for thou shalt not go over this Jordan (KJV).

When he finished reading, Lincoln said:

My dear Father Chiniquy, let me tell you that I have read these strange and beautiful words several times, these last five or six weeks. The more I read them, the more, it seems to me, that God has written them for me as well as for Moses.

Has He not taken me from my poor log cabin, by the hand, as He did of Moses in the reeds of the Nile, to put me at the head of the greatest and most blessed of modern nations just as He put that prophet at the head of the most blessed nation of ancient times? Has not God granted me a privilege, which was not granted to any living man, when I broke the fetters of 4,000,000 men and made them free? Has not our God given me the most glorious victories over my enemies? Are not the armies of the Confederacy so reduced to a handful of men, when compared to what they were two years ago, that the day is fast approaching when they will have to surrender? . . .

Yes! Every time that my soul goes to God to ask the favor of seeing the other side of Jordan . . . there is a still solemn voice which tells me that I will see those things only from a long distance. . . .

Why did God Almighty refuse to Moses the favor of crossing the Jordan, and entering the Promised Land? It was on account of the nation's sins! . . .

When I look on Moses, alone, silently dying on the Mount Pisgah, I see the law, in woe of its most sublime human manifestations, and I am filled with admiration and awe.

But when I consider that law of justice, and expiation in the death of the Just, the divine Son of Mary, on the Mount of Calvary, I remain mute in my adoration. The spectacle of the Crucified One which is before my eyes is more than sublime, it is divine! Moses died for his people's sake, but Christ died for the whole world's sake! Both died to fulfill the same eternal law of the Divine justice, though in a different measure.

Now, would it not be the greatest of honors and privileges

bestowed upon me . . . that I might die as they did, for my nation's sake![18]

A few days later, Lincoln's cabinet was meeting when they learned of Lee's surrender to Ulysses S. Grant at Appomattox, Virginia, on April 9, 1865. There were no shouts, no cheers, no smiles. At the president's suggestion, they all dropped to their knees and offered thanks to God for preserving the Union and guiding them to abolish slavery.

General Lee surrendered on April 9. Lincoln died on April 15, Good Friday, after glimpsing the restoration of the Union. Lincoln was the Moses whom God had called to free the slaves. And Lincoln was only too correct about the drama that would unfold. He would not see the end of the war nor celebrate it for more than a couple of days.

ABOVE THE FRAY

Lincoln's voice was different from that of most of his contemporaries. He didn't believe that God was for the North or for the South. He believed that God was the ruler of nations, that he would accomplish his will through the war. This is the kind of faith Lincoln had in his God:

> The will of God prevails. In great contests each party claims to act in accordance with the will of God. Both may be, and one must be, wrong. God can not be for and against the same thing at the same time. In the present civil war it is quite possible that God's purpose is something different from the purpose of either party—and yet the human instrumentalities, working just as they do, are of the best adaptation to effect His purpose. I am almost ready to say this is probably true—that God wills this contest, and wills that it shall not end yet. By His mere quiet power, on the minds of the now contestants, He could

have either saved or destroyed the Union without a human contest. Yet the contest began. And having begun He could give the final victory to either side any day. Yet the contest proceeds.[19]

Is it just coincidental that the slaves considered themselves in a situation similar to the Israelites in Egypt and prayed for deliverance while Lincoln believed that God had given him a mission like that of Moses? Moses led the children of Israel through the wilderness to the Promised Land, but God told Moses he could not enter the Promised Land. Moses died after glimpsing the beauty of the land from afar. Isn't that like the death of Lincoln?

What was the miracle of answered prayer during the Civil War? The slaves were given their request: freedom. Lincoln saw his requests granted: that the Union would not split but remain united and that the slaves would be freed. At the same time, although it happened through the horror of war, hundreds of thousands of young men entered the kingdom of heaven through faith in Christ—an answer to the prayers of those who prayed for revival and those army leaders who prayed for their men!

So what have we learned? The consequences of harboring sin are harsh. Many families were devastated by the Civil War, and racial injustice has continually plagued our national history. But God's sovereign hand turned the prayers of all Americans into a miraculous display of divine power for the good of the nation and its people. That is overwhelming evidence of the power of prayer in our national history!

But God was not through yet. The Third Great Awakening and the revivals that had spread throughout the Northern and Southern armies would continue to bear fruit. One man in particular who had been honed through these two great spiritual events would continue the prayer effort for decades. That man was D. L. Moody. He was a faithful servant who kept the prayer flame burning until the next awakening stirred the hearts of Americans toward God.

For Discussion and Reflection

Adult Discussion

Before class, use an eye dropper to write the words *secret sin* with lemon juice on several sheets of paper, one for every three people in your class. Bring along an incandescent lamp.

Form groups of three, and have each group look at one piece of paper to see if they can identify the secret words. Then have each group hold the paper near the lightbulb on the lamp so that the words show up. Give time for each group to complete this activity. Ask:

- ★ Why did the "secret sins" show up when the paper was put near the lightbulb?
- ★ How is this like the way God sometimes reminds us of secret sins in our lives?
- ★ Why did Lincoln, in the midst of the Civil War, ask that people pray and confess their sins to God?

Form groups of four, and have people read Psalm 32. Then have them discuss the following questions. Ask:

- ★ What did David see as the benefits of confessing secret sins?
- ★ What might Abraham Lincoln have seen as the benefit of Americans' unitedly confessing sins to God?
- ★ What might be the value of Christians' confessing secret sins to God today?

Have groups report on their discussions; then say: "We often have a lot to say about the sins of our world, but we seldom think much about the sins in our lives. Let's take a few minutes now to privately confess any secret sins to God and to ask him to help us turn from those sins and remain true to him."

Allow several minutes for silent meditation and prayer. Then wrap up your session with a prayer that Christians around the nation repent and turn to God with pure hearts.

Youth Discussion

Bring plain paper to class. Form trios, and have each trio design a paper airplane that will fly a long distance. Give groups five minutes to complete their airplanes. Then have one person from each group throw the plane from a given line.

Now give each group time to develop another plane using the ideas from the design of other groups' airplanes. Give groups five minutes; then fly the airplanes again. Ask:

* How did it feel when your plane didn't go the farthest the first time?
* What did you learn from the first time that helped make your plane go farther the second time?
* How is this like the way we sometimes learn from mistakes in life?

Have the kids discuss the following questions in their trios:

* What would you do if you failed to win in eight consecutive elections?
* What did Abraham Lincoln do in that situation?
* How might our nation be different if Lincoln had given up and not run for president?

Have the groups report on their discussions; then read 1 Peter 4:12-13. Ask: "What do these verses say we should do about our trials?"

Read James 1:2-12. Ask:

- ★ What do these verses say our struggles do for us?
- ★ What can we learn from these passages and from the life of Abraham Lincoln?
- ★ What does James 1:5 say we can do if we don't know what to do?

Say, "No matter what happens, we can trust that God is with us. He's promised to give us wisdom, and if we look to him in prayer, he'll show us what to do."

NINETEEN

Igniting
the Fires

In the second half of the nineteenth century, two huge fires swept through Chicago. On an October Sunday evening in 1871, flames began eating block after block of homes. The Great Chicago Fire destroyed much of the city and was probably the worst disaster in the city's history.

The other fire—a spiritual one—was ignited by the preaching of one man: D. L. Moody. In 1859, Moody started a Sunday school that attracted hundreds of children—fifteen hundred at its height. Moody's work became so well known that President Lincoln stopped to visit the school on his way to Washington to begin his first term of office as president.

What kind of man was Moody? A man who believed deeply in prayer. As a shoe salesman and then as a Christian who worked tirelessly for his Lord, his time was always at a premium. Yet this is what he said about prayer: "If you have so much business to attend to that you have no time to pray, depend upon it that you have more business on hand than God ever intended you should have."[1]

During the Great Chicago Fire of 1871, Moody lost his church, the Chicago YMCA he had launched, and even his home. The Chicago Fire finally died out, but Moody's spiritual fire kept going until his death in 1899. And his inner fire—his love for God—never died. He once said:

> Some day you will read in the papers that Moody is dead. Don't you believe a word of it. At that moment, I shall be more alive than I am now. . . . I was born in the flesh in 1837; I was born of the Spirit in 1855. That which is born of flesh may die. That which is born of the Spirit shall live forever.[2]

One night God kindled a fire in Moody's soul that led him to give up a promising career in the shoe business to serve God full-time. This is how Moody tells the story:

> I had never lost sight of Jesus Christ since the first day I met Him in the store in Boston, but for years I really believed I could not work for God. No one had ever asked me to do anything. When I went to Chicago, I hired four pews in a church, and used to go out on the street and pick up young men and fill these pews. I never spoke to those young men about their souls; that was the work of elders, I thought. After working for some time like that, I started a mission Sabbath-school. I thought numbers were everything, so I worked for numbers. . . .
>
> Then God opened my eyes. There was a class of young ladies in the school who were without exception the most frivolous set of girls I ever met. One Sunday the teacher was ill, and I took that class. They laughed in my face, and I felt like opening the door and telling them all to get out and never come back.
>
> That week the teacher of the class came into the store where I worked. He was pale, and looked very ill. "What's the trouble?" I asked. "I have had another hemorrhage of my lungs. The doctor says I cannot live on Lake Michigan, so I am going to New York State. I suppose I am going home to die." He seemed

greatly troubled, and when I asked the reason, he replied, "Well, I have never led any of my class to Christ. I really believe I have done the girls more harm than good." I had never heard anyone talk like that before, and it set me thinking. After awhile I said: "Suppose you go and tell them how you feel. I will go with you in a carriage, if you want to go."

He consented, and we started out together. It was one of the best journeys I ever had on earth. We went to the house of one of the girls, called for her, and the teacher talked to her about her soul. There was no laughing then! Tears stood in her eyes before long. After he had explained the way of life, he suggested that we have prayer. He asked me to pray. True, I had never done such a thing in my life as to pray God to convert a young lady there and then. But we prayed, and God answered our prayer.[3]

Moody said that he and the teacher went to each of the other homes and talked to the other girls. Since they had to climb stairs at many of the places, the teacher was usually out of breath when he told the young lady what he had come to talk about. Each one of the girls received Christ as her Savior.

It took more than one day to visit all the homes because the teacher's strength wore out. But after ten days, all the girls had entered the kingdom of God. The night before the teacher had to leave Chicago, Moody called the class together for a prayer meeting. He later wrote:

There God kindled a fire in my soul that has never gone out. The height of my ambition had been to be a successful merchant, *and if I had known that meeting was going to take that ambition out of me, I might not have gone.*

But how many times I have thanked God since for that meeting! The dying teacher sat in the midst of his class and talked with them, and read the fourteenth chapter of John. We tried to sing "Blest Be the Tie That Binds," after which we knelt down to pray. I was just rising from my knees when one of the class began to pray for her dying teacher. Another prayed, and another, and before we rose *the whole class had prayed!* As I went out I said to myself, "O God, let me die rather than lose the blessing I have received tonight!"[4]

The next night Moody went to the train station to see the teacher off. One by one the entire class came. The little group tried to sing, but all they could do was cry. The teacher boarded his train, and as the train pulled out of the station, he stood on the rear car, pointed his finger upward, and told them all he would meet them in heaven.

THE WORLD HAS YET TO SEE

That prayer meeting was a miraculous event that had far-reaching results. It set Moody on a course that would change the lives of millions. As he preached in America and Europe, he ignited revival wherever he went.

While on his first trip to England, he met a wholesale butcher named Henry Varley, who remarked, "The world has yet to see what God will do with a man fully consecrated to Him."[5] Those words stuck with Moody, and he decided that he would be that man.

Moody's ministry was deeply affected by the prayers of one woman—"Auntie" Sarah Cooke, who attended Moody's church. In 1871, she and her friend Mrs. Hawxhurst were at one of Moody's camp meetings. They informed him that they were praying for him to be baptized with the Holy Ghost. He met with them in Farwell Hall every Friday afternoon to pray. Cooke said that on the Friday before the Great Chicago Fire, "Mr. Moody's agony was so great that he rolled on the floor and in the midst of many tears and groans cried to God to be baptized with the Holy Ghost and fire."[6]

While on a trip to New York a few days later, he felt such a sense of the Holy Spirit that he said, "Hold, Lord, it is enough!"[7]

What influence did Moody have on his era? For one thing, he encouraged R. A. Torrey to join his ministry. Torrey, also a revivalist who held evangelistic meetings, pastored Moody's church and authored at least forty books, one of which is the classic *The Power of Prayer.* Moody also established many schools, including the still-prominent Moody Bible Institute in Chicago, which has sent out thousands of missionaries and educated many other Christian workers.

Moody helped establish two publishing companies: Fleming H. Revell (named after Moody's brother-in-law) and Moody Press. Editor Allen Fisher writes, "Perhaps Moody, more than any other person, deserves to be called the father of this influential medium [book publishing] that ministers to both Evangelicalism and American society."[8]

Moody's preaching inspired many to go out as missionaries. During one evangelistic service, Presbyterian pastor Arthur T. Pierson spoke about how the great commission could be fulfilled by the year 1900. Moody was so impressed with Pierson's ideas that he carried on the challenge that led to large missions conferences.

It is estimated that one hundred million people heard Moody speak during his lifetime.[9]

THE FIRST DAY OF WINTER

Moody, like George Whitefield before him, didn't go out of this life with a whimper. He preached until his energy was spent. In November 1899, he preached a series of services in Kansas City to crowds in the huge convention hall. But Moody had to quit after five days because he suffered a heart attack. He took the train back to Northfield, Massachusetts, where giant maples nestled around the house where he had been born. There he was put to bed near a window, where he could see the familiar valley scenes he loved. Moody died on December 22, 1899.

It was the end of an era. A new century beckoned, and social forces were beginning to dampen America's enthusiasm for God. But once again Christians began to pray.

FROM BASEBALL TO EVANGELISM

So far we have seen how God has used ordinary men and women to form our country through the power of prayer. The diversity of the people God has used is amazing. For example, the foremost American evangelists were from completely different backgrounds: Jonathan Edwards was one of the greatest minds of his century and an educated theologian. Charles Finney was a country lawyer. Moody began his ministry as a shoe salesman. And now another man would be used of God to transform thousands of lives during the Fourth Great Awakening—a major-league baseball player. . . .

Billy Sunday and a few friends were sitting around a table in a smoke-filled bar. The lights were dim, and the men were laughing and talking loudly about the Chicago White Sox game they had just won.

"You're the fastest runner I ever saw!" one of the men remarked to Billy. "How fast are you?"

"The coach timed him running the bases last week," the big

man sitting across from Billy bragged. "Fourteen seconds flat. The coach checked his stopwatch twice."

As they all joked about Billy's speed, the sound of band music blared in from outside the door. "Hey, look!" the pitcher exclaimed. "It's the Pacific Garden Mission band."

"They're looking for converts," the big man joked.

The men took their drinks and sauntered outside to see what was going on. One by one they sat down on the curb to listen to the mission group sing gospel hymns. As Billy leaned back and closed his eyes, the songs took him back to the log cabin in Ames, Iowa, where he had grown up. He could hear his mother singing those old hymns as she worked. He also heard the congregation in his old church bellowing out the words on a Sunday morning. Their voices were ordinary, but the joy in the words shone through.

Billy began sobbing. *I've strayed so far from my godly past,* he realized. The more he thought about his sinfulness, the more he sobbed. His friends just stared at him.

Finally a young man from the Pacific Garden Mission group crossed the street and spoke to Billy. "We're going down to the Mission. Won't you come, too? I'm sure you'll enjoy it."

Billy stood up. He had made his decision. Turning to his teammates, he announced, "I'm through. I am going to Jesus Christ. We've come to a parting of ways."

"Yeah, right," the big man sneered. "You're gonna get religion."

The others laughed.

"There goes your baseball career," someone else jeered.

But Billy turned his back on them and walked the distance to the mission. When inside, he found a quiet place and sank to his knees. "Oh, Jesus, forgive me of my sins!" he cried.[10]

HOME-RUN PREACHER

After his conversion, Billy Sunday was a changed man. He gave up drinking, betting, and going to the theater. He kept working as a major-league baseball player for another four years, but in 1891, he quit his position and accepted a full-time job with the YMCA.

God used Billy Sunday in a miraculous way. In just over a quarter of a century of preaching, Billy Sunday delivered his message twenty thousand times. Two million people proclaimed their new faith in Christ as a result. In New York City, a million and a half people came to hear Billy Sunday preach during a single ten-week campaign.

One of Sunday's earliest campaigns was conducted in Burlington, Iowa, near his hometown of Ames. The city was awash in saloons and liquor stores. The citizens received him with antagonism. But after five weeks of meetings, Burlington was a changed place. Papers across Iowa headlined: "Burlington Is Dry: Sunday Has Made Graveyard out of Once Fast Town." This is a portion of an article that appeared in the Burlington *Hawkeye:*

> Rev. W. A. Sunday's labors of five weeks closed in Burlington amid a scene of wild enthusiasm. A half acre of handkerchiefs and cheers from six thousand throats, shouting in a delirium of feeling, after twenty-five hundred persons had been added to the membership of Burlington churches, with hundreds more giving notice of their coming a little later. After this staid old city, firm in the conservatism of a one-time capital of Iowa, had been faced about and given such an uplift of moral standard that the observer within its gates who saw its intense antagonism six weeks ago, is overwhelmed with amazement at the change."[11]

Billy Sunday helped further the Fourth Great Awakening into the early years of the new century.

A NEW GENERATION

The future looked uncertain as America turned the corner into the twentieth century. New forces such as atheism, evolution, liberal religious thinking, and materialism began to infiltrate American society, and they began attacking the Christian faith. Within the church, a social gospel was taking root, which shifted the emphasis from winning people to Christ to addressing the needs of society.

But not all was dark. In 1901, Christians at Moody Bible Institute, at the Keswick Convention in England, in Melbourne, Australia, in the Nilgary Hills of India, and at Onsam in Korea began praying for a worldwide revival. Because of their prayers, R. A. Torrey planned a worldwide evangelistic tour along with his soloist, Charles M. Alexander. Torrey and Alexander began in Australia. In his opening message in Melbourne, Torrey announced: "I believe that a worldwide revival has begun. I know of five thousand people outside of Australia who are praying for the success of this mission."[12] Torrey also preached in Tasmania, New Zealand, China, Japan, India, and finally London.

THE WELSH REVIVAL

To get a clear picture of the religious forces at work just after the turn of the century, we must travel to Wales and discover the momentum behind the great Welsh revival. It began in 1904 with a young coal-miner-turned-student named Evan Roberts. He was a spiritual young man who was praying for revival in his country. One day, he attended a service led by Seth

Joshua, a Presbyterian evangelist. Joshua prayed, "Oh, God, bend us," and gave an invitation for others to follow him. Dr. J. Edwin Orr relates what happened next:

> Evan Roberts went forward and prayed with great agony, "Oh, God, bend me." He couldn't concentrate on his studies. He went to Principal Phillips, the principal of his college, and said, "I hear a voice that tells me I must go home and speak to our young people in my own home church. Mr. Phillips, is that the voice of the devil or the voice of the Spirit?"
>
> And Phillips answered very wisely, "The devil never gives orders like that. You can have a week off."
>
> [Roberts] went back home to Lochlure and announced to the pastor, "I've come to preach."[13]

The pastor allowed Roberts to address anyone who agreed to stay after the Monday prayer meeting. Seventeen people stayed.

Roberts told them, "I have a message for you from God. You must confess any known sin to God and put any wrong done to man right. Second, you must put away any doubtful habit out of your life. Third, you must obey the Spirit promptly." Finally he said, "You must confess your faith in Christ publicly."[14]

All seventeen responded.

Because of this response, the pastor asked Roberts to speak again. Then he asked him to stay for another week of meetings. During those meetings, a break came, and people all over the area began flocking to hear the young man speak.

The revival spread like wildfire, first to North Wales, then to the rest of the country. The social impact was astounding. Crime plummeted. Judges retired because they had so few cases to try. There were virtually no rapes, robberies, murders, burglaries, or embezzlements. Drunkenness and the illegitimate birth rate dropped by half. Also, a wave of bankruptcies hit the area—nearly all of them taverns.

That meant that the police had nothing to do. The district consuls held emergency meetings to discuss the role of the police now that they had so little to do.

The awakening kept on spreading—to Europe, Africa, Australia, and Asia. It truly became a worldwide awakening—just what the prayer warriors had asked God to send.

THE FOURTH GREAT AWAKENING IN AMERICA

In late 1904, churches in the United States began hearing about the Welsh revival. As we discovered earlier, Christians were already praying for an awakening, but now the denominations renewed their efforts. The revival began in a small Welsh church in Wilksburg, Pennsylvania, where there were 123 converts in the services.

The Fourth Great Awakening spread to Scranton, then all over the state. As it rippled into New Jersey, it was so encompassing in Atlantic City that, according to Dr. Orr, only fifty unbelievers were left out of a population of fifty thousand.[15]

The revival hit New York, then spread to all parts of New England. It also affected the South. In Florida, Mordecai Ham began a revival ministry that many years later would touch the life of a very special high school student from North Carolina—Billy Graham.

Almost every area of the country was changed through the Fourth Great Awakening. In Chicago, pastors heard of the conversions in Michigan, so they met to pray for God's leading to promote the revival in their city. The revival came.

In Portland, Oregon, 240 department stores signed an agreement to close daily between eleven o'clock and two o'clock for prayer. In Denver, Colorado, all businesses closed for two hours at midday for prayer and fasting. The mayor proclaimed a Day of Prayer, and the state legislature closed for prayer. Imagine an entire city in the middle of a busy weekday, pausing to ask for God's blessings!

In April 1906, a black Holiness preacher named William J. Seymour began prayer meetings in a home in Los Angeles. As more people came, the meetings were moved to a run-down Methodist church on Azusa Street. For three years, thousands of people, both black and white, crowded into the church. This was the beginning of the Pentecost Revival, an offshoot of the Fourth Great Awakening. This revival led to the growth of Pentecostal denominations.

Meanwhile, the American-linked Welsh revival in the British Isles drew one hundred thousand people to the Christian faith during a five-month period. The social impact was so astounding that it has never been equalled to this day.

What was the social impact of the Fourth Great Awakening in America? There was renewed social consciousness for political honesty and against business double-dealings. This changed the outcome of many elections and produced civic reform in many areas. This awakening would have an effect all the way up to World War II.

What have we learned from the four awakenings that kept bringing America back to God? First, they were always preceded by prayer and accompanied by prayer. Not only did church members pray for revival—which brought on an unusual work of God and spread through the power of the Holy Spirit without the need for human organization—but prayer also moved key people to fit into the work God called them to do. Second, social reform naturally grew out of revival. Abolition, women's suffrage, and other causes naturally sprang from the Christian church. Third, even during times of deep revival, God's people refused to acknowledge some sin, which brought on severe consequences. The Civil War was the most devastating result of unrepentance by the church. And last, our nation has been formed and propelled through decades of history through the intervention of God's power in the spiritual life of our national leadership and citizenry.

As we turn a historical corner and begin to look at the modern era of our prayer heritage, we will once again see what happens when God's people forget the lessons they learned in the past. But we will also see the birth of movements that have shaped not only our country but the world as well. Once again we will discover the prayer miracles at work in history through ordinary people filled with the power of God!

For Discussion and Reflection

Adult Discussion
Bring in small slips of paper and a container to collect them in. Pass out three slips of paper to each person. Ask everyone to write a favorite hobby or interest on each slip of paper. Gather the slips of paper and have someone write the various hobbies on a chalkboard or large piece of paper as you read them. Ask:

> ★ What was it like seeing all these different hobbies listed?
> ★ Why do you think there are so many different ones?
> ★ How were the spiritual leaders in this chapter different from each other?
> ★ How were they similar?

Form groups of four, and make sure each person has a Bible. Say: "Now we're going to explore the differences among biblical leaders. In your groups, list differences and similarities between John, Peter, and Paul. Use your Bibles to help you."

After about ten minutes, let groups report their findings. Then ask:

★ How was God able to use John, Peter, and Paul even though they were so different?
★ How might God be able to use some of our differences?

In their groups, have people go over the list of hobbies and interests and choose ones God might be able to use in their lives to further his work in their community.

Youth Discussion

Bring in sand, rocks, and magnifying glasses. Form groups of three. Give each group some sand, a rock, and a magnifying glass. Tell groups to study the sand and rock and write down characteristics about them. When groups finish, ask:

★ What was it like looking carefully at the sand and rocks?
★ How were the rocks and sand similar?
★ How were they different?
★ How were the spiritual leaders in this chapter different?
★ Why do you think God chose such different people to serve him?

Read 1 Corinthians 12:12-18. Ask:

★ What does this passage say about the different gifts and abilities we all have?
★ What kinds of people can God use?
★ What kinds of tasks can God use people to perform?
★ Do you think everyone is able to do something to serve God? Why or why not?

Have the kids form pairs. Tell partners to share things they think God might enable them to do to serve him. Have partners pray for each other to follow through on doing what they think God wants them to do for him.

THE EVANGELICALS

★ ★ ★

TWENTY

When God Intervenes

As late as 1892, in the landmark decision of *The Church of the Holy Trinity v. the United States,* the Supreme Court declared:

> [N]o purpose of action against religion can be imputed to any legislation, because this is a religious people. . . . [T]his is a Christian nation. . . . [W]e are a Christian people, and the morality of our country is deeply engrafted upon Christianity. . . . There is no dissonance in these declarations. There is a universal language pervading them all, having one meaning; they affirm and reaffirm that this is a religious nation.

Those are powerful words, but they were written more than one hundred years ago. Are those ideas still true today? Are we a Christian nation? Would the Supreme Court stand by that ruling today?

The difficulties of the twentieth century were ones that Christians had never faced before. But God once again chose men and women of faith to lead our country through the storms and difficulties we would experience. Several forces combined to challenge the growth of the church in America. The rise of modernism—which denied the supernatural work of God, the virgin birth of Christ, his resurrection, and many other historical doctrines—affected the spiritual beliefs of many. Materialism and secularism also weakened the spiritual life of our country. America's prosperity grew until it surpassed the expectations of almost everyone. But wealth usually does not bring people to God; it causes them to become self-sufficient and selfish.

In this section, we will look at several areas in which we can see answers to prayer and the Spirit of God orchestrating events that affected the entire world during the century that is now drawing to a close. In this chapter, we will learn how God answered prayer in many ways during the two world wars. In the remaining chapters, we will see ways in which our national leaders considered prayer an essential part of our national life and how God has worked through men and movements in America during the twentieth century.

THE WAR TO END ALL WARS

World War I occurred during a time when America still had much religious zeal. Although evolution, modernism, and materialism were already rearing their heads, they hadn't yet become the forces they would later grow to be. Historian Robert S. Alley writes of Woodrow Wilson, America's president during those years:

> Wilson's Christian faith was the driving force of his life. No one in the history of the White House could equal his mastery of the Bible, nor could anyone surpass his knowledge of theology.[1]

Within months of Wilson's election to a second term, German submarines torpedoed and sank five American ships. On April 2, 1917, Wilson addressed the U.S. Congress in a war message:

It is a fearful thing to lead this great peaceful people into war, into the most terrible and disastrous of all wars. . . .[2]

To such a task we can dedicate our lives and our fortunes, everything that we are and everything that we have, with the pride of those who know that the day has come when America is privileged to spend her blood and her might for the principles that gave her birth and happiness and the peace which she has treasured. God helping her, she can do no other.[3]

When the U.S. Congress declared war on Germany on April 6, 1917, American churches got behind the war effort. Local Red Cross units met in church buildings; ministers went to train as chaplains; war commissions were formed by most church denominations to raise and contribute money to the war effort, usually to help the government support chaplains; the government commissioned the YMCA to provide chaplains for camps in the U.S. and overseas. Church women knitted socks and sweaters for soldiers enduring the horrible conditions of European trench warfare. Laymen sold Liberty Bonds and war-savings stamps to raise money. And many people prayed fervently.[4]

Most Americans believed that World War I would be the "war to end all wars" and that our troops were making the world safe for democracy. On November 11, 1918, an armistice, a temporary peace agreement, was signed. President Wilson described God's role in the Allies' victory when he presented the proposed peace treaty to the U.S. Senate on July 10, 1919:

The stage is set, the destiny is disclosed. It has come about by no plan of our conceiving, but by the hand of God who led us into this way. We cannot turn back. We can only go forward, with lifted eyes and freshened spirit, to follow the vision. It

317

was of this that we dreamed at our birth. America shall in truth show the way. The light streams on the path ahead and nowhere else.[5]

AFTER THE WAR

After the war ended victoriously for the United States, America began moving forward again. Christians were exuberant. "The Star-Spangled Banner," with its strong references to God in its latter verses, was chosen as our national anthem in 1931.

Right after the armistice of 1918 was signed, the Executive Committee of the Board of Foreign Missions of the Presbyterian Church in the U.S. called for a united drive to evangelize the world. One hundred thirty-five representatives of mission boards and agencies met to organize the Interchurch World Movement. The Interchurch World Movement planned to raise 336 million dollars and become one of the most glorious achievements in the history of the church.

But the bubble of optimism soon burst. Normally, spiritual fervor cools after a war, and once again the churches began to decline at the end of the war. By mid-May of 1920, the Interchurch World Movement had collapsed.[6]

Throughout the 1920s, a spiritual depression was affecting American churches. Interest in missions waned; the Student Volunteer Movement lost its steam. Then the stock market crashed in 1929. At times it looked as if the evangelical church in America would never recover. Was God dead, as philosopher Nietzsche claimed?

The amazing story of the power of prayer is that the Spirit of God has purposes and plans far beyond what humans can imagine. Time after time in American history, the church has redefined and adapted its methods to changing times while holding sacred its essential biblical message. In the midst of the poverty of the Depression Era, God was still moving. Many Christians expected the hard times of drought, bank crashes, and unemployment to bring on another great revival. That didn't happen. But some quieter movements were under way that were all but invisible at the time. Ruth Tucker writes:

> It was during that decade [the 1930s] that Clarence Jones and some of his visionary colleagues initiated the earliest attempts to establish missionary radio [forerunner of the Religious Broadcasters Association], that William Cameron Townsend [founder of Wycliffe Bible Translators] began training missionary linguists, that Joy Ridderhof implemented her ideas for gospel records [forerunner of the Christian music industry], and that others were testing the practicality of aviation on the mission field. World War II, however, frustrated the plans of many of these missionary activists, and it was not until the end of the war that the real thrust of missionary specialization got under way.[7]

World evangelization began to take on many different forms. No longer did the majority of missionaries strike out as evangelists. Instead, new strategies were planned to reach more people with the gospel. This would transform the way Americans viewed missions.

One important ministry whose seeds were sown during these years between the wars was the Navigators, founded by Dawson Trotman. God was preparing this little group for an immense trial that loomed just over the horizon. Let's take a look at Trotman's ministry.

THE SAILOR'S SALVATION
By the mid-1930s, Trotman had started his struggling ministry to servicemen. His foremost priority was prayer. He was

known for spending hours in prayer, within groups and alone. He kept an extensive notebook in which he wrote prayer requests and answers. This is a June 1933 prayer entry in his journal:

> Had a truly blessed time alone with the Lord. Early this morning. Again have I had the matter of prayer brought definitely to my attention as being vitally connected with accomplishing much business for God. I set my face again to pursue and persevere in habits of much time with Him. Truly our most difficult work, as refreshing and as wonderful as it is—Prayer.[8]

His first recruit, Les Spencer, a sailor on the USS *West Virginia,* started a Bible class aboard ship. Trotman, who remained behind, often climbed the hills above the San Pedro harbor near Long Beach and prayed for the men on every ship he saw.

Prayer miracle after prayer miracle built Trotman's tiny ministry. Then in April 1940, almost the entire fleet of Navy ships left for maneuvers in Hawaii. Trotman visited the islands and began training Christians to evangelize and train new believers in their faith. This established a strong work near Pearl Harbor, which had become the home base for the U.S. Naval Fleet.

In response to Trotman's prayers and those of his men, God was helping the Navigators establish a Christian on every ship. One of the Navigators witnessed to a writer who worked for *Collier's* magazine. On September 13, 1940, a lengthy article about the Navigators' work appeared in the magazine. In it, the writer quoted a chief bos'n mate who described the Navigators' ministry:

> We've got 12 of them on the *California*—maybe 15. You can't tell. Today you've got 12, maybe 15. Tomorrow you've got

maybe 18 or 20. They're always working on the wicked, converting sinners, holding revivals, praying with lost souls. Every ship in the fleet's got some—I don't know how many in all and they ain't saying.[9]

Each month, more Navigators were being trained aboard ship—and only God knew how much they would be needed in the next four years. The importance of prayer and evangelism was soon apparent, however.

On December 7, a group of thirty Navigators met early in the morning for Bible study at the Honolulu Navigator Home. This would be no ordinary Bible study. . . .

As the men closed their Bibles and had second cups of coffee, Petty Officer Herb Goeldner pushed back his chair and stood. "If you'll excuse me, I have a Bible class at 0800 on the ship," he said.

"We'll see you later," Gunner Jim Downing said as Goeldner headed for the door.

Goeldner got into his car and gently put it into gear. As he drove along, the sunshine warmed the arm he had resting on the open window. Then he heard rifle fire and explosions in the distance. *What on earth is that?* he wondered as he tromped the gas pedal and sped toward the navy yard gate. What he saw when he braked at the gate took his breath away. In the harbor, Japanese aircraft were dropping bombs! Smoke and burning debris were everywhere. Goeldner quickly turned his car around and raced back to get the other Navigators.

When he reached the house, the others had already heard an alert on the radio. Several of them crowded into his car, and he sped toward the main gate. When Goeldner reached the main gate, he was waved through immediately. Once inside, he parked and everyone spilled from the car. Then everyone stood stock-still.

Eight huge battleships had been peacefully docked on Battleship Row at Ford Island in the harbor. Now the *West Virginia* was listing to port while fires swept across her decks. The *Arizona* was a mass of exploded wreckage as she showered flaming debris in all directions. The *Oklahoma* floated bottom up, and the *California* was sinking. Flaming oil blanketed the water while enemy aircraft screamed overhead, strafing everything that moved.

Wounded sailors were running for their lives. Men were jumping from the burning wreckage. Others were trying to help any way they could.

Downing and Chief Yeoman Watters raced for the landing, where they tried to hail a boat going to Ford Island. In their hands they carried their Bibles and notebooks. "Looks like we'll need both hands," Watters commented dryly. Both men stashed their books inside an equipment box on the dock. "Glad I'm caught up on my praying," Watters told Downing. Then the men each ran his separate way to help wherever he could. . . .[10]

The Navigators put all their energy into helping. Author Betty Skinner writes about the aftermath of the bombing of Pearl Harbor for one of the ships:

> Sorting through the mail those first days, Jim [Downing] had the sad duty of returning letters addressed to the dead or missing. He reviewed the list of the 105 *West Virginia* men and could account for nearly all having heard the Gospel from their shipmates. In most cases they had said, "Yes, I'd like to make this decision—later." When it was discovered later that some of the men trapped in the sunken ship lived till after Christmas, Jim

hoped that in those dark weeks of waiting they had reconsidered the Scripture and accepted the offer of peace with God.[11]

The Lord had prepared a small army of godly men who would be assigned strategic places during this lengthy and costly war. Who could better witness to God's love and forgiveness than soldiers who had earned the trust of their fellow servicemen?

THE GOVERNMENT PROMOTES SPIRITUAL GROWTH

During the war, chaplains once again took center stage. In past conflicts, the government had commissioned nonmilitary groups to handle the recruitment and training of chaplains. In 1940 the U.S. government instituted a policy of providing one chaplain for every 1,200 soldiers. The Most Reverend William R. Arnold, a Roman Catholic, assumed the position of chief of chaplains. In 1941 Congress appropriated $12,816,880 to build 604 chapels for the troops. A special book, *A Song and Services Book, Army and Navy for Field and Ship,* was published. It contained hymns, Scripture, and prayers. The American Bible Society distributed Bibles and Testaments within the armed services. President Franklin Roosevelt wrote the foreword:

> As Commander-in-chief, I take pleasure in commending the reading of the Bible to all who serve in the armed forces of the United States. Throughout the centuries men of many faiths and diverse origins have found in the Sacred Book words of wisdom, counsel and inspiration.[12]

Each American war has had many miracles and lasting effects, and World War II was no exception. Sometimes the prayer miracles were seen nationally, but most often individuals had their own miracles to share with their families. The following accounts are a few examples of how God's leading changed the course of individual lives and our history.

THE MIRACLE OF THE SEAGULL

During World War II, American airpower came of age, and Captain Eddie Rickenbacker became America's leading air ace for shooting down twenty-six enemy planes in airborne dogfights. In 1942, Rickenbacker was assigned a mission to deliver an important message to General MacArthur, who was headquartered in New Guinea. He handpicked a crew and took off in a B-17. But somewhere over the South Pacific, the crew got lost and were out of reach of radio. When their fuel ran low, they ditched their plane in the ocean. The B-17 stayed afloat long enough for the eight men to board three rafts. For the next month, they fought water, sun, and weather. At night they drove off sharks, which were ramming their rafts.

But the crew's biggest problem was food. After eight days on the raft, their rations ran out. As the days slipped by without any rescue, they began to realize that they were going to starve to death. Only a miracle would save them. And that's just what happened. . . .

It was hot, so hot that the men felt lethargic and tired. The raft slowly bobbed up and down; the sun shone off the waves, sending spears of light in all directions.

Captain Rickenbacker raised his head as Captain William Cherry began to speak. Through the haze in his head, Rickenbacker realized that Cherry was reading the usual service for the afternoon. When he finished reading, he offered a prayer for deliverance. At first it seemed that the rest of the men had not heard him, but a few moments after his amen, they all began singing a hymn of praise. Rickenbacker sang, too. Their voices floated weakly over the waves. Rickenbacker was amazed that the men still praised God.

When the hymn had wafted away, the men started talking to one another. Rickenbacker began to doze off, too weak to stay awake. *I wonder when it will all end. God must do something soon or we'll all die,* he thought. He pulled his hat brim lower over his eyes.

Suddenly he felt something heavy and scratchy on his head. Somehow, even with his eyes closed, he knew that a seagull had landed on his head. *Food! If I can catch the gull, we can eat it!* he realized.

He didn't hear another sound as he felt the thin feet flex over his hat. Rickenbacker peered from under his hat brim without moving his head. The other men were staring at him, their faces tense but hopeful. He realized that they were waiting for him to grab the bird. He planned his next move, hoping that the gull wouldn't fly off, leaving their hopes dashed. Rickenbacker's hands tensed. Then he grabbed for the legs.

The next thing he knew, he felt the huge thrust of the gull's body as it tried to escape his grasp. The bird lunged, but Rickenbacker held on with all the strength he had. He felt the raft rock wildly; then he opened his eyes to see the men sitting nearest him grab for the bird, too. Within moments, they had the screeching gull pinned to the raft. . . .

The men ate that bird, and they used its intestines for bait to catch fish. And of course their spirits were lifted by this miraculous answer to prayer. After all, why would a lone seagull be hundreds of miles from shore if it were not sent by the hand of God?

Eventually the airmen were found, after spending over a month at sea adrift in their life rafts. They survived due to God's miraculous answer to their persistent prayers. . . .[13]

THE MIRACLE OF THE CLOUD

Early in March 1945, the U.S. Army's 35th Infantry Division, 137th Infantry, Company I, was making its way through the dense woods of the German Rhineland. The soldiers had orders to take the town of Ossenburg. Finally they reached a clearing where a handful of wounded American soldiers huddled behind a large stone house. They had tried to cross the clearing but had met a barrage of bullets from three nests of German machine guns. The nests were impenetrable, protected by a small hill.

The Americans had to cross that clearing to reach their objective, but that would mean the loss of many lives. Spencer January, a twenty-four-year-old infantryman, was faced with the possibility that he would never reach home again to kiss his wife or hold his five-month-old son.

In desperation, he dropped to his knees and pleaded with God to do something about the suicidal situation. A short time later, the order to move ahead was given. Spencer grabbed his M-1 rifle and started forward. Just before he stepped into the clearing, a miracle happened. A long, fluffy, white cloud appeared out of the clear, sunny sky. It moved in over the trees and obscured the Germans' machine-gun nests.

The American soldiers ran for the other side of the clearing, dragging the wounded with them. When they reached the trees, they threw themselves under cover. As soon as the last man had reached safety, the cloud disappeared. The day was once again bright and sunny. Spencer thought, *This has to be God's doing. I'm going to see what happens now.*

The German soldiers, not realizing that the Americans had escaped, resumed their shooting. Moments later the stone house that had sheltered the American soldiers on the other side of the clearing was blown to bits by artillery. But the Americans went on to capture the city.

Two weeks later, Spencer received a letter from his mother. She told an amazing story. A member of her church in Dallas, Texas, a Mrs. Tankersly, was a prayer warrior. She had telephoned Spencer's mother one morning from the defense plant where she worked, saying that the Lord had awakened her at one o'clock in the morning to pray for Spencer. She prayed until six o'clock, when she had to get ready for work. Just before she got up from her knees, she asked the Lord to cover Spencer with a cloud!

Spencer calculated the time difference and discovered that Mrs. Tankersly had prayed at exactly the same time that he was approaching that deadly clearing! And 6:00 A.M. Dallas time was the same time that Company I made its dash for safety, covered by a cloud. The Lord had sent the cloud at the request of Mrs. Tankersly, just in time! Spencer January writes, "From that moment on, I intensified my prayer life. . . . I am convinced there is no substitute for the power of prayer."[14]

THE MIRACLE OF D-DAY

On June 6, 1944, the largest invasion force in the history of the world was preparing for a massive assault on the coast of France. The invasion involved 250,000 men; 11,400 aircraft; 3,300 assault ships; 6 battleships; and countless destroyers. The Allies had to win this battle, called the D-Day Invasion. Today we know its final outcome, but most of us don't realize how God performed a great miracle that answered many American prayers.

D-Day was originally scheduled for June 5. General Eisenhower explained what occurred to change the day of the invasion:

> The final conference for determining the feasibility of attacking on June 5 was scheduled for 4:00 A.M. on June 4. . . . Some of the attacking contingents had already been ordered to sea. . . . On the morning of June 4 the report we received was discouraging. Low clouds, high winds, and formidable wave action were predicted to make landing a most hazardous affair. The meteorologists said that air support would be impossible, naval gunfire would be inefficient, and even the handling of small boats would be rendered difficult.
>
> At three-thirty the next morning our little tent was shaking and shuddering under a wind of almost hurricane proportions. It seemed impossible that in such conditions there was any reason for even discussing the situation. Bad conditions predicted the day before for the coast of France were actually prevailing there, and if we had persisted in the attempt to land on June 5, a major disaster would almost surely have resulted. This told us to inspire more confidence in their [the meteorologist staff's] next astonishing declaration, which was that by the following morning [June 6], a period of relatively good weather, heretofore completely unexpected, would ensue, lasting probably thirty-six hours. The long-term prediction was not good but this short period of calm weather would intervene between the storm we were then experiencing and the beginning of the next spell of bad weather.
>
> I quickly announced the decision to go ahead with the attack on June 6.[15]

Back home in the United States, the American people were in a somber religious mood. President Franklin Roosevelt spoke to the nation in his usual radio address on the evening of D-Day with a simple prayer for the American Armed Forces:

> Almighty God: Our sons, pride of our Nation, this day have set upon a mighty endeavor, a struggle to preserve our Republic, our religion, our civilization, and to set free a suffering humanity.
>
> They will need Thy blessings. Their road will be long and hard. The enemy is strong. He may hurl back our forces, but we shall return again and again.
>
> They fight not for the lust of conquest. They fight to end conquest. Help us, Almighty God, to rededicate ourselves to renewed faith in Thee, in this hour of great sacrifice.
>
> Many people have urged that I call the Nation into a single day of special prayer. But because the road is long and the desire is great, I ask that our people devote themselves in a continuance of prayer.[16]

Across the Atlantic, King George VI called the British Empire to prayer also:

> That we may be worthily matched with this new summons of destiny, I desire solemnly to call my people to prayer and dedication. We are not unmindful of our own shortcomings, past and present. We shall ask not that God may do our will, but that we may be called to do the will of God; and we dare to believe that God has used our nation and empire as an instrument for fulfilling His high purpose.[17]

Not only were the U.S. national leaders praying, but others, such as General George Dempsey, commander of the British and Canadian forces, met in Portsdown Parish church with four hundred officers and men and prayed for an hour in what he called one of the most moving experiences of his life. All over America and Great Britain, people were following the lead of their great leaders and falling to their knees to pray. And God listened.

As dawn approached on June 6, winds were at near-hurricane proportions. An attack in the midst of these winds would end in certain disaster. But delaying the attack would force the troops to wait until June 18 for the right tidal conditions. That's when God intervened. General Eisenhower described what happened:

> I made the most agonizing decision of my life. If there were nothing else in my life to prove the existence of an almighty and merciful God, the events of the next twenty-four hours did it. . . . The greatest break in a terrible outlay of weather occurred the next day and allowed that great invasion to proceed, with losses far below those we had anticipated.[18]

The good weather lasted thirty-six hours, just enough time. God also seemed to blind the Germans to a possible attack. Their weather service told them an invasion would be impossible, so many of the high-ranking officers, including General Erwin Rommel, went to a birthday party.

The victorious battle of D-Day accelerated the defeat of Hitler and the Nazis. It also prevented their having enough time to perfect their newest weapon—the atomic bomb. And if the Allies had waited until June 18 to attempt the invasion, they would have encountered the worst storm to hit the English Channel in eighty years!

AT HOME DURING THE WAR YEARS
At home, God was also working. During World War II, successful religious rallies were organized in major cities such

as New York and Chicago. The resulting revival was carried on by an organization formed in 1945 called Youth for Christ. Billy Graham, a young Wheaton College graduate, became its first full-time evangelist. Nearly nine hundred rallies were held, which about one million people attended.[19]

Also during the war years, Charles E. Fuller built the largest radio audience in the country with his program *The Old-Fashioned Revival Hour.* In 1947 he founded Fuller Theological Seminary in Pasadena, California. In 1942 a coalition of denominations and individuals was formed called the National Association of Evangelicals (NAE). By 1947 the NAE represented 1.3 million members.[20]

With the end of the war came jubilation and a return to normalcy. Once more our citizens were open to hearing about God's work in the lives of men and women committed to his cause. This openness would eventually result in a much different kind of fruit—a multiplication of God's Word that would circle the globe.

But another trend gained momentum, one that would produce disastrous results in the lives of our families, schools, and government. In the next chapter, we'll see how America turned away from God's principles and abandoned the power of prayer in the latter half of this century. At the same time, some national leaders have expressed a deep commitment to God and prayer, as have many citizens. These two opposing forces are battling to win the hearts and souls of Americans. Many times it seems as if anti-God sentiments will win the day. Does this mean there is no hope? Are Christians in America today at the mercy of those who would prefer a godless society?

For Discussion and Reflection

Adult Discussion

Bring in one bucket and one small rubber ball. If you have more than fifteen people, bring in multiple buckets and balls and form groups of ten. Set the bucket near a wall, and place a masking-tape line at least ten feet away. Have people stand behind the line and take turns trying to get the ball into the bucket. Let every person have at least two tries. Then ask:

- ★ How difficult was it to get the ball into the bucket?
- ★ How difficult is it to pray?
- ★ Why did Dawson Trotman describe prayer as our most diffi-cult work?
- ★ What is refreshing and wonderful about prayer?

Have people form pairs and read 1 Timothy 2:1-8. Then have them discuss the following questions. Ask:

- ★ What were Paul's first instructions to Timothy?
- ★ Who should we include in our prayers?
- ★ What makes it so hard today to persevere in spending time with God?
- ★ What are ways we can solve this problem?

Have pairs report on their discussion; then have each pair join another pair to form a foursome. Have them spend time in prayer as a group, praying for the things mentioned in 1 Timothy 2. Then encourage them to spend time in personal reflection, asking God for a renewed desire to spend more time with him in prayer.

Youth Discussion

Form groups of eight to ten. Have each group form a circle by standing shoulder to shoulder. Tell the kids to turn to their right as they take one step into the circle. They should be standing close together. Have everyone place their hands on the waist of the person in front of them. At the count of three, everyone will sit down on the knees of the person behind them, keeping their own knees together to support the person in front of them. Tell the students to hold this position as long as possible, trying to outlast the other groups. When one circle caves in, have everyone return to their seats.

Ask:

- ★ How did you feel while trying to keep your circle together?
- ★ How did you respond when a group collapsed?
- ★ How is this like being consistent in spending time with God?

Have the kids form groups of four. Ask:

- ★ What things in your life make it hard for you to spend regular time in prayer?
- ★ What are ways you can make time for God?
- ★ Read 1 Timothy 2:1-8. What kind of priority does Paul place on prayer in this passage?
- ★ How can we give prayer that kind of priority in our lives?
- ★ Timothy mentions praying for leaders. Who are leaders today that we should be praying for?

Have the groups report on their discussions; then have them pray together for the leaders they suggested. As you close your class, encourage the kids to make this kind of prayer a regular practice as they seek to draw closer to God through prayer.

TWENTY-ONE

A Spiritual Malaise

Since 1950, many positive and negative trends have existed side by side in our country and have affected the lives of Americans. The trends reflect God's power for righteousness and the enemy's battle to defeat the American church. Although it would be impossible to describe all these swirling forces, we can see many ways in which they have changed our society.

Not long after World War II, our code of moral conduct began to be replaced by moral relativism—the belief that there is no absolute right or wrong. This concept attempts to replace biblical principles with situational ethics—the idea that if something feels good or seems right at the time, it's acceptable behavior. This led to a number of setbacks for Christians, including a lack of consensus on how to run our government, schools, and families.

During the same time period, our country experienced sporadic revivals. They weren't as widespread as previous awakenings, but they resulted in new surges of evangelicalism in America. Many of these revivals occurred in Christian colleges in 1949 and 1950. Timothy Beougher, assistant professor of evangelism at Wheaton College Graduate School, writes of one:

Billy Graham, at that time president of Northwestern Bible Schools in Minneapolis, held a prayer meeting in his office, which included J. Edwin Orr, Armin Gesswein, Jack Franck, and William Dunlap. They met after midnight to pray for a spiritual awakening among college students. Within a week, a powerful revival had broken out at Bethel College in St. Paul, Minnesota.[1]

Many campuses experienced new spiritual fervor, including Wheaton College, North Park College, Houghton College, Asbury College, Seattle Pacific University, Multnomah School of the Bible, Westmont College, John Brown University, Northern Baptist Theological Seminary, and Fuller Theological Seminary. *Life, Newsweek, Time,* and many newspapers covered the revivals.[2]

Several well-known Christian leaders, including Billy Graham, Carl F. H. Henry, Harold Ockenga, Robert Cook, Bill Bright, and Richard Halverson, who served as chaplain of the U.S. Senate for many years, got their start during this time of spiritual renewal. In 1953 Dr. Edwin Orr wrote:

> It appeared as if the Holy Spirit had begun to raise up a new generation of revived leaders, who, when they reach places of responsibility in their respective denominations, will lend their influence to the support of a program of revival and cooperative evangelism.[3]

Many official government acts emphasized the importance of prayer in our national life. One of the most significant was the establishment of the National Day of Prayer in 1952. President Truman signed the National Day of Prayer bill under the direction of the Eighty-second Congress. In the next chapter, we will learn more about this vital legislation and the miracles God performed to bring it to national attention decades later.

TURBULENT TIMES

During the 1960s, cold winds of unrest began to blow over the face of America. As these trends gathered force, they became the cause of many of our modern problems. Timothy Beougher writes:

> To label the 1960s in America as a "turbulent" decade is no exaggeration. In this era filled with drugs, sex, violence, tear gas, shootings, arson, bombings, the Vietnam War, riots, and assassinations, colleges and universities were scenes of frequent demonstrations, many resulting in the destruction of property. Conditions grew so bad that by 1970, several schools cancelled commencement services because of fear of violence.[4]

THE TREND CONTINUES

During his presidency, Jimmy Carter recognized the spiritual darkness in our country. On July 15, 1979, he gave what many called his Malaise Speech: "We are confronted with a moral and spiritual crisis. . . . In a nation that was proud of hard work, strong families, close-knit communities, and our faith in God, too many of us now tend to worship self-indulgence and consumption. Human identity is no longer defined by what one does, but by what one owns."[5]

One lasting legacy of the sixties that has had far-reaching impact was the 1962 Supreme Court ruling abolishing prayer in public schools. The First Amendment of our Constitution states, "Congress shall make no law respecting an establishment of religion, or prohibiting the free exercise thereof."[6] In 1962, through a case brought before the United States Supreme Court by Madalyn Murray O'Hair on behalf of her son William Murray, the Court struck down teacher-led school prayer and banned other religious expression from public schools on the grounds that they violated the Constitution's First Amendment.

The Founding Fathers, however, never intended the First Amendment to abolish religion from public life. Justice Joseph Story, who was appointed to the Supreme Court in 1811 and is considered one of the foremost authorities on the Constitution and its framers, wrote:

> The real object of the First Amendment was not to countenance, much less advance, Mohammedism, or Judaism, or infidelity, by prostrating Christianity; but to exclude all rivalry among Christian sects, and to prevent any national ecclesiastical establishment which should give to a hierarchy the exclusive patronage of the national government. It thus cut off the means of religious persecution (the vice and pest of former ages), and the supervision of the rights of conscience in matters of religion which had been trampled upon almost from the days of the Apostles to the present age.[7]

Until now, the First Amendment had always meant that Congress was prohibited from establishing a national religious denomination. But suddenly the Supreme Court began seeing the words *the church* not as a denomination but as any religious activity.

This led to the Court's fateful ruling on school prayer in 1962. Here is the Supreme Court's summary:

> Because of the prohibition of the First Amendment against the enactment of any law "respecting an establishment of religion," which is made applicable to the States by the Four-

teenth Amendment, state officials may not compose an official state prayer and require that it be recited in the public schools of the State at the beginning of each school day—even if the prayer is denominationally neutral and pupils who wish to do so may remain silent or be excused from the room while the prayer is being recited.[8]

There was only one dissenter to this ruling, and that was The Honorable Judge Justice Potter Stewart. Here are excerpts from his dissenting opinion:

A local school board in New York has provided that those pupils who wish to do so may join in a brief prayer at the beginning of each school day, acknowledging their dependence upon God and asking His blessing upon them and upon their parents, their teachers, and their country. The Court today decides that in permitting this brief non-denominational prayer the school board has violated the Constitution of the United States. I think this decision is wrong.

The Court does not hold, nor could it, that New York has interfered with the free exercise of anybody's religion. For the state courts have made clear that those who object to reciting the prayer must be entirely free of any compulsion to do so, including any "embarrassments and pressures." But the Court says that in permitting school children to say this simple prayer, the New York authorities have established "an official religion."

With all respect, I think the Court has misapplied a great constitutional principle. I cannot see how an "official religion" is established by letting those who want to say a prayer say it. On the contrary, I think that to deny the wish of these school children to join in reciting this prayer is to deny them the opportunity of sharing in the spiritual heritage of our Nation. . . .

For we deal not here with the establishment of a state church, which would, of course, be constitutionally impermissible, but with whether school children who want to begin their day by joining in prayer must be prohibited from doing so. Moreover, I think that the Court's task, in this as in all areas of constitutional adjudication, is not responsibly aided by the uncritical invocation of metaphors like the "wall of separation," a phrase nowhere to be found in the Constitution.[9]

For the first time in our history, our Supreme Court ruled against God!

Having won the victory of removing prayer from our schools, secular humanists tried to remove other Christian symbols and activities from public education. In 1980, *Stone v. Graham* made it illegal for the Ten Commandments to be displayed in a public-school classroom. Can you imagine how George Washington would have responded to this ruling? Going even further in 1982, *Beck v. McElrath* disallowed even a moment of silence. The Court feared that this silence might be interpreted as prayer. *Lubbock Civil Liberties Union v. Lubbock Independent School District* in 1982 forbade students from meeting before and after school to read the Bible. Most recently, the U.S. Supreme Court struck down the Religious Freedom Restoration Act, which would protect religious liberties guaranteed by the U.S. Constitution. This decision of the Court was made in spite of the fact that Congress had overwhelmingly approved the act.[10]

What does William Murray, the son of Madalyn Murray O'Hair say about these anti-God actions of our government and antireligious trends?

Thirty years ago my atheist mother, Madalyn Murray O'Hair, attempted to defect to the Soviet Union. Why? She wanted to live in a godless country. She wanted to live in a nation where the government was god. Today my mother is happy with America. She no longer wants to leave the United States be-

340

cause America has become what she wanted it to be—a god-less nation![11]

What effect has all this legislation had upon our schools and our nation? Before 1962 polls among educators listed the primary problems in public schools as talking, chewing gum, making noise, running in the hall, getting out of turn in line, wearing improper clothing, and not putting paper in waste-baskets. By 1982, a mere twenty years later, the top public-school offenses were rape, robbery, assault, burglary, arson, bombings, murder, suicide, vandalism, extortion, drug and alcohol abuse, gang warfare, pregnancy, abortion, and venereal disease.[12] This only confirms what George Washington said in his farewell address following his second term as president:

> Religion and morality are indispensable supports. . . . And let us with caution indulge the supposition that morality can be maintained without religion . . . reason and experience both forbid us to expect that national morality can prevail in exclusion of religious principle.[13]

Not only did antireligion legislation affect morality, but it also affected students' learning. Student academics are measured by the Scholastic Aptitude Test (SAT), which has been administered since 1926. Before 1962 the average achievement level was 970 points. But after 1962 the average dropped significantly. In 1986 the average was 915 points—a dramatic decline, never seen before. Today the United States is twenty-first out of twenty-two industrialized nations when it comes to quality of education.[14] According to Project Literacy U.S.A., the United States has the highest illiteracy rate among the industrial nations. Twenty-six million American adults cannot read or write; up to seventy-two million cannot read or write above the fifth-grade level.[15] What a change from 1765, when John Adams observed that "a native American, especially in New England, who cannot read and write is as rare a phenomenon as a comet."[16]

Our schools, which previous generations attended with pride and anticipation, have become armed camps, with teachers being threatened and even assaulted. We watch our children go to school, often with fear. And we have reason to fear—look at these horrifying statistics:

According to a recent Gallup poll, 63 percent of the students will experience assault during school hours.[17] Government sources tell us that 57 percent of all illegal drugs are sold on school campuses, with a corresponding rise in violent youth crime.

A child who watches an average of two to four hours of television per day will have witnessed 8,000 homicides and 100,000 other acts of violence by the time he or she reaches junior high. That child will have seen 20,000 homicides by high school graduation.[18]

In 1984 a government study revealed that teachers spend 30 to 80 percent of their time enforcing discipline. Three million high school students in 1984 were victims of in-school crimes each month. Also, each month, 1,000 teachers required medical attention because of in-school assaults and 125,000 teachers were threatened.[19]

Nearly 135,000 guns are brought to school every day.[20] One in five suburban high school boys owns a gun. There are an estimated 71 weapon-carrying incidents per 100 students per month.[21] A Gallup poll found that 21 percent of students said they had been attacked with a knife or a gun. Overall, assaults were reported by 63 percent of students.[22]

Between 1965 and 1992, the number of twelve-year-olds arrested for violent crimes—murder, rape, robbery, and aggravated assault—rose 211 percent; the number of thirteen- and fourteen-year-olds arrested rose 301 percent; and the number of fifteen-year-olds arrested rose 297 percent![23]

Millions of marriages will end in divorce, leaving children with deep emotional scars and turning millions into latchkey kids, left to fend for themselves for several hours each day. Thirty-one percent of all births in the United States are to unmarried women. Nearly 69 percent of all black births occur out of wedlock.[24] Since 1973 abortion has been legal in the U.S., and it has become one of the biggest moral controversies ever to arise in our country.

In 1989 the number of HIV/AIDS cases in the youth population was estimated at one in one hundred. Types of sexually transmitted diseases have gone from a half dozen a decade ago to fifty-five, and they are spreading quickly through the youth and adult populations. There are seven thousand alcohol-related deaths each year among the more than three million teenage alcoholics.[25] Four hundred thousand teens attempt suicide—one every eighty seconds![26]

All across America, our churches and synagogues are being desecrated and burned. Movies, books, and videos that assault our sensibilities with the most vile language and visual scenes are not only readily available but are even part of the so-called mainstream media and are widely acclaimed.

Doesn't that send a message that something is wrong? Is it just a coincidence that all these problems began to escalate after this twenty-two-word prayer, the one used in the school attended by William Murray, was challenged by Ms. O'Hair?

> Almighty God, we acknowledge our dependence upon Thee, and we beg Thy blessings upon us, our parents, our teachers, and our country.[27]

How amazing that the four things mentioned in that simple prayer—"us, our parents, our teachers, and our country"—have been under attack in the years since 1962.

And these are just the visible results. Even more sinister is the greed, political corruption, and dishonesty that's hidden from view. What's worse, there's an overwhelming sense that we are powerless to do anything about these problems.

So what do we do? The problems are obviously bigger than any one of us. Is this the end of our Christian heritage, the one built for so many years on the prayers of our people? Has our country decided that prayer is no longer important? Has God been put on a shelf like a discarded idol? Have the prayers of the few stopped making a difference in our national history?

The answer is an emphatic no! *Prayer still works.* In the next two chapters, we'll look at some hopeful signs that indicate that our nation may once again return to God before it's too late. Then in the following chapter, we'll identify the trends that indicate that we may truly be on the road to a Fifth Great Awakening!

For Discussion and Reflection

Adult Discussion

Bring to class a cassette player and a tape of someone speaking. If you have (or can make) a tape of someone giving a positive message about a relationship with God through Jesus, that would be best. Say: "In a moment, I'm going to play several seconds of this tape, and I want you to do anything you can do to avoid hearing what the speaker says. You can plug your ears, make noise, or do whatever you want to avoid hearing the message." When everyone is ready, play several seconds of the tape at a normal speaking volume. Then have people turn their attention to you. Ask:

- ★ Did you catch the message on the tape?
- ★ What was it like to intentionally avoid hearing what was said?
- ★ How is this like the way people in our country have deliberately avoided God in their lives in the past few decades?
- ★ How is this like the way Christians sometimes isolate God from their everyday lives and confine God to Sundays at church?
- ★ What has been the result of our society's deliberate isolation from God?
- ★ What has been the result of Christians' isolating God to Sundays at church?

Have people form pairs and read 1 Thessalonians 5:16-18. In their pairs, have participants discuss the following questions. Have pairs list possibilities; then have them share their answers with the class. Ask:

- ★ What does it mean to pray constantly?
- ★ How can we do that when we have so many other things to do?
- ★ What effects might praying continually have on our daily lives?

Then have people reflect silently on the following questions:

- ★ What are some ways in which you might be isolating yourself from God?
- ★ What positive things could happen in your life if you opened yourself fully to God every day of the week?

345

Youth Discussion

Bring to class a cassette player and a tape of Christian music. Say: "In a moment, I'm going to play several seconds of this tape, and I want you to do anything you can do to avoid hearing what the music says. You can plug your ears, make noise, or do whatever you want to avoid hearing the message." When the kids are ready, play several seconds of the tape at a fairly low volume. Then have the kids turn their attention to you. Ask:

★ Did you hear the message on the tape?
★ What was it like isolating yourself from the music?
★ How is this like the way many people today isolate themselves from God?
★ How is this like the way some Christians confine God to Sunday mornings?
★ How has our world been affected by people isolating God from their lives?

Form pairs, and have them discuss the following questions:

★ In what ways do Christian teens live for themselves during the week?
★ What are ways you have found to get God into your everyday school week?
★ Read 1 Thessalonians 5:16-18. What does it mean to pray without ceasing?
★ How can we do that?
★ How might it change our lives?

Say: "Take a moment to reflect privately. Are you confining God to Sundays? What evidences would your classmates give that you have a relationship with God? Spend a few moments praying silently. Ask God to help you find ways to include him more completely in your daily life."

TWENTY-TWO

Rays
of Hope

Prayer can change things! Even though the picture of our society looks bleak, there have been positive things happening during the second half of the twentieth century. One of these is the fact that some of those who have served in Congress and the Oval Office in recent years have been true to God. They have prayed together and helped pass positive legislation. Let's look at what they did.

In 1942 members of the United States Senate and House of Representatives began meeting privately to talk, think, and pray together once a week. Those meetings continue today. In 1953 members of Congress invited President Dwight D. Eisenhower to join them for a fellowship breakfast. This was the beginning of the National Prayer Breakfast. President Ronald Reagan spoke of the history of these prayer breakfasts in 1985:

> Back in 1942, at the height of World War II, a handful of
> Senators and Congressmen discussed how they might be of
> personal and spiritual support to one another. If they could
> gather now and then to pray together, they might discover an
> added resource, which would be of sustaining value. And so,
> very informally, they began to meet.
>
> In time, in both the House and Senate groups, some infor-

mal rules evolved. The members would meet in the spirit of peace and in the spirit of Christ, but they need not be Christians. All members would be welcome, regardless of their political or religious affiliation. Sincere seekers, as well as the deeply devoted, all on a common journey to understand the place of faith in their lives and to discover how to love God and one's fellow man.

They wouldn't publicize the meetings, nor would they use them for any kind of political gain. The meetings would be off the record. No one would repeat what was said. And, above all, the members could talk about any personal problem on which they needed guidance, any sadness for which they needed prayer.

Well, the two groups met quietly and with no fanfare for ten years. And then President Eisenhower, as we've been told, came into the story. In 1952, when he was running for president, one of his most important strategists . . . was a fine man, a Senator named Frank Carlson. . . . One night out on the campaign trail, Eisenhower confided to Senator Carlson that during the war, when he was commanding the Allied forces in Europe, he had had a spiritual experience. He had felt the hand of God guiding him and felt the presence of God. And he spoke of how his friends had provided real spiritual strength in the days before D-Day. Senator Carlson said he understood, that he himself was getting spiritual strength from members of a little prayer group in the Senate.

A few months later, just a few days after he was sworn in as president, Eisenhower invited Frank Carlson to the White House. He said, "Frank, this is the loneliest house I've ever been in. What can I do?" And Carlson said, "I think this may be a good time for you to come and meet with our prayer group." And Eisenhower did. In 1953 he attended the first combined Prayer Breakfast. And the presidents have been coming here for help ever since. And here I am. . . .

Some wonderful things have come out of this fellowship. A

number of public figures have changed as human beings, changed in ways I'd like to talk about, but it might reveal too much about the membership. Fellowships have begun to spring up throughout the Capitol. They exist now in all three branches of the Government, and they have spread throughout the capitals of the world to parliaments and congresses far away.[1]

Each year near the opening of Congress, members of the Senate and House of Representatives invite people from every state and almost every nation to join the U.S. president for this prayer breakfast.

The first governor's prayer breakfast was held in 1959. In 1989 similar breakfasts were held in more than five hundred cities. These prayer breakfasts are the result of small prayer groups that meet weekly at all levels throughout our nation.

In 1954 Congress added a phrase to the Pledge of Allegiance so that it says, "one Nation *under God,* indivisible, with liberty and justice for all." The phrase echoes the words *In God We Trust,* which were put on coins in 1865. Also in 1954, Congress approved a joint resolution to establish a room with facilities for prayer and meditation for the use of members of the Senate and House of Representatives.[2] This Congressional Prayer Room, which is just off the Capitol rotunda, is always open during congressional sessions. Inside is an altar with an open Bible. A stained-glass window shows George Washington kneeling in prayer. This room is reserved for members of Congress and is not open to the public.

THE NATIONAL DAY OF PRAYER

In 1952 a joint resolution of Congress called upon each president to set aside one day each year when people "may turn to

God in prayer and meditation at churches, in groups, and as individuals." It was called the National Day of Prayer.

Unfortunately, when President Eisenhower attended services on the 1957 National Day of Prayer, he found only a handful of people praying. When he investigated why only a few observed this day, he found that only the religious press gave it notice. The secular press did not print anything about it. More efforts were made the next year to encourage observance of the National Day of Prayer, but when Eisenhower and his wife went to their church, they found it nearly empty again.

For the next two years, Eisenhower tried to popularize the Day of Prayer, to no avail. During the thirty years following Eisenhower's presidency, various groups continued to promote the National Day of Prayer. More churches began to pray on that day, and campaigns were initiated to make people more aware of it, but the observance never seemed to get off the ground. One of the reasons for the meager response was the lack of opportunity to inform the nation from year to year about the date. Since the president could proclaim a different date every year, people couldn't plan for it in advance and lost track of when it would be celebrated the following year. The problem could be resolved if the National Day of Prayer was established as a regular day on the national calendar.

In 1982 the National Prayer Committee, an affiliation of leaders seeking to mobilize prayer worldwide, decided to form the National Day of Prayer Task Force. Vonette Bright, cofounder of Campus Crusade for Christ International, accepted the responsibility of chairing the Task Force and making the public aware of the National Day of Prayer. Pat Boone was cochairman, and there were liaisons from Protestant, Catholic, and Jewish religious communities. For six years the National Day of Prayer Task Force saw tremendous results, but their greatest accomplishment was helping establish the National Day of Prayer as a permanent day on the national calendar.

On June 17, 1987, Strom Thurmond introduced Bill S.1378 into the Senate to amend the Joint Resolution of Congress so that the National Day of Prayer would be observed every year on the first Thursday of May. Beginning in January 1988, letters supporting the permanent date began to flow to senators, congressmen, and other contacts. On April 14, 1988, the Senate bill was passed into the Judiciary Committee. The Task Force began calling and writing to the committee members to encourage them to approve the bill. Then the day for the vote arrived. Would the bill pass in time to be enacted for 1988?

As Vonette Bright and her staff met early on that sunny morning, she reminded them, "This is the day the committee will vote. Today, we'll know whether the bill will live or die. Let's spend some time praying that it passes."

The staff quietly sat in a circle as they prayed one by one. After an extended time together, they quietly went back to work.

At eleven o'clock, Vonette received a telephone call from Senator Howard Metzenbaum's secretary. He was one of the crucial committee members. "The senator has some reservations about the bill," the secretary explained, "because he feels it violates the separation of church and state. At this point, he will not be voting for it." When Vonette hung up the phone, she announced the disturbing news to her staff, and they all began making telephone calls to urge friends and colleagues of Senator Metzenbaum to call him and encourage him to support the bill. One of the people Vonette called was Rabbi Joshua Habermann, the National Day of Prayer Task Force's Jewish liaison.

Mrs. Habermann picked up the phone.

"May I speak to your husband?" Vonette asked.

"I'm sorry, but he isn't home right now. May I give him a message?"

Vonette quickly explained the problem to her. "Is there any way we can reach him before the committee meeting at 2:00 P.M.?"

"I'm sorry. He's out until two o'clock and is unreachable unless he calls me. But if he does call, I will be sure to give him the message."

As soon as all the other telephone calls had been made, the staff once more met for prayer. They prayed that the rabbi would call home, for a change of heart for Senator Metzenbaum, and mostly that God would be glorified in whatever happened.

At one-thirty the telephone rang. Vonette quickly answered. "It's Rabbi Habermann," Vonette informed the staff. The staff began to pray silently as the rabbi conversed with Vonette. He explained that he rarely called home when he was out, but for some reason he had called that afternoon. He had then immediately called Senator Metzenbaum. "I explained to the senator how the bill supports interreligious cooperation without violating the traditional line between church and state. By the way," he added, "I don't know if you know this, but just a year ago, I officiated at his daughter's wedding."

The staff marveled at how God's hand had guided the selection of this specific rabbi as the Jewish liaison several years earlier. The rabbi's call to Senator Metzenbaum must have made the difference because at two o'clock the Senate Judiciary Committee passed the bill unanimously!

The bill now had to be presented to the whole Senate with the committee's endorsement. The bill reached the Senate floor on Friday, April 22, and was passed unanimously by voice vote. As the bill was completing its round in the Senate, Congressmen Tony Hall, Carlos Moorehead, Robert Garcia, and Frank Wolf prepared for its arrival in the House of Representatives, which also had to vote on the bill.

Monday afternoon, the call came into the National Day of Prayer office that the bill was officially in the House and would be headed to the Post Office and Civil Service committee. Vonette Bright asked Susan Sorensen, "Do you have a list of the members of the House committee? I'd like to pray for each member by name."

Susan found the list, and Mrs. Bright took it into her office for prayer. A few minutes later, she rushed out. "It says on this committee list that they meet every Wednesday. If it is approved this Wednesday, the bill might just make it to the president's desk by the National Day of Prayer!"

What an event that would be! Vonette quickly made calls to the congressmen. Susan called the committee secretary and explained the situation. The secretary was annoyed about putting a bill on the agenda with 152-too-few cosigners and outside the forty-eight-hour time limit.

In the meantime, the congressmen networked. The aides and secretaries tried to find a way to get the discussion onto the agenda. Vonette and her team prayed. A few hours later, the same committee secretary who was so upset earlier called back. "The bill made it onto the agenda for Wednesday, April 27," she said. That was only eight days before the National Day of Prayer! Could this mean that the bill would be passed in time for this year's National Day of Prayer?

Everyone kept working furiously. The committee passed the bill on Wednesday. Then Vonette and Susan found out that the bill could come before the House of Representatives only at the beginning of the week, which was just a few days away.

Many people helped to get the bill onto the House agenda. At 1:00 P.M., just three days before the National Day of Prayer, the bill came up under an agenda section called "unanimous consent." It passed by voice vote.

Many details and lots of paperwork had to be completed before the bill could land on President Reagan's desk for the last signature. With more prayer effort and lots of work, the bill was completed on time.

On the afternoon of Thursday, May 5, 1988, a nervous group was waiting to enter the Oval Office. After a few moments, Vonette Bright; Pat Boone; Susan Sorensen; Congressmen Tony Hall, Frank Wolf, and Carlos Moorehead; Rabbi Joshua Habermann; and Father John V. O'Connor walked across the carpet to the president's desk. One by one, each person shook the president's hand and then paused for a quick photo.

As the president greeted the group warmly, the press with its flashing cameras and the presidential staff and bodyguards standing nearby were forgotten. The president gathered the group behind his beautifully carved desk. The president took his seat as the group gathered for another round of photos. President Reagan, Vonette Bright, and Pat Boone talked about the importance of the bill and how it would change the observance of the National Day of Prayer. "I certainly need people to uphold me in prayer," the president said. Then he signed several copies of the bill, handing the pens to those surrounding him to be used as mementos of that significant day. . . .[3]

That Thursday, President Reagan signed the bill at four-thirty in the afternoon—on that year's National Day of Prayer! This observance became one of only thirty-two annual commemorative dates celebrated on specific days in our nation! That year, observances were held all over the nation as 38 governors and 150 mayors proclaimed a Day of Prayer.

Another positive part of America's recent prayer history is the faith of the godly men who have sat in the Oval Office. Through spoken words and deeds they have honored God in many ways. Lets look at a few examples:

PRESIDENT GERALD FORD

Gerald Ford believed in prayer. As a congressman he was a member of a weekly prayer group. When he became vice president, he continued to meet weekly with his prayer group. On the night he learned of Nixon's resignation and realized that he would be president, he prayed with his wife, Betty. He described that prayer time:

> I concluded with a prayer from the 5th and 6th verses of Chapter 3 of the Book of Proverbs: "Trust in the Lord with all thine heart, and lean not unto thine own understanding. In all thy ways acknowledge Him, and He shall direct thy paths."
>
> Fifty years before, I had learned that prayer as a child in Sunday school. I can remember saying it the night I discovered that my stepfather was not my real father. I had repeated it often at sea during World War II. It was something I said whenever a crisis arose.[4]

The biggest decision of Ford's presidency was whether to pardon former president Richard Nixon for his part in the Watergate conspiracy. Ford went to prayer to help make his decision and publicly asked for prayers for guidance. He explains:

> I wanted to go to church and pray for guidance and understanding before making the announcement. So at eight o'clock Sunday morning, I attended services at St. John's Episcopal

Church of Lafayette Square. I sat alone in the Presidential pew, took Holy Communion, and then returned to the Oval Office.[5]

PRESIDENT JIMMY CARTER

Jimmy Carter attended Sunday school at Plains Baptist Church from his earliest childhood. He was a member of the Royal Ambassadors—a missionary education group for young boys. He professed his faith in Jesus Christ and was baptized into church membership at age eleven. He was ordained a deacon in 1958.

During his presidency, Jimmy Carter was deeply concerned about our nation's sins. He ardently felt that the only solution for America was for our people to humble themselves and pray. He wanted to include this theme in his inaugural address, but his staff advised him to change it. He spoke about the incident at a National Prayer Breakfast on January 27, 1977:

> The first draft of my Inaugural speech did not include the reference to Micah's admonition about justice, mercy, and humility. But I had chosen instead 2 Chronicles 7:14, which Congressman Wright quoted this morning: "If my people who are called by my name, shall humble themselves, and pray, and seek my face, and turn from their wicked ways; then will I hear from heaven, and will forgive their sin, and will heal their land."
>
> When my staff members read the first draft of my speech, they rose up in opposition to that verse. The second time I wrote my Inaugural draft I had the same verse in it. They came to me en masse and said, "The people will not understand that verse. It is as though you, being elected president, are condemning the other people of our country, putting yourself in the position of Solomon and saying that all Americans are wicked."

So, correctly or wrongly, I changed to Micah. I think this episode, which is true, is illustrative of the problems that we face. Sometimes we take for granted that an acknowledgment of sin, an acknowledgment of the need for humility, permeates the consciousness of our people. But it doesn't.[6]

PRESIDENT RONALD REAGAN

Ronald Reagan was outspoken about his belief in God. After giving a speech to the National Association of Evangelicals in which he talked about "the focus of evil in the modern world," a flurry of headlines ran about his speech. The *Washington Post* said that the focus on evil was, as their writer put it:

> An intriguing subplot of the Reagan administration, a debate between the president and his critics over the morality and spirituality of his policies.
> Not since the Vietnam war and the civil rights movement have churchmen been so involved or played such a key role in the dialogue over public policy.[7]

Historian Henry Steele Commager said this of the Reagan speech: "It was the worst presidential speech in American history, and I've read them all. No other presidential speech has ever so flagrantly allied government with religion. It was a gross appeal to religious prejudice."[8]

This harsh criticism didn't stop Reagan from continuing his agenda. He spelled it out very clearly in a speech to the National Association of Evangelicals one year later:

> Here at home, I believe there are three basic tasks that we must accomplish. First, we must . . . find positive solutions to the tragedy of abortion. Second, we must restore education in basic values to America's schools. . . . We must make certain

that we not only improve instruction in math and science, but in justice, religion, discipline, and liberty. . . . And third, school prayer. . . . I firmly believe that the loving God who has blessed our land and made us a good and caring people should never have been expelled from America's classrooms.[9]

Throughout his eight years as president, Reagan tried to reverse the rulings concerning the removal of school prayer. In each of his National Day of Prayer speeches, he alluded to this. He believed in prayer and in the fact that it belonged in our schools and government. Reagan proposed an amendment to reinstate prayer in schools, but the Congress would never pass it.

PRESIDENT GEORGE BUSH

While George Bush was in office, the bicentennial of the presidency of the United States was celebrated. He felt there was no better way to observe it than to proclaim a National Day of Prayer and Thanksgiving. He said: "As I assume the office of President, I am humbled before God and seek His counsel and favor on our land, and join with our first President who said 'it would be peculiarly improper to omit in this first official act, my fervent supplications to that Almighty Being who rules over the universe . . . that his benediction may consecrate to the liberties and happiness of the people of the United States, a government instituted by themselves for these essential purposes.' "[10]

In 1990 George Bush signed a special proclamation to make 1990 "The Year of Bible Reading." In many locations within the United States and in several foreign countries, including Israel, Christians read the complete Bible from cover to cover in round-the-clock marathons. Each of these events was opened and closed with prayer. Christians personally placed Bibles in the hands of many world leaders during The Year of Bible Reading as well.

Not only have White House leaders called people to pray in recent years, but many other government leaders in different positions have also been praying, with remarkable results. In many instances, God's power has been revealed in miraculous ways. One example is the prayer experience of Governor Guy Hunt of Alabama.

PRAYER MIRACLE IN ALABAMA

In 1988 a drought created severe hardship in the Southern states. Alabama was one of the states affected. For four years, far less than the normal amount of rain fell. In some sections of the state, the precipitation was fifty-five inches below normal. The groundwater level was dropping, and farmland was producing little more than dust. National Guard tanker trucks provided water for whole communities. The local news reported Governor Hunt's statewide plea:

> Alabama is in the grips of one of the worst droughts our state has ever seen. Some sections are fifty-five inches below normal in rainfall for the last four years. The situation has become critical. Today I ask all Alabamians to join together for a statewide "Day of Prayer" next Wednesday. I ask that God-fearing people across our state pray that God will send life-giving rain.[11]

Governor Hunt, a former Baptist pastor, believed the solution to the problem was prayer. On June 25, 1988, in his weekly radio address, he said:

> Today I ask all Alabamians to join together for a statewide day of prayer next Wednesday, June 29th. I ask that God-fearing people across our state put aside time next Wednesday to pray

that God will send life-giving rain to our state and our nation. I encourage all Alabamians to pray in whatever manner they choose.

Throughout American history, the importance of prayer has been recognized by our great leaders. Benjamin Franklin during the Constitutional Convention of 1787 called on Congress to remember the Nation's religious roots. Franklin said: "We have been assured in the sacred writings that, except the Lord build the house, they labour in vain that build it."

In the Bible it is written "all things whatsoever ye shall ask in prayer, believing, ye shall receive."

Let's all believe that the drought will end.[12]

The news media widely ridiculed Governor Hunt, and one columnist said that if the governor was going to call a prayer meeting, he should have waited until a weather front was approaching the area.

The situation was desperate. Farmers had already lost 50 percent of their crops. Commercial river navigation was at a standstill in some areas. The state of Alabama asked the federal government to declare all sixty-seven counties disaster areas. The drought stood out as the worst in a century. But Governor Hunt went ahead with his plans. He wrote this in his proclamation:

Prayer has been vital to our country since our beginnings. . . . Many of our great leaders in our nation and state have not been hesitant to acknowledge their dependence on God. God tells us to seek Him and He will 'hear from Heaven . . . and heal our land' and pour His blessings upon His people.[13]

On that Wednesday, June 29, with no rain in the forecast, Governor Hunt opened five of his private and public meetings with prayer. At the start of a meeting with legislators at the governor's mansion, he prayed: "Many of our people are suffering. We would ask thee, Heavenly Father, if it be according to thy gracious will, that thou would bless our state, our lands with a bountiful rain, that the fruits of this earth, if it is of thy blessings, might come forth for the benefit of thy people."[14] Churches also organized prayer services, and individuals held prayer meetings statewide.

Within forty-eight hours, God answered! The entire state of Alabama received rainfall, while the adjacent states of Mississippi and Georgia barely got a sprinkle! Governor Hunt reported the rainfall results at his news conference a few days later:

> I am happy to report today that our prayers have been answered. . . . The Lord has been good to us in the last couple of weeks and given us rain. In the last ten days, some sections, a lot of rain. Auburn, for instance, got more than eight inches of rain over the period. Demopolis more than five inches and Tuscaloosa more than three inches.

When we interviewed Governor Hunt for this project, he told us that after so much rain fell, the news columnists suggested he hold a prayer meeting to stop the rain, which continued for several days.

God hasn't given up his call to our nation. As we have seen, in the past he has shown his power in the outcome of our national conflicts. Even today he is still showing mercy and grace in the face of our national sin and unrepentance. We can see his mercy once again as it was displayed during 1991's Gulf War.

PRAYER STORM IN THE DESERT

The Gulf War was different from other American conflicts because the nation watched it unfold on their TV screens—from the very first air strikes. It also only lasted one hundred hours. Yet within that brief period of time there were significant answers to prayer. Some would even argue that the brief span of the actual battle and the small number of casualties were the most convincing proofs of the incredible power of prayer. But there were other examples, too.

Two men deserve credit for leading us to victory in the Gulf—General Colin Powell and General Norman Schwarzkopf. Colin Powell was born in Harlem to immigrant parents from Jamaica. As a child, he attended St. Margaret's Episcopal Church with his family. Later he joined the army and fought in the jungles of Vietnam. While living in Gainesville, Florida, he attended a Baptist church, and he taught a fifth-grade Sunday school class in another Episcopal church in another city. He served as a Pentagon aide in the Carter administration and as a battalion commander in Korea. He was the mastermind of Desert Storm.

Norman Schwarzkopf was born into a military family. His father was a West Point graduate, and he followed suit. Schwarzkopf put in two tours of combat duty in Vietnam and served as a deputy commander of the Grenada Invasion in 1983. With this experience under his belt, he rose to lead the troops in the Gulf War.

On Christmas Eve, just weeks before the war began, Schwarzkopf attended a Christmas Eve service in Saudi Arabia with his troops. The service was held in a huge tent and held a packed crowd—and the congregation joined to sing "Oh, Come, All Ye Faithful."[15]

In 1990 United States military personnel were in the Persian Gulf preparing to go to war against Saddam Hussein's Iraqi army. As the troops moved into Saudi Arabia before the Desert Storm conflict, most of them celebrated Christmas in the desert. Schwarzkopf, a working general, also found himself in that lonely place over the holidays. He attended Christmas Eve services and received a call from President Bush. The president said, "I couldn't let this day go by without calling to wish you and all the men and women under your command a Merry Christmas. I know that you are far away from your loved ones, but I want you to know that our thoughts and prayers are with you. You know the course we are on. Our prayers will stay with you during the coming days."[16]

Once again a president was calling on God before the country went to war.

As the final preparations for the battle were made, Schwarzkopf wrote a letter home to his family in which he lamented the fact that he must command his troops into conflict. He also said that if God called on him to sacrifice his life, he would be thinking of his family.[17] As an encouragement to his men as they went into battle, he sent this letter to his troops:

> Soldiers, sailors, airmen, and marines of United States Central Command: This morning at 0300 we launched Operation Desert Storm, an offensive campaign that will enforce United Nations resolutions that Iraq must cease its rape and pillage of its weaker neighbor and withdraw its forces from Kuwait. The President, the Congress, the American people, and indeed the world stand united in their support for your actions. You are a member of the most powerful force our country, in coalition with our allies, has ever assembled in a single theater to face such an aggressor. You have trained hard for this battle and you are ready. During my visits with you, I have seen in your eyes a fire of determination to get this job done and done quickly so that we may return to the shores of our great nation. My confidence in you is total. Our cause is just! Now you

must be the thunder and lightning of Desert Storm. May God be with you, your loved ones at home, and our country.[18]

Churches across our country called prayer meetings. Millions of individuals in America were praying. Military chaplains continually encouraged the men and women to pray for themselves and their comrades. God answered the prayers of Americans and their leaders through many miracles. Here are two of them. . . .

THE MIRACLE WELL

Marine Major General Charles Krulak was responsible for supplying the Allied frontal assault against Iraqi troops. One thing they desperately needed was lots of water for decontamination to counteract chemical warfare if they encountered it. Krulak was glad that the troops had wells available that could supply the needed 100,000 gallons a day.

His well-laid plans were disrupted when his troops were ordered seventy-four miles away to the northwest, to an area called "the gravel plains." The soldiers desperately dug for water at their new site but found only dust. Experts were called in to help, but no matter how hard they searched, they couldn't locate a water source.

General Krulak had made it a practice since 1977 to meet with his staff officers for morning prayers. One Sunday morning shortly before the ground attack, the critical need for water became the focus of the prayers in one of those meetings. A colonel interrupted the prayer session to ask Krulak to come see something.

The colonel took Krulak down a road constructed by the Marine Corps and pointed out a pipe rising out of the ground about thirty to fifty yards from the road. A crossbar on the pipe made it look like a cross. At the base of the pipe were a green diesel generator, a red pump, four new batteries, and a tank containing one thousand gallons of diesel—a fuel not used by U.S. forces. Who could have dug this well? Why hadn't it been discovered earlier?

Krulak pushed the ignition button, and the generator popped into use. The well began supplying water—within ten gallons of the 100,000 needed per day.

What a miracle! Twenty thousand troops, and the general, had traveled this road, and not one of them saw this well until Sunday morning. General Krulak later said, "There was no way anyone could have driven down that road and not seen the well and equipment painted in multiple colors. That well was the result of prayers of righteous men and women praying in America . . . and the prayer miracles didn't end with finding the well."[19]

CHANGING WINDS

From the start of the Gulf War, military leaders were certain that the Iraqi forces would use biological as well as chemical warfare. This could have had deadly consequences for American troops. Millions of Americans at home and many soldiers in the field were praying for a miracle to prevent a potential Armageddon.

The ground attack was planned for about four o'clock in the morning on February 24. But the big problem was that the prevailing wind would blow any harmful chemicals directly into the faces of the American troops. Then the second amazing prayer miracle of the war occurred. At 3:45 A.M., as the troops readied for battle, the winds suddenly shifted from the south-west to the northwest. This unprecedented wind shift meant that any poisonous gas used by the Iraqis would blow back at them. The attack went forward.

On February 28 General Schwarzkopf ordered a cease-fire. Minutes later the wind shifted back to its usual direction! Christians who were present called it an extraordinary answer to prayer.

Just as in many other American conflicts, chaplains played an integral part in the spiritual outcome of the war. During the Gulf War campaign, chaplains held Bible studies nightly. Bibles were everywhere, and worship was common. Men and women professed Christ in remarkable numbers. Chaplain (Col.) David P. Peterson, who supervised more than four hundred chaplains of all faiths, said: "There is a spiritual hunger among all our people like I have never seen before."[20] The U.S. chaplains and military officers gave the credit for this great spiritual movement to the prayers of the American people back home.

These two miracles are just the tip of the iceberg. Thousands of families whose husbands, wives, sons, and daughters have marched off to war can tell of their own personal miracles of prayer. President Harry S. Truman said it so well while the Korean War raged in Asia:

> All of us—at home, at war, wherever we may be—are within the reach of God's love and power. We all can pray. We all should pray. We should ask the fulfillment of God's will. We should ask for courage, wisdom, for the quietness of soul which comes alive to them who place their lives in His hands.[21]

Truman put his finger on a central truth: that our prayers can change events.

We could list so many other prayer miracles across our great country precipitated by our leaders in national, state, and local government. Against the backdrop of our declining morals and the war against religion in public life, these leaders lift up a prayer banner that we can all see if we look for it. Surely God has noticed the prayers of these men and women, and perhaps we can credit the tremendous blessings we still enjoy in our country to their prayers.

But they can't do it alone. It is our responsibility to follow their examples and pray for our country and our leaders and to participate in corporate prayer events such as the National Day of Prayer.

Many ordinary people are also turning to prayer for our country. In the next chapter, we will turn our attention to grassroots prayer movements in our lifetime. In these prayer efforts are the seeds of change and power for the future.

For Discussion and Reflection

Adult Discussion

Form groups of three or four. Give each group paper, a pencil, and a blindfold. One at a time, have all members of each group draw a picture of a house with their eyes covered. The group can help support them by directing their hand, etc.

When everyone finishes, ask:

- ★ What went through your mind as you drew?
- ★ How did it work out to have people helping you?
- ★ How is this like the way we help and support each other through prayer?
- ★ How have senators and congressmen been supporting each other since 1942?

★ What difference do you think their prayers have made in our nation?

Have people discuss the following questions in their groups:

★ Why is a prayer group such a powerful support to us?
★ What are some examples of ways a prayer group has made a difference in your life?
★ Read Proverbs 3:5-6, a passage President Gerald Ford quoted during times of crisis. How do these verses relate to prayer?
★ What would you say to a friend to encourage him or her to be part of a prayer group?

Youth Discussion

Bring marbles, scissors, books, construction paper, and tape to class. Form groups of three or four. Make the materials available, and explain that groups will have five minutes to construct roller coasters for marbles. The object is to get a marble to travel the fastest and farthest along a given path.

When time is up, let groups demonstrate their roller coasters. Then ask:

★ How would you have felt if you were the marble traveling along your path?
★ How did your roller coasters direct the marbles?
★ How is this like the way God sometimes directs our lives?
★ How is it different?

Say: "President Reagan talked about godly paths. He said that 'the freedom to choose a godly path is the essence of liberty.'"[22]

Have the kids discuss the following questions in their groups:

★ What is the meaning of this statement: "Freedom to choose a godly path is the essence of liberty"?
★ Read Proverbs 3:5-6. What do we need to do to have God direct our paths?
★ What role does prayer play in following God's path?
★ Read Proverbs 2:13-15. In what ways are you as a Christian teen enticed from the path of righteousness?
★ How can you keep on the right path?

Have the kids pray together, committing to help each other keep following God on the path he puts before them.

TWENTY-THREE

Carrying On the Mantle of Prayer

Throughout this book we have seen the spirit of revival and awakening as it transformed our country over and over again. Time after time, someone took up the mantle of prayer and passed it on to the next generation. Jonathan Edwards and George Whitefield took the mantle from the Pilgrims and Puritans. Lyman Beecher and Charles Finney picked it up next and passed it on to the prayer warriors of the 1857 revival. D. L. Moody carried the mantle to the brink of the twentieth century, and Billy Sunday took it from him. Other spiritual leaders have taken the mantle into the twentieth century and onward to the present.

God has raised up ordinary men and women to further his kingdom in our time. There are so many extraordinary examples that we don't have room to list them all. We have selected three couples who represent many of the powerful ways God is moving among his people in this century. Each couple—ordinary people made extraordinary through the power of prayer—took up the mantle of service for God, much as the prophet Elisha took up Elijah's mantle and carried on God's work.

CARRYING THE MANTLE OF MASS EVANGELISM

If you ask any American, "Who is the most respected and well-known religious figure in our country?" he or she will most likely reply, "Billy Graham." For more than fifty years, this world-renowned evangelist and frequent minister to United States presidents has called Americans to repentance, prayer, and decisions for Christ in crusades across America and throughout the world. He has also spoken to millions of people through his radio and television broadcasts. According to the Billy Graham Evangelistic Association, Reverend Graham has preached to 210 million people in live audiences in more than 185 countries, resulting in 3 million people making faith commitments.

We read earlier that Billy Graham made a decision to follow Christ in 1934 during evangelistic services held by Mordecai Ham. In 1943 Graham married Ruth Bell, the daughter of a Presbyterian missionary couple.

Billy Graham built his crusades on prayer. Author William Martin describes the preparations for the 1949 Los Angeles crusade, which set the pattern for his other mass-evangelism events:

> Nine months before the meetings began, the organizers engaged veteran revivalists J. Edwin Orr and Armin Gesswein to conduct preparatory meetings throughout the Los Angeles area. As a result of their efforts, nearly eight hundred small groups were meeting regularly to pray for the campaign long before it began in September. Then, two weeks before opening night, Grady Wilson flew in from South Carolina to organize still more prayer meetings, some lasting all day or night, and around-the-clock prayer chains involving hundreds of people.[1]

Ruth Bell Graham has taken a role behind the spotlight as wife and mother and as her husband's support line. Born in a

Presbyterian hospital three hundred miles north of Shanghai, China, Ruth describes her years as a missionary kid as basic training for her future. In her autobiography, *It's My Turn,* she explains her feelings just before she first traveled to Korea to live in a missionary boarding school:

> The thirteen-year-old girl lay in the stifling heat of the old missionary home at Number Four Quinsan Gardens, in the port city of Shanghai, China, praying earnestly that she would die before morning.
>
> Dawn broke over the great, gray city, and obviously, God had not seen fit to answer my prayer.[2]

Those were the years of learning how to depend on God in tough times, which helped her later when she and her husband faced the stresses that come with worldwide renown. She has been the prayer support behind his many years of ministry.

CARRYING THE MANTLE FOR MISSIONS AND EVANGELISM

Have you ever heard of Coweta, Oklahoma? That's the small rural town where both Bill and Vonette Bright grew up. After making separate commitments of faith to Jesus Christ, they married and settled down in Los Angeles. In 1951 they decided to make a contract with the Lord. One Sunday afternoon, they went into separate rooms, and each listed the things they most wanted out of life. Then, together, they wrote and signed a contract to the Lord, surrendering everything they desired to him and to each other. That contract was the foundation of the ministry they cofounded—Campus Crusade for Christ International. Bill Bright explains what happened a short time after they signed the contract:

373

One evening at about midnight, during my senior year in seminary, I was studying for a Greek exam. There was nothing unusual about the setting or about the circumstances. Vonette was asleep in a nearby room. Suddenly, without warning or without an indication of what was going to happen, I sensed the presence of God in a way I had never known before. Though it could not have lasted more than a few seconds, I suddenly had the overwhelming impression that the Lord had flashed on the screen of my mind His instructions for my life and ministry.[3]

That was the vision for ministry that has carried Bill and Vonette Bright through almost fifty years of serving God. The center of their ministry is evangelism—fulfilling the great commission as Jesus gave it in Matthew 28:18-20. Their first effort was on the UCLA campus, where they organized a twenty-four-hour prayer chain, which was divided into ninety-six periods of fifteen minutes each, so that Christians could pray around the clock for the ministry.

By 1960 the Campus Crusade for Christ staff included more than a hundred people working on forty college campuses in fifteen U.S. cities and in Korea and Pakistan. Today the ministry serves in 172 countries.

In recent years, Bill Bright has helped launch a fasting and prayer movement to bring our country back to its righteous beginnings. He writes:

In the providence of God, I believe the power of fasting, as it relates to prayer, is the spiritual atomic bomb of our moment in history to bring down the strongholds of evil, bring a great revival and spiritual awakening to America, and accelerate the fulfillment of the Great Commission.

On the basis of His Holy Word and divine assurances He has placed in my heart, I am absolutely convinced that our Sovereign God is going to send a great revival to our nation and world so that the Great Commission will be fulfilled.[4]

Vonette Bright has also been active in organizing prayer efforts. In 1972 she launched the Great Commission Prayer Crusade, which became a worldwide movement, to mobilize women to pray. In 1984 she was one of the leaders in a prayer gathering called the International Prayer Assembly, which was held in Seoul, Korea. As we learned in the previous chapter, her most recent national prayer effort was serving as chairperson in 1988 for the National Day of Prayer and helping it become a permanent day on our national calendar.

CARRYING THE MANTLE FOR FAMILY VALUES

Dr. James and Shirley Dobson got their start in ministry through the power of prayer also. After Dr. Dobson graduated from medical school, he worked at Children's Hospital at the University of Southern California in the Los Angeles area. Soon he began a speaking career through which he tried to bring Christians back to biblical family values.

Through what some might see as a coincidence, he and Shirley entertained Francis and Joyce Heatherly in their home in 1970. Francis was then director of marketing for one of the largest Christian publishing houses in the United States. This contact led to a contract for Dobson to write *Dare to Discipline,* the book that jump-started his ministry, Focus on the Family. Dobson's good friend and colleague Rolf Zettersten describes how Jim and Shirley prayed over the book:

> Dr. and Mrs. Dobson requested 250 copies of their newly published book to send to influential people and to his professional colleagues. Jim personally autographed all the books, and then

together, he and Shirley laboriously packaged them, addressed the envelopes, stamped them all, and wrote, "Special Fourth Class Mail, Book" 250 times on the labels. There in the family room of their first little house, they then got down on their knees and laid their hands on the pile of books. Jim prayed a prayer of dedication, asking God to bless his labor in the work of the kingdom. Finally, they carefully carried the packages to his Volkswagen and headed for the post office.[5]

Focus on the Family grew exponentially over the next few years. But in 1985 the ministry—and Dr. Dobson—experienced a time of crisis. Prayer was the solution to the problem.

It began when Dr. Dobson accepted appointments to several national government boards, including the Attorney General's Commission on Pornography. For fifteen months, he suffered under the oppression of viewing pornographic material and also of criticism and attacks from supporters of the pornography industry. At the same time, contributions to Focus on the Family fell dramatically. Dobson began to question the future of the ministry.

Then he received a letter from his uncle's sister, Mrs. Aleen Swann. She told a story about Dobson's uncle, Dr. James McGraw, who had lain dying of cancer in 1977. Dobson's father, a pastor, began to pray for the dying man. Both Rev. James Dobson Sr. and McGraw were ministers who had dedicated themselves to spreading the gospel. For two days and nights, Rev. Dobson pleaded with God to spare his friend's life so he could keep serving him. Rolf Zettersten explains what happened on the third day:

God spoke to [Rev. Dobson]. It was not an audible voice, but the message was unmistakable. He said, "I have heard your prayers. I know that you love Me and are concerned about My people and My kingdom. I have seen your compassion, and I am going to answer your petitions in a way you could never have imagined. You are going to reach literally millions of people for Me, from coast to coast and around the world. But it will not be through your efforts or the work of James McGraw. It will be through your son!"[6]

That afternoon Dr. James McGraw went to be with the Lord. The next day, Rev. Dobson had a heart attack from which he never recovered.

Aleen Swann finished her letter by encouraging Jim Dobson in his work: "The end is not yet!" Her story changed Dobson's view, and he determined to continue on in the ministry. The next month, contributions increased dramatically, and since then the ministry has achieved nationwide prominence and has became an advocate for the family from individual homes to the nation's capital.

Through all these years, Shirley Dobson has been at her husband's side. But God called her to a ministry outside Focus on the Family. She became an advocate for prayer in our country when she assumed the leadership of the National Day of Prayer after Vonette Bright stepped down. Today Shirley is a well-known speaker on behalf of prayer. Her efforts have greatly benefited and increased grassroots participation in the National Day of Prayer observances.

God is not a respecter of persons. He raises up ordinary people who see miracles happen as a result of prayer. No matter who we are, we can have an impact in our homes, neighborhoods, communities, and nation that is far beyond anything we can do in our own strength—through the power of prayer.

THE SCIENCE OF PRAYER

Prayer is so much more than a onetime plea to God. Did you know that prayer can be a scientifically proven healer that brings peace and joy to life? Most of us wouldn't even try to approach the subject of prayer in what might be described as a "scientific" manner. Prayer is just too spiritual and too deeply personal to be subjected to that sort of mundane scrutiny. Besides, those of us who pray don't really need scientific justification. But even the scientific community has begun to realize the power of prayer.

Dr. Larry Dossey has experienced the healing power of prayer in his medical practice. He tells us that researchers have determined scientifically that prayer really does help people. These studies have proven that people who pray and have prayers said on their behalf are healthier, live longer, and have fewer stress-related illnesses. He writes:

> The experimental data on prayer that I turned up caught me off guard. I really wanted nothing to do with it. Meditation was acceptable, but the thought of "talking to God" in prayer was reminiscent of the fundamental Protestantism I felt I had laid to rest. Yet the results of prayer experiments kept forcing themselves into my psyche.
>
> These studies showed clearly that prayer can take many forms. Results occurred not only when people prayed for explicit outcomes, but also when they prayed for nothing specific.[7]

Ronna Harris and Mary Dew agree. As counselors and professors of psychiatry, they began a study called "Coping with Transplantation" in the fall of 1989 to determine why some heart-transplant recipients and their caregivers coped so much better than others. But they soon stumbled upon something they had not considered when designing their study:

It was not our original intention to study the role of religion and faith as coping strategies for these transplant-related stresses. However, time and again the recipients and family members whom we interviewed told us about the tremendous impact of their faith during the entire transplant process and afterwards. We realized that we were missing something important in our research plan, and we decided early on in the study to ask a series of carefully designed questions to examine the impact of religion directly.[8]

What these researchers found was that a person's commitment to religious faith had a strong correlation to how competent he or she was at managing disease and coping with stress. One year after the transplant, "74 percent of the recipients and 80 percent of the caregivers spend regular time in prayer."[9] The study concluded that prayer and other evidences of deep faith were "strong predictors of which recipients and which caregivers would go on to have a less rocky road in the long term after transplant."[10]

Science, it seems, is finally discovering what many of us already know: Prayer works!

We could cite thousands of examples of how God has intervened in all kinds of situations to help and comfort his people. To illustrate the incredible power of prayer in everyday life, let's look at two stories. The first is about the miraculous airplane experiences of Alan and Sandi Frye. The second is the astounding rescue of a drowning baby.

POWER OVER FEAR

Three days after the Valujet DC9, Flight 592, disappeared into the muck of the Florida Everglades with all passengers on board, Alan and Sandi Frye of Lake Mary, Florida, prepared to board a Mexican airline charter flight. They were traveling to Cancún, Mexico, on a much-needed vacation for their fifteenth anniversary. Their good friends Ken and Doris Frasier were with them. Sandi had wanted to take a cruise, but Alan had persuaded her that this trip was just what they needed.

As they walked up the steps of the airplane, Sandi thought about how she had prayed to overcome her long-standing fear of flying. For the past year, she and Alan had immersed themselves in prayer, both in their church prayer group and in their personal lives. They were involved in a home-fellowship Bible study, where Sandi had asked the group to pray that she would depend on God instead of giving in to emotion. She had also made her fear a matter of prayer during her devotional times.

As she boarded Flight 401, she almost conquered the fear still lurking beneath the surface of her mind. After all, what were the chances of something terrible happening?

Sandi leaned back in the seat and closed her eyes. *The takeoff wasn't too bad,* she decided as the muffled roar of the engines vibrated through the cabin. *I'm so glad Alan's right here beside me.* She glanced at him but noticed that his face seemed pinched with worry. He glanced out the window and looked down at the wide expanse of blue beneath the DC9.

"What's wrong?" Sandi asked, her fear starting to bubble up again.

"We've been in the air too long," he said. "It's only a one-and-a-half-hour flight to Cancún, and we've been in the air for two hours. And we seem to be circling."

Sandi's fear reared its ugly head. "What do you think is wrong?"

Just then, an ashen-faced flight attendant picked up the cabin microphone. He stumbled over his words and seemed short of breath. "Ladies and gentlemen, ladies and gentlemen. May I have your attention, please? The captain has declared an emergency. He's lost radio contact with the airport and has flown off course. We're short on fuel, and we'll be forced to land on the water. We need to prepare for an emergency landing."

For a moment, the cabin was silent; then cries and sobs broke out everywhere. "The plane will break up in the ocean waves," one man screamed. "We'll all drown."

Sandi felt Alan's strong hand on hers. She bent her head toward him, and they began praying together. After a few moments, she looked across the aisle at Doris. Tears were brimming over her friend's eyelids.

Suddenly a mysterious confidence rose up inside Sandi, which erased her fear. "We're not going into the Gulf," she exclaimed. "We're going to be in church on Sunday morning giving our testimony to the glory and saving power of Jesus Christ!"

Alan and Sandi knelt in the aisle next to Ken and Doris. All four of them joined hands and began praying as the plane rumbled on for another tense sixty minutes. Most of the passengers were paralyzed with fear, but Ken and Doris and Alan and Sandi were rejoicing in the peace God had given them. They continued to pray aloud.

Meanwhile, Sandi's father, W. H. Roberson, was driving along the city streets in Lake Mary. Suddenly a feeling of fear for his daughter came over him. He began to pray for her safety until that feeling of fear left him.

Back on the plane, the flight attendant made another announcement. "The pilot has made contact with an air-traffic controller at the air force base in Tampico, Mexico. The control tower said we can land on the airstrip if we have enough fuel to make it that far. Right now, FAA inspectors at the Orlando airport are calculating our fuel load. But it looks as if we may fall short of land by eighty miles."

Sandi and Alan began to pray that the fuel would be extended. They had confidence that God had everything under control.

Sandi and Alan began talking about their three kids at home in Florida. Sandi's faith was unshakable. She knew that the Lord was in control and that they would see their kids again. She and Alan began singing a praise song to the Lord.

Twice the pilot requested permission to put the plane in the water because he feared for the safety of his passengers if he tried to make it to land. But the air-traffic controller at the air base said, "No, keep coming. Keep coming."

The flight attendants began preparing the passengers for the emergency landing. "Please stow all your belongings under the seats. Fasten your seat belts securely; then lean over and grab your ankles."

"You'll have to put away your Bible now because we're going down," Alan told Sandi.

She ran her hand over its cool pages. Then she closed it with a snap, set it on the floor, and put her feet on top of the cover. She grabbed her ankles. She was standing firm on the Word of God!

The plane ran out of fuel over the Gulf. The pilot banked the craft, trying to make it to the airstrip. With a jolt, the DC9 lost all airspeed and began dropping quickly, two hundred yards short of the runway. As the plane flew along the shore, it hit the ground violently. With a terrifying sound, the nose gear was ripped off, and the right wing dug into the ground.

All around Sandi and Alan, people were being tossed like rag dolls. Some were yanked out of their seat belts by the force;

arms and legs flailed wildly. But Sandi and Alan felt as solid as rocks in their seats.

With a shower of sparks and the scream of twisting metal, the plane spun around and stopped abruptly. For a second, no one inside the cabin moved. Then people began jumping up to escape the smoke-filled cabin.

Sandi grabbed her Bible and ran toward the rear exit, but it was a mass of mangled metal and thick smoke. She turned around and headed for the wing exit. Then she and Alan jumped out onto the firm, solid earth.

"Praise God! Praise God!" she shouted as she ran a safe distance from the aircraft. All around her, people were crying and screaming hysterically. With a peaceful state of mind, she and Alan went from group to group giving the praise to God for saving them.[11]

Later, Sandi and Alan found out that the FAA had determined that the jet would crash into the Gulf of Mexico 80 to 120 miles from land! Although the aircraft had been loaded with just enough fuel to make the one-and-a-half-hour flight to Cancún, it had traveled three hours and ten minutes—710 miles more than planned.

Alan and Sandi escaped unhurt from their ordeal, and there were only minor injuries among the other passengers. The power of prayer had saved the lives of all on board!

THE MIRACLE BABY

It was a beautiful Saturday afternoon in Nebraska. Jim Day and his mother were flying a kite with Jim's four-year-old son near the shores of a quiet, horseshoe-shaped lake. Kristen was in her mother-in-law's house, fixing lunch for fifteen-month-old Jessica.

Suddenly Kristen heard her husband scream. Looking out the window, she saw him race toward the lake. Panicked, she realized that little Jessica had fallen into the lake. About fifteen feet from shore, Jim saw white clothing and a figure under several feet of water.

Jim dived in after the baby and pulled her from the water. Kristen ran to his side and was horrified to see her baby's yellow skin and blue lips. Jessica wasn't breathing! There wasn't a sign of life.

Jim began doing CPR on the baby. Her lifeless eyes just stared straight up, and her belly was swollen with water. Desperation gripped Kristen as she fell to her knees and cried out in prayer to God to save her baby. Jim kept doing CPR, but there was no response. Kristen just kept praying, asking for the life of her baby girl. For almost fifteen minutes, there was no sign of life. Then the baby began making groaning noises and grinding her teeth, but her eyes were still vacant.

Because the lake was twenty miles away from town, it took the ambulance nearly half an hour to arrive. After what seemed like an eternity, the siren screamed into the yard. Kristen removed the baby's wet clothes and wrapped her in a blanket; then the EMT team took over.

Jim and Kristen flew down the country roads, following the ambulance to the small rural hospital. When they arrived, the doctor took one look at the baby and her vital signs and called for an emergency helicopter. "We're sending her to the nearest large hospital, about seventy-five miles away. But the baby doesn't look good. After that much time with no vital signs, she probably has neurological or brain damage."

When the helicopter arrived, Kristen was horrified to find out that she couldn't ride with her baby. She and Jim would have to drive. But Jim had disappeared. When she found him, he told her that he had called their former church in Southern California as well as Pastor John Leech at their Colorado church and asked that Jessica's recovery be put on the prayer chain immediately. Then Jim and Kristen ran for their car, knowing that church members and friends were praying for Jessica.

It took them more than an hour to drive those seventy-five long miles, but when they arrived at the hospital, the doctor was all smiles. "She's not the same baby," he said. "The description we got from the other hospital was of a baby in serious condition. But when Jessica arrived here, she was alert. She's a miracle baby." Kristen knew that it was an answer to prayer!

After the chaos had settled down, Kristen held baby Jessica. As she rocked the little form, she thanked God for saving her baby. Then it was as if God spoke to her: "Kristen, I gave her back to you."

"You did?" Kristen answered.

"Yes, I did."

That night, Jessica was doing so well that the doctor removed all her tubes except one IV. Jessica recovered fully, without a sign of neurological or brain damage—a true miracle of prayer![12]

During each century and each awakening in our country, it wasn't the power of a single man or woman or even of a group or committee that changed our country; it was the many men, women, and children who lived normal, everyday lives but also rose above their routine through prayer.

Each of us has access to God's power. He is waiting for us to tap into his power. The world teaches us that the burden of maintaining our peace and freedom rests squarely on our own shoulders. Yet worrying about our future, our children, and our jobs robs us of our joy. In trying to control the uncontrollable, we exhaust ourselves.

We can continue to worry and fret, or we can ask God for help through the simple act of falling on our knees in prayer. Each of us makes a difference. Indeed it is not too late to awaken the nation to a complete renewal of faith and prayer. In recent years, thousands of people have begun to gather in small and large prayer groups to do just that. In the next chapter, we want to show you how you can be a part of this swelling movement of God.

For Discussion and Reflection

Adult Discussion

Form groups of three. Give each group a pencil and paper, a small block of wood, sandpaper, and a sheet of newspaper. Have group members sand the wood with the sandpaper, holding it over the newspaper to catch the sawdust. Ask the group members to observe the procedure and write down the things that happen or change.

Gather as a large group and list the changes the groups observed on a large piece of paper. Here are some possible observations: the wood became smoother; the sandpaper got worn down; the wood got hot.

Have the groups discuss the following questions. After each question, have them report on what they discussed.

  ★ How is what happened to the wood similar to what happened during the twentieth century when anti-God and religious forces met?

★ What resistance do you find when you talk to others about Jesus?
★ How can prayer help you be courageous in those situations?

Read John 16:33 aloud. Ask:

★ How might this verse encourage you about the current problems in our culture?
★ How might this verse help you in talking with your friends about your faith?

Youth Discussion

Form groups of three. Give each group a pencil and paper, a small block of wood, sandpaper, and a sheet of newspaper. Have group members sand the wood with the sandpaper, holding it over the newspaper to catch the sawdust. Ask the groups to observe the procedure and write down the things that happen or change.

Gather as a large group and list the changes the groups observed on a large piece of paper. Here are some possible observations: the wood became smoother; the sandpaper got worn down; the wood got hot.

Have the groups discuss the following questions. After each question, have them report on what they discussed.

★ How is what happened to the wood similar to what happened during the twentieth century when anti-God and religious forces met?
★ How does this apply to the situations you find at school and with your friends and to the temptations you face today?
★ What might happen if you resist our culture's declining morality? How is that like our sandpaper experiment?

★ What resistance do you find when you talk to others about Jesus?
★ How can prayer help you be courageous in those situations?

Read John 16:33 aloud. Ask:

★ How might this verse encourage you about the current problems in our culture?
★ How might this verse help you in talking with your friends about your faith?

TWENTY-FOUR

The Power of Ordinary People

Isn't God's power impressive? Viewing what he has done over the past five hundred years gives us an awesome picture of how he works with men and nations—making ordinary people extraordinary through the incredible power of prayer. But we must ask ourselves: How can we carry on the tradition of prayer so that we can experience a Fifth Great Awakening in America and turn our country back to God? Perhaps more than ever before, we must look to ourselves, not just our leaders, to reawaken our trust in Jesus Christ. There is a great need for ordinary Americans to realize the importance of prayer. In the final analysis, it is neither the court nor the government that determines the blessings that are bestowed by heaven. Only when each of us calls upon God will we make a difference in our home, community, and nation. We can count on this truth from the Psalms: "Unless the Lord builds a house, the work of the builders is useless" (Psalm 127:1).

But what most of us forget is that a house is built brick by brick, nail by nail, board by board. It isn't put together with just the beams. It requires every little and every large piece to make it a whole. It takes big prayer miracles and mundane day-to-day events. It also takes all kinds of people praying individually and in small and large groups.

We have seen how God has used ordinary people to accomplish great things throughout the five hundred years of our national history, but they could not have done anything without the help of thousands of Christians who didn't achieve fame but turned their lives into powerhouses of prayer.

Unfortunately, merely recognizing the spiritual malaise in our country today will not solve our problems.

As we have looked at the prayer heritage of our country, we have noticed three trends that generally occurred before God sent a spiritual awakening: (1) Small revivals often preceded a great awakening. This was true for the First Great Awakening in the 1700s. (2) A greater unity between denominations and other religious groups was forged. That was evident when the circuit riders began reaching the West with the gospel regardless of the denominations of their listeners. (3) Widespread prayer movements rose up spontaneously. The first example of this was Jonathan Edwards and the Concert of Prayer during the First Great Awakening. Of course the most dramatic example was the Prayer Revival just before the Civil War.

Are these trends occurring in our country today? Yes! Is God preparing to send a Fifth Great Awakening that will bring our country back to its godly roots? Much depends on how we respond to God's call to prayer and revival. Let's look at these trends today and then discover how we, too, can help bring on the Fifth Great Awakening.

THE MOVEMENT OF SMALL REVIVALS
As in many of the revivals in the past, students were the first to experience the moving of God in 1995 when a revival spread

to many areas of our country, resulting in changed lives and renewed churches.

Henry Blackaby, director of the Office of Prayer and Spiritual Awakenings for the Home Mission Board of the Southern Baptist Convention, coauthored a book with Claude King called *Experiencing God,* which served as a catalyst for this renewal. Pastor John Avant introduced Blackaby's material to his church in Brownwood, Texas, where a revival broke out in January 1995. The revival spread to nearby Howard Payne University, a Baptist school of about fourteen hundred students.

The Howard Payne revival spread to Southwestern Seminary in Fort Worth, Texas. Many churches in the area were also impacted. Then the students at Wheaton College (Illinois) caught the spirit of revival. From there the revival spread to campuses and churches in many areas of the country, including Massachusetts, California, Alabama, Indiana, Oregon, Georgia, Michigan, Minnesota, Pennsylvania, New York, and Connecticut.[1] During the same time period, a revival occurred at the National Convocation on Revival in Little Rock, Arkansas. This led to further spread of revival in churches and on campuses.

A revival also occurred at the biennial staff training of Campus Crusade for Christ at Fort Collins, Colorado, in July 1995. Nancy Leigh DeMoss spoke on brokenness, igniting a week of repentance and renewal among the more than four thousand attendees. The revival was so powerful that scheduled conference events were canceled as people prayed from early in the morning until midnight.

THE MOVEMENT TOWARD UNITY

All over our country, we can see the move toward unity. Denominations, parachurch organizations, and other groups are coming together to try to reach the world for Christ. In the spirit of this new unity, groups are retaining their distinctiveness while working together on the many areas of doctrine and religious experience they share. We will mention just two examples of this trend.

The *JESUS* film, one of the most effective evangelistic tools in the history of Christianity, was Bill Bright's vision beginning back in 1950. He prayed for God to help Campus Crusade produce a film that could deliver the message of Christ to the world's millions. But it wasn't until the mid-1970s that God answered that prayer. For five years, a team of five hundred scholars and leaders from secular and Christian organizations planned the project. In 1978, the film was produced for six million dollars. The script was taken directly from the Gospel of Luke, and it was filmed on location in Israel. Warner Brothers distributed the film to theaters in 1979. Today *JESUS* is the most-translated film in the history of motion pictures. As of January 1, 1996, the film was available in 342 languages, with 445 Christian agencies using the film. More than 732 million people had viewed the film in 217 countries.[2]

An interdenominational effort that sprang from the use of the *JESUS* film is the CoMission. It began after the premiere of the film in Soviet bloc countries, when government leaders asked Western Christians to help train public-school educators to teach morality in classrooms all over Eastern Europe and Russia. It was a humanly impossible task, but in answer to prayer, God began to put together a group of organizations and agencies to cooperate in sending teams to hold convocations for teachers in 1991. The first three organizations were Campus Crusade for Christ International, Walk Thru the Bible, and the Association of Christian Schools International. The spirit of interdenominational cooperation is evident in the CoMission's goal: to call together the body of Christ to share resources to fulfill the great commission in the former Soviet Union.

As of June 1996, more than 38,000 teachers had attended 125 convocations held in 10 countries in the former Soviet Union. The organization estimates that more than 7.1 million students and their families have been affected. To accomplish this result, 84 organizations are working together and have sent more than 1,500 CoMissioners as team members to these convocations.

THE MOVEMENT OF PRAYER

Today a host of prayer movements have sprung up all across our country. In the spring of 1980, more than 500,000 Christians gathered on the Mall in Washington, D.C., for the first Washington for Jesus Rally. Called the nation's largest prayer meeting, it was put together so that Americans could repent and pray for their nation. In 1988, a second rally brought together one million people to repent and to pray for their churches. And in 1996, a third rally called for prayer for the youth of this country and for the return of the nation to faith in God.

Another indicator of a spiritual renewal in this country is the phenomenal success of a Christian men's movement called Promise Keepers. It all started in 1990. University of Colorado football coach Bill McCartney was driving to Pueblo, Colorado, with his friend Dave Wardell, who was the state chairman of the Fellowship for Christian Athletes. McCartney, whose Colorado team had just won the national championship, shared his dream to see the stadium in Boulder, where the University of Colorado plays its home games, filled to capacity with men honoring God and learning how to become men of integrity.

Later that year, seventy-two men began to fast and pray. Their prayer desire was to have thousands of men coming together for Christian renewal. They developed a group called Promise Keepers, whose goal was to urge men to pray and commit to keeping seven promises that encompass everything from serving God and family to supporting one's local minister and influencing the world for Christ.

The following year, four thousand men gathered at the University of Colorado's basketball arena for the first Promise Keepers Conference. By 1993 Promise Keepers filled the university's fifty-thousand-seat Boulder stadium, and in 1995 Promise Keepers filled thirteen stadiums with more than seven hundred thousand men. In 1996 attendance hit one million men. In 1997 an estimated half a million men traveled to Washington, D.C., in September for a Stand in the Gap gathering—possibly the biggest group ever to assemble there.[3] The assembly received news headlines all over our country. Today Promise Keepers is the fastest-growing men's movement in America.

No country can hope to experience spiritual renewal without involving its youth. That's just what began to occur at a youth evangelism conference in Dallas, Texas, in 1990. The student participants decided to meet at their school's flagpole to pray. That was the beginning of an annual event known as "See You at the Pole." Every third Wednesday of September since then, students have gathered at school flagpoles to pray for their schools, teachers, families, and friends. It has become the largest student prayer gathering in history.

Another developing sign of national prayer renewal is the rapidly growing annual Fasting and Prayer Conference. In 1994 the first Fasting and Prayer Conference was held in Orlando, Florida. Hundreds of our nation's religious leaders attended. Since then, each year in November, the conference is held in a different city. Recently churches and other groups have been linked by satellite to enable more Christians to participate in the conferences. The most recent event encompassed two hundred parachurch organizations and utilized TV broadcasts potentially reaching 32 million households. The results of these gatherings, scheduled each year in mid-November, are already becoming apparent as scores of college campuses and hundreds of churches are experiencing spiritual awakening through fasting and prayer.

In the 1980s, God gave David and Robyne Bryant a longing to help precipitate a spiritual awakening in our country through prayer. In December 1981, they led the first Concerts of Prayer gathering in the twentieth century in our country. Today thousands of Concerts of Prayer rallies take place through Concerts of Prayer International. That organization has helped begin many other local prayer gatherings and organizations.

Other important groups or movements are also holding prayer gatherings. A few are

- ★ U.S. Prayer Track and Pray USA!
- ★ National Children's Prayer Network
- ★ Mission America
- ★ Celebrate Jesus 2000

Could these spontaneous prayer efforts springing up all over our country be a harbinger of the Fifth Great Awakening?

THE CHALLENGE
If the evidence of answered prayer over the past five hundred years has taught us anything, it's that God answers the prayers

of his people. Each of us can change our world through the power of prayer, for the Bible says, "The earnest prayer of a righteous person has great power and wonderful results" (James 5:16).

We would like to challenge you to be part of this prayer effort. Just think about what your prayers can do for your life, for your community, for our country!

Perhaps you have experienced a prayer miracle in your life. Perhaps you have seen the healing power of prayer, too. Through our own personal answers to prayer, we have all seen what God can do to change our circumstances and to help us become more like his Son, Jesus. Therefore most of us believe that prayer will transform our lives, but do we believe that God can still bring another awakening in spite of our country's hardened, sinful condition? Bill Bright says a resounding yes. He writes:

> If awakenings of the past foreshadow events to come, I believe that we will see the fire of the Holy Spirit break out in the churches and spread to every nook and cranny in the land. We will see revival begin with God's people, but millions of unbelievers everywhere—in government, education, the media, Hollywood—will turn to Christ in unprecedented numbers. That is the nature of true revival. It is never contained within church walls.[4]

But how can we pray in such a way that we will help bring on this revival? Dan Hayes, in his book *Fireseeds of Spiritual Awakening,* gives several steps we can take to prepare for a revival:

> First, God's people must recognize the need for revival. Second, God's people must humble themselves before Him. Third, God's

people must confess their sins and repent of them, making resti-
tution where necessary. Fourth, God's people must begin to
pray fervently and consistently for spiritual awakening. Fifth,
God's people must call others to pray as well.[5]

If we obey God's call to revival, what results we will see!
Can you imagine crime rates dropping so drastically that po-
licemen have time to form quartets and sing in churches? How
about if millions of people gather during the National Day of
Prayer each year to confess our national sins and repent of
them? If America would once again return to its Christian
roots, we could close prisons, darken courtrooms, cut down
on the need for foster homes. We could solve our national debt
and live in safety and peace. We could see racial reconciliation
and tackle the other social problems our country faces. We
could generate the human and financial resources to change
the world for Christ in our generation.

Remember William Arthur's book *The Tongue of Fire,* published in 1856, just before the Prayer Revival? At the end of his
book, he offered a prayer asking God to send a revival to America. One year later, the great Prayer Revival swept our country.

We, too, want to end with a prayer for revival. We believe in
the power of prayer. We are sure that God is waiting to send us
his power when we humble ourselves and pray fervently. We
want to obey God's command as given in the book of Joel in
the Old Testament:

> The Lord says, "Turn to me now, while there is time! Give me
> your hearts. Come with fasting, weeping, and mourning.
> Don't tear your clothing in your grief; instead, tear your
> hearts." Return to the Lord your God, for he is gracious and
> merciful. He is not easily angered. He is filled with kindness
> and is eager not to punish you. (Joel 2:12-13)

We urge you to join us as we pray for the Fifth Great Awakening to descend on our nation. Pray the following prayer, asking that God will change our nation as he has changed it so many times before:

> Father God, full of mercy and love, we have sinned against you. We have disobeyed your Word. We have not dwelled in a spirit of unity with our brothers and sisters in the Lord, and we have chosen to go our own way. But we realize the error of our ways. We repent of the evil we have done. We humble ourselves before you, asking for your mercy and your power.
>
> Forgive us for the many sins we have committed. Please heal our land and cleanse it of sin. Help us to repent so that you can send your revival fire. Give us godly counsel and your wisdom. We ask that you would raise up men and women who can lead us to righteousness. We pray for our leaders in government and the leaders in our churches.
>
> We earnestly desire that your Word be preached to all people in our lifetime. Make us a righteous people who will go anywhere at your command to reach those who have never heard your name.
>
> We thank you for your graciousness, your kindness, and your patience for our land. We pray this in the name of our Lord Jesus Christ, to the glory of God. Amen.

We encourage you to join one or two of the many prayer efforts in your area. Spread the news to your friends about God's desire to remake our nation into a powerhouse of righteousness. Your heartfelt participation in a call for spiritual renewal will make a difference!

OUR LEGACY IN STONE

Our prayer heritage is truly one of our most precious national treasures. As we have seen in the prayer history of our country, it is easy for each new generation to forget its spiritual roots. Our forefathers gave us a remembrance to help us keep our heritage in mind. It is a legacy written in stone to help us remember God's work in our midst.

We like to think of this legacy as giving credit where credit is due. Do you remember the last time you watched a movie? At the end, the credits roll, often for several minutes. That part of the film documents everyone who had a significant part in making the movie what it is.

We have a roll of credits for our country also. In the concluding chapter, we would like to show how our country honors the people who shaped our nation and led our people into righteous living. Amazingly, this honor roll also gives credit to an even higher power—our awesome God! As we close this exploration of the incredible power of prayer, we'll take one final look at the Christian prayer heritage of America through the buildings and monuments of our nation's capital.

For Discussion and Reflection

Adult Discussion
Bring in a damp paper towel and several marbles or rocks for every three people in your class. Form groups of three. Have two people hold the damp towel, and have each person estimate how many marbles or rocks they can pile on the towel before it breaks. Then have the third group member place each marble or rock onto the towel one at a time until it breaks.

When the groups are finished, compare the number of marbles or rocks the towels held. Then ask:

★ How was the addition of marbles like continuing, prevailing prayer for our country?

★ What does it mean to persist in prayer?
★ Why does it make a difference to God?

In their trios, have people study Luke 11:5-13. Give the groups the following questions to guide their discussion. Encourage people to share personal experiences of the results of persistent prayer. Ask:

★ How is the neighbor in the passage like God?
★ How is the neighbor different from God?
★ What do boldness and persistence in prayer have to do with God's answering prayer?

Bring the class back together, and have the groups report on their discussions. Then ask:

★ Why does God want us to continue in prayer until we receive an answer?
★ What would persistent prayer mean for us in our daily lives?
★ What issues are worth taking to God in prayer on a consistent basis?

Challenge your class to prevail in prayer this week over issues of the most concern to them. Then discuss how we can use consistent prayer to bring revival to our nation.

Youth Discussion

Bring small wrapped candies to class. Put several out in front of the class. Pick a number between one and one thousand. Tell the students to each write a number on a piece of paper and hold it up so you can see it. Whoever guesses the number first wins the candy.

When a student guesses correctly, give him or her the candy. Then ask:

- ★ How did it feel to keep guessing without winning?
- ★ What did it take to win the candy?
- ★ How is this like praying a long time for something? How is it different?

Form groups of four, and have the kids read Luke 11:5-13. Give the groups the following questions to guide their discussion:

- ★ How is the neighbor in the passage like God?
- ★ How is the neighbor different from God?
- ★ What do boldness and persistence in prayer have to do with God's answering prayer?

After the groups report on their discussions, have each person make a list of things they'd like to see happen. Suggest that the kids come up with a prayer request for each of the following categories: themselves, America, the church, their families. When the kids complete their lists, ask, "What difference might consistent prayer make in each of these situations?"

Wrap up the class with prayer, and encourage the kids to commit to praying for their long-term concerns faithfully throughout the month. Emphasize that revival will come only when Christians continue to pray faithfully for their country.

TWENTY-FIVE

Standing Stones

If you travel through the Middle East, you will notice unusual piles of stones in various places. They are called "standing stones," and they are reminders of God's significant work or of tragedies that occurred because of the nations' sinfulness. Sometimes stones are piled beside a road to remember an accident that occurred there. If an unusual happening occurs, a pile of stones will often be left behind. Even in death, stones are left to remember the great things that occurred in a person's life. For example, President Bill Clinton placed stones on the grave of former Israeli prime minister Yitzhak Rabin.

Americans, too, practice this tradition, but we do it by building monuments. These monuments help us remember important men, women, and events in our history. Washington, D.C., contains many of the more well-known national monuments. Vast numbers of Americans tour these sites each year. God's significant work in the making of this great nation is often forgotten by these visitors and never mentioned by tour guides, but if they would look closely, they would find the signposts of God's miraculous intervention in the monuments to these famous lives and situations.

Take a mental tour with us as we show you a few of these monuments and point out the telltale evidence of God's significant work that the builders left behind.

George Washington, a man of prayer, is honored with a

555-foot monument. The words *Praise to God* are on the capstone. In the interior, on carved blocks lining the walls of the stairwell, are biblical quotations and Christian references such as "Search the Scriptures," "Holiness to the Lord," "Train Up a Child in the Way He Should Go," and "In God We Trust." What a fitting memorial for a man who spent time on his knees before God every day!

The Lincoln Memorial is often described as "a sacred religious refuge" where one can find inspiration. That, too, is suitable for this man of God. He was often seen praying and searching the Scriptures. He relied on God in some of the tensest moments in our country's history!

As you look at his large, chiseled-granite face, you can almost hear him speak the words etched on the walls that surround him. Those words—spoken by him—remind us of his deep faith in God. The south wall contains the Gettysburg Address: "That this nation, under God, shall have a new birth of freedom—and that government of the people, by the people, for the people, shall not perish from the earth."

His second inaugural address is on the north wall. It speaks of "God," the "Bible," "providence," "the Almighty," and "divine attributes." It also says, "As was said 3,000 years ago, so it still must be said, 'The judgments of the Lord are true and righteous altogether.'"

The third memorial is to Thomas Jefferson, author of the Declaration of Independence, founder of the University of Virginia, and third president of the United States. This Founding Father, perhaps the most brilliant American statesman who has ever lived, was not a devout Christian, but he acknowledged reverence for God as necessary for the prosperity of America. From the Jefferson Memorial on the south banks of Washington's tidal basin, Thomas Jefferson still speaks through this inscription: "God, who gave us life, gave us liberty. Can the liberties of a nation be secure when we have removed a conviction that these liberties are the gift of God? Indeed I tremble for my country when I reflect that God is just, that his justice cannot sleep forever."

The Robert E. Lee Memorial Home is located above the Arlington National Cemetery. The Arlington Memorial bridge links this memorial with the Lincoln Memorial, across the Potomac River. It symbolizes the reconciliation that these two great men of God sought between the North and the South.

Thousands of American soldiers have been buried around Robert E. Lee's former home, noted for its family prayer parlor. The Lee mansion at Arlington National Cemetery overlooks Washington, D.C., and the graves of President John F. Kennedy and his brother Robert.

Both of the Kennedy memorials are inscribed with famous statements from the men's speeches, as well as references to prayer and seeking God's guidance. John F. Kennedy's memorial says: "Let us go forth to lead the land we love, asking His blessing and His help." The Robert Kennedy memorial says: "Let us dedicate ourselves to that and say a prayer for our country and our people."

In the Capitol building, there is a large room called Statuary Hall. Each state contributes two statues representing the most outstanding individuals from that state's history. These honored people represent the best in that state's leadership and character.

These one hundred special Americans, memorialized in marble or bronze in the Capitol building, include not only some of America's greatest leaders but also some of our Christian leaders. Many of these statues could also be considered "standing stones," reminding us of God's significant work in America's history and his many answers to prayer.

Father Junipero Serra, the great Franciscan missionary to the Indians, represents California. We read earlier about his great sacrifice and answered prayers as God performed a significant work through him to establish a series of missions throughout California. This was a herculean task, especially since Father Serra was already in his fifties and suffered from a chronic ulcer on one leg.

One of Connecticut's representatives is Governor Jonathan Trumbull, the only Colonial governor to support the American Revolution. He was Washington's good friend and declared days of prayer and fasting in support of the Revolutionary cause.

Father Damien, a priest who dedicated his life to helping lepers on the Hawaiian island of Molokai, represents Hawaii. In the 1870s he accomplished amazing feats in the area of leprosy care, in addition to building six chapels plus homes for boys and girls. He died of leprosy after sixteen years of undaunted dedication.

Frances Willard, a Christian social reformer who pioneered the women's Christian temperance movement in the 1880s and promoted higher education, represents Illinois. She was associated with evangelist Dwight Moody, and her statue was the first to honor a woman in Statuary Hall.

Starting in 1856, Mother Joseph from the state of Washington was directly responsible for establishing eleven hospitals, seven academies, five Indian schools, and two orphanages in the Pacific Northwest. She left a legacy of humanitarian service that has never been equaled.

From the state of Oklahoma comes the Cherokee Indian Sequoya, whose memory is perpetuated in the name of two species of California giant-redwood trees. Sequoya invented the Cherokee alphabet prior to 1820, enabling the Cherokees to read and write the Scriptures.

From Massachusetts comes John Winthrop, the Colonial governor for twelve terms. He arrived in Boston in 1630 with eighteen hundred Puritan settlers. He developed a form of government compatible with Puritan beliefs and ideals.

Roger Williams founded Rhode Island Colony in 1636. His greatest gift to the colonies was the authorship of the Declaration of the Principle of Religious Liberty.

Do you recall the Pennsylvanian Reverend John Muhlenberg? He told his Woodstock, Virginia, congregation one Sunday morning during the Revolutionary War, "There is a time to preach and a time to pray." And then, in a voice that sounded like a trumpet blast, he exclaimed, "There is a time to fight, and that time has now come." Laying aside his ministerial robe, he stood before his flock in the full uniform of an American colonel. Almost the entire male audience, nearly three hundred men, enlisted that day and followed him into battle for American freedom.

God is also honored in many of the buildings in our capital. They, too, serve as a reminder of God's work in this great country of ours through the years.

The first building constructed in the nation's capital was the White House. The cornerstone was laid in 1792 during George Washington's presidency, and the magnificent structure was completed during the term of our second president, John Adams. A prayer authored by President John Adams is carved into the marble facing of the State Dining Room fireplace. It reads: "I pray Heaven to bestow the best of blessings on this house and on all that shall hereafter inhabit it. May none but honest and wise men ever rule under this roof."

Our Capitol building also reflects God's steady guidance in our country and the faith of our Founding Fathers. It shows that our country was founded not just as a nation "under God" but as a nation of Christians. Even today every session of the House and Senate begins with prayer.

The United States Capitol's foundation was laid in 1793 by George Washington. Inside, the 180-foot-high Capitol rotunda, so large it could house the Statue of Liberty, displays paintings that depict our Christian heritage. One is the landing of Columbus, which shows him giving thanks to God. Another shows the Christian baptism of the Indian princess Pocahontas. Next to that painting is one depicting the departure of the Pilgrims for America. On the sail of the small ship can be seen the phrase "God with Us."

Entombed in one of the cornerstones of this great building is Daniel Webster's famous speech containing the words "God save the United States of America."

In an alcove located just off the main rotunda of the Capitol is the Congressional Prayer Room. It is reserved for the private prayer and meditation of members of Congress. Just as our past leaders used prayer to help guide them in the formation of our country and its leadership, many of our present leaders also pray in that room.

The central feature of the Congressional Prayer Room is the beautiful stained-glass window. Called "Washington's Gethsemane," the window depicts the kneeling figure of George Washington at Valley Forge, praying to God for his soldiers and his country. Behind him are etched the words from Psalm 16:1: "Preserve me, O God, for in Thee do I put my trust." Above Washington are the words "This Nation under God."

Situated on a busy street across from our nation's Capitol is the Supreme Court. Above the east entrance to the Court is a carved relief of Moses. He is holding the tablets of the Ten Commandments, serving as a reminder that the foundation of our law is the Bible. Also above the main entrance to the Supreme Court building, the words "Equal Justice under the Law" are engraved. This is a biblical concept dating back to the time of Moses.

The Ten Commandments are inscribed on the huge oak doors of the entrance to the Supreme Court chambers. In the Supreme Court chamber, each session opens with this simple prayer: "God save the United States and this Honorable Court."

The Library of Congress, the world's largest library, with a collection of over 110 million items, is growing at the rate of 2 million new items per year. In the library, numerous Scriptures can be found on the walls. One of the eight inscriptions in the main reading room reminds Americans of what God asks of us. Taken from Micah 6:8, it says, "What doth the Lord require of thee, but to do justly, to love mercy and walk humbly with thy God?"

The men who built these monuments, statues, and buildings recognized God's blessing and rule in our nation. God truly did answer many prayers and work through countless miracles to bring us to where we are today—untold numbers of amazing stories of ordinary people who changed history through prayer! The Israelites remembered God's significant works and answered prayers with "standing stones," and we need to do the same. As we view the monuments and remember the great men and moments behind them, we need to also think about the answered prayers that made the difference.

But we don't have to travel to our nation's capital to build reminders of our prayer heritage. We'd like to conclude our book by suggesting a few simple activities you can do in a group, with your family, or by yourself to help keep our American prayer heritage alive. Make the focus of your prayer the spiritual awakening of America and a personal revival within your life.

It's true. The incredible power of prayer is still alive today!

For Discussion and Reflection

The stories of the incredible prayer history of our country are truly astounding. We pray that as a result of hearing these accounts, you, too, will begin to pray consistently for our country. Only through our prayers will our people turn from their sins, as stated in 2 Chronicles 7:14, and pursue godliness. The following activities will help you pray in a meaningful way individually or as a group.

"STANDING STONES"

Choose three or four things to pray for on a regular basis. Start out with at least ten small rocks (about two or three inches high), and paint them. When an answer to a prayer occurs, write it on a small slip of paper and tape it to the rocks. Or take snapshots if appropriate, and paste them onto the stones. Display the rocks on a shelf.

PERSONAL PRAYER REMINDERS

You can take the first activity further by making "standing stones" for yourself and/or your family. Think back on the last year. Recall prayers God answered for you and/or your family. Often we forget how awesome God is because we don't think of his past goodness to us. Erect a pile of stones in a place you walk by frequently. Each time you pass the stones, thank God for the incredible power of prayer.

PRAYER JOURNAL

Just like Dawson Trotman, you can make a prayer journal. Divide your journal pages into two columns. As you write in each request, date it in the first column. When the request is answered, fill in the second column and date it, too. Go back each month and see how many prayers God has answered!

PRAYER BANNER OR PRAYER BULLETIN BOARD

Choose three or four requests and pray for them. When a request is answered, post it on your bulletin board or draw and write it on a prayer banner you've created. See how long the banner becomes or how full the board is after a year!

ABOUT THE AUTHORS

David W. Balsiger is a television field producer-director, advertising executive, and author of thirty-eight major literary works, including twenty-two books. He is the director of the media division of Group Publishing in Loveland, Colorado. His best-selling books include *In Search of Noah's Ark* (Sunn), *The Incredible Discovery of Noah's Ark* (Doubleday-Dell), *The Lincoln Conspiracy* (NAL), and *Ancient Secrets of the Bible* (Dell/Group). These books have sold from 250,000 to more than one million copies each. Three of the books have been on secular and religious national best-sellers lists.

Joette Whims has worked as a writer for many years and has been an editor for several publishing firms. She has coauthored several books, including books on prayer for children for the National Day of Prayer and Michigan Family Forum. She has also taught adult groups in her church and community. She and her family live in San Bernardino, California.

Melody Hunskor taught public school for fourteen years. She has written several books on active learning. She and her sister, Joette Whims, coauthor history newspapers for public schools in several parts of the country and a newspaper column called "A Touch of Home." She and her family live in Stewartville, Minnesota.

NOTES

Chapter 1: The Transforming Power of Prayer

1. David Barton, *America: To Pray or Not to Pray* (Aledo, Tex.: Wallbuilder Press, 1988), 82.
2. "Insight" newsletter, published by Family Research Council, Washington, D.C., 17 November 1997.
3. This re-creation adapted from videotaped interview of Roger Morrison by John Stocker, Resurrection Fellowship Church, 10 October 1995.

THE EXPLORERS
Chapter 2: The Impossible Proposal

1. Thomas S. Giles, "Did You Know?" *Christian History Magazine: Columbus & Christianity,* 35:2.
2. Christopher Columbus, *Libro de las Profecias (Book of Prophecies).* Quoted in William J. Federer, *America's God and Country: Encyclopedia of Quotations* (Coppell, Tex.: FAME Publishing, Inc., 1994), 112–13.
3. Kevin A. Miller, "Why Did Columbus Sail?" *Christian History Magazine: Columbus & Christianity,* 35:11.
4. This re-creation adapted from Peter Marshall and David Manuel, *The Light and the Glory* (Old Tappan, N.J.: Fleming H. Revell Company, 1977), 32; and George Grant, *The Last Crusader* (Wheaton, Ill.: Crossway Books, 1992), 95–96.
5. This re-creation adapted from John Eidsmoe, *Columbus and Cortez: Conquerors for Christ* (Green Forest, Ark.: New Leaf Press, 1992), 84; and Marshall and Manuel, *The Light and the Glory,* 35–36.

Chapter 3: The Lure of Gold

1. This re-creation adapted from Marshall, *The Light and the Glory,*

37–38; Eidsmoe, *Columbus and Cortez*, 106; and Miller, "Why Did Columbus Sail?" 9.

2. Samuel Eliot Morison, *Admiral of the Ocean Sea* (Boston: Little, Brown and Company, 1942), 171. Quoted in Eidsmoe, *Columbus and Cortez*, 106–7.

3. Eidsmoe, *Columbus and Cortez*, 17.

4. Miller, "Why Did Columbus Sail?" 9.

5. This re-creation adapted from Marshall and Manuel, *The Light and the Glory*, 39–40; Eidsmoe, *Columbus and Cortez*, 108; and Miller, "Why Did Columbus Sail?" 11–13.

6. Quotation from Marshall and Manuel, *The Light and the Glory*, 41. Re-creation adapted from Marshall and Manuel, *The Light and the Glory*, 40–41; and Eidsmoe, *Columbus and Cortez*, 108.

7. Marshall and Manuel, *The Light and the Glory*, 42.

8. Eidsmoe, *Columbus and Cortez*, 112–13.

Chapter 4: Poverty, Prayer, and Service

1. Marshall and Manuel, *The Light and the Glory*, 71.

2. This re-creation adapted from Eidsmoe, *Columbus and Cortez*, 166–75.

3. Ibid.

4. This re-creation adapted from Don DeNevi and Noel Francis Moholy, *Junipero Serra* (San Francisco: Harper & Row Publishers, 1985), 22–28.

5. Marshall and Manuel, *The Light and the Glory*, 77.

6. This re-creation adapted from Marshall and Manuel, *The Light and the Glory*, 78.

THE COLONISTS
Chapter 5: Jamestown Colony

1. This re-creation adapted from Marshall and Manuel, *The Light and the Glory*, 82–83.

2. *Strange Stories, Amazing Facts* (Pleasantville, N.Y.: The Reader's Digest Association, Inc., 1976), 340.

3. Benjamin Hart, *Faith and Freedom* (San Bernardino, Calif.: Here's Life Publishers, 1988), 139.

4. Ibid.

5. This re-creation adapted from Marshall and Manuel, *The Light and the Glory,* 83–85; and Hart, *Faith and Freedom,* 140.

6. Marshall and Manuel, *The Light and the Glory,* 87.

7. Hart, *Faith and Freedom,* 141.

8. Ibid.

9. John Smith, *Description of Virginia.* Quoted in George Willison, *Behold Virginia* (New York: Harcourt, Brace, and Company, 1952), 80. Quoted in Marshall and Manuel, *The Light and the Glory,* 94–95.

10. John Smith, *Description of Virginia.* Quoted in Willison, *Behold Virginia,* 106. Quoted in Marshall and Manuel, *The Light and the Glory,* 99.

11. Hart, *Faith and Freedom,* 144–45.

12. Marshall and Manuel, *The Light and the Glory,* 100.

13. Ibid., 91.

Chapter 6: An Unlikely Beginning

1. Cotton Mather, *Life of William Bradford.* Reprinted in *The Story of Pilgrim Fathers* (Boston and New York: Houghton Mifflin Company, 1897; New York: Klaus Reprint Company, 1969), 40. Quoted in Marshall Foster and Mary-Elaine Swanson, *The American Covenant: The Untold Story* (Santa Barbara, Calif.: Foundation for Christian Self-Government, 1981), 73.

2. William Bradford, *Of Plymouth Plantation: 1620–1647.* Reprinted in *The Modern Library,* Samuel Eliot Morison, ed. (New York: Random House, Inc., 1969), 326. Quoted in Foster and Swanson, *The American Covenant,* 71.

3. Bradford, *Of Plymouth Plantation: 1620–1647.* Quoted in Verna M. Hall, *The Christian History of the Constitution of the United States of America* (San Francisco: Foundation for American Christian Education, 1976), 190. Quoted in Foster and Swanson, *The American Covenant,* 73.

4. Hart, *Faith and Freedom,* 69.

5. This re-creation adapted from Hart, *Faith and Freedom,* 69–72.

6. William Bradford, *A History of Plymouth Plantation.* Quoted in Hart, *Faith and Freedom,* 70.

7. Ibid.

8. Bradford, *Of Plymouth Plantation: 1620–1647.* Quoted in Marshall and Manuel, *The Light and the Glory,* 110.

9. Jasper Rosenmeier, "Bradford's *Of Plymouth Plantation,"* in *Typology and Early American Literature,* Steve Bercovitch, ed., 76. Quoted in Marshall and Manuel, *The Light and the Glory,* 110.

10. Bradford, *Of Plymouth Plantation: 1620–1647.* Quoted in Marshall and Manuel, *The Light and the Glory,* 111.

Chapter 7: The Incredible Journey

1. John Robinson, personal letter. Quoted in Hart, *Faith and Freedom,* 73.

2. Ibid., 73–74.

3. Bradford, *Of Plymouth Plantation: 1620–1647.* Quoted in Marshall and Manuel, *The Light and the Glory,* 116.

4. Marshall and Manuel, *The Light and the Glory,* 117.

5. This re-creation adapted from Marshall and Manuel, *The Light and the Glory,* 118–19.

6. Jean Poindexter Colby, *Plimoth Plantation: Then and Now* (New York: Hastings House Publishers, 1970), 38.

7. Bradford, *Of Plymouth Plantation: 1620–1647.* Quoted in Marshall and Manuel, *The Light and the Glory,* 120–21.

Chapter 8: The Plymouth Settlement

1. William Bradford and Edward Winslow, *Morte's Relation.* Quoted in Alexander Young, *Chronicles of the Pilgrim Fathers* (Boston: Charles C. Little and James Brown, 1841), 158–59. Quoted in Marshall and Manuel, *The Light and the Glory,* 123–24.

2. Bradford and Winslow, *Morte's Relation.* Quoted in Marshall and Manuel, *The Light and the Glory,* 124.

3. Bradford, *A History of Plymouth Plantation.* Quoted in Hart, *Faith and Freedom,* 79.

4. Bradford, *A History of Plymouth Plantation.* Quoted in Foster and Swanson, *The American Covenant,* 28.

5. Hart, *Faith and Freedom,* 80.

6. Marshall and Manuel, *The Light and the Glory,* 136.

7. Edward Winslow, quoted in Alexander Young, *Chronicles of the Pilgrim Fathers,* 347–50. Quoted in Marshall and Manuel, *The Light and the Glory,* 142.

8. Ibid., 143.

9. Ibid.

10. This re-creation adapted from Kate Waters, *Sarah Morton's Day: A Day in the Life of a Pilgrim Girl* (New York: Scholastic, Inc., 1989), and Marshall and Manuel, *The Light and the Glory,* 141.

Chapter 9: The Puritans Arrive

1. John Winthrop, *History of New England from 1630–1649,* James Savage, ed. (New York: Ayer, 1972, reprint of 1825 ed.). Quoted in Hart, *Faith and Freedom* (San Bernardino, Calif.: Here's Life, 1988), 88.

2. Ibid., 89.

3. Ibid., 90.

4. Marshall and Manuel, *The Light and the Glory,* 157.

5. *The Winthrop Papers, Vol. II, 1623–1630* (Boston: Massachusetts Historical Society, 1931). Quoted in Marshall and Manuel, *The Light and the Glory,* 161–62.

6. Edmund S. Morgan, *The Puritan Dilemma* (Boston: Little, Brown and Company, 1958), 58. Quoted in Marshall and Manuel, *The Light and the Glory,* 167.

7. Charles E. Hambrick-Stowe, "Ordering Their Private World," *Christian History Magazine: The American Puritans,* 41:17.

8. Ibid., 18.

9. Sanford H. Cobb, *The Rise of Religious Liberty in America,* 162. Quoted in Marshall and Manuel, *The Light and the Glory,* 185.

10. This re-creation was adapted from George W. Harper, "New England Dynasty," and J. I. Packer, "Theology Tested by Trial," *Christian History Magazine,* issue 41.

Chapter 10: Trials of Faith

1. Horton Davies, *The Worship of the American Puritans, 1629–1730,* (New York: Peter Lang Publishing, Inc., 1990), 140–41.

2. John Eliot, quoted in Cotton Mather, *Magnalia Christi Americana,* 1852. Reprinted as *The Ecclesiastical History of New England* (New York: Russell and Russell, 1967). Quoted in Iain Murray, *The Puritan Hope* (London: The Banner of Truth Trust, 1971), 93.

3. Cotton Mather, *Magnalia Christi Americana,* 495.

4. Cotton Mather, quoted in Robert Flood, *America: God Shed His Grace on Thee* (Chicago: Moody Press, 1975), 55.

5. Ola Elizabeth Winslow, *John Eliot, "Apostle to the Indians"* (Boston: Houghton Mifflin Company, 1968), 179. Quoted in Ruth Tucker, *From Jerusalem to Irian Jaya* (Grand Rapids, Mich.: Zondervan Publishing House, 1983), 89.

6. Bradford, *Of Plymouth Plantation: 1620–1647,* quoted in Stephen Foster, *Their Solitary Way,* 50. Quoted in Marshall and Manuel, *The Light and the Glory,* 216.

7. John Winthrop, *History of New England from 1630–1649,* James Savage, ed. (Boston: Little, Brown and Company, 1853). Quoted in Marshall and Manuel, *The Light and the Glory,* 217.

8. Cotton Mather, *Magnalia Christi Americana,* 1852. Reprinted as Cotton Mather's *Ecclesiastical History of New England* (New York: Russell and Russell, 1967), 2:355.

9. Winthrop, *History of New England from 1630–1649.* Quoted in Marshall and Manuel, *The Light and the Glory,* 217.

10. *Old Sudbury* (Boston: Pinkham Press, 1958), 23. Quoted in Marshall and Manuel, *The Light and the Glory,* 228.

11. This re-creation adapted from Marshall and Manuel, *The Light and the Glory,* 228–29.

12. Leo Bonfanti, *The Witchcraft Hysteria of 1692* (Burlington, Mass.: Pride Publications, Inc., 1992), 2:39.

13. Ibid., 41.

14. Ibid., 45–46.

15. Hambrick-Stowe, "Ordering Their Private World," 18.

Chapter 11: Wake the Sleeping Giant

1. Hart, *Faith and Freedom,* 218.

2. Martin E. Marty, *Pilgrims in Their Own Land: 500 Years of Religion in America* (Boston: Little, Brown and Company, 1984), 113.

3. Jonathan Edwards, *A Faithful Narrative of the Surprising Work of God* (Grand Rapids, Mich.: Baker Books, 1979), 14.

4. Jonathan Edwards, "Some Thoughts Concerning the Revival," in *The Great Awakening,* C. C. Goen, ed., vol. 4 of *The Works of Jonathan Edwards* (New Haven: Yale University Press, 1972). Quoted in Edward Charles Lyrene, "The Role of Prayer in Revival Movements, 1740–1860," (Ph.D. diss., Southern Baptist Theological Seminary, 1985), 41–42.

5. Benjamin Franklin, "Autobiography," from *A Benjamin Franklin Reader,* Nathan Goodman, ed. Quoted in Keith J. Hardman, *Seasons of Refreshing: Evangelism and Revivals in America* (Grand Rapids, Mich.: Baker Books, 1994), 91.

6. A. D. Belden, *George Whitefield, the Awakener* (Nashville, 1930). Quoted in Hardman, *Seasons of Refreshing,* 92–93.

7. Marshall and Manuel, *The Light and the Glory,* 252.

8. Ibid., 253.

9. Ibid.

10. This re-creation adapted from Harry S. Stout, "Heavenly Comet," *Christian History Magazine* 12, no. 2:14–15; and Marshall and Manuel, *The Light and the Glory,* 252–53.

11. Rev. Jonathan French, "Thanksgiving Sermon, November 29, 1798," quoted in Verna M. Hall, *The Christian History of the American Revolution* (San Francisco: Foundation of American

Christian Education, 1976), 51. Quoted in Foster, *The American Covenant,* 40.

Chapter 12: In God We Trust

1. Noah Webster, *The History of the United States* (Ann Arbor, Mich.: University Microfilms, 1975), 207–208.
2. Harry Stout, "Preaching the Insurrection," *Christian History Magazine: The American Revolution,* 50:12.
3. Patrick Henry, quoted in Mark Couvillon, "Christians in the Cause," *Christian History Magazine: The American Revolution,* 15, no. 2:18–19.
4. This re-creation adapted from Mark Couvillon, "Fighting Words," *Christian History Magazine: The American Revolution,* 13.
5. Stout, "Preaching the Insurrection," 13.
6. Cassandra Niemczyk, "Little-Known or Remarkable Facts about Christianity and the American Revolution," *Christian History Magazine: The American Revolution,* 2.
7. Mark A. Beliles and Stephen K. McDowell, *America's Providential History* (Charlottesville, Va.: Providence Foundation, 1989), 123–25.
8. Hall, *Christian History of the American Revolution,* 407.
9. Ibid.
10. Courtesy of the Massachusetts Historical Society.
11. Marshall and Manuel, *The Light and the Glory,* 278.
12. Ibid., 281.
13. Courtesy of the Library Company of Philadelphia.
14. From brochure entitled *"With United Hearts . . ."* (Dallas: Thanks-Giving Square Foundation, 1975), 4.
15. Hall, *Christian History of the American Revolution,* 543–44.
16. Marshall and Manuel, *The Light and the Glory,* 296.
17. Beliles, *America's Providential History,* 162.
18. Ibid., 147.
19. Ibid., 142.
20. Ibid., 147–48.

21. Ibid., 149.
22. B. F. Morris, *Christian Life and Character of the Civil Institutions of the United States* (Philadelphia: George W. Childs, 1864), 537.
23. Daniel L. Dreisbach, *Real Threat and Mere Shadow* (Westchester, Ill.: Crossway Books, 1987), 67.
24. Taken from the one-page flyer, "The Thanksgiving Proclamation" (Buena Park, Calif.: Americanism Education League, n.d.).

Chapter 13: A Man of Prayer

1. William White, *Washington's Writings,* quoted in *Maxims of Washington,* John F. Schroeder, ed. (Mt. Vernon: Mt. Vernon Ladies Association, 1942), 406. Quoted in Federer, *America's God and Country,* 665.
2. John Marshall, *The Life of George Washington,* abridged edition, 2 vols. (1832; first edition in 5 vols., 1804–1807), 445. Quoted in Federer, *America's God and Country,* 664.
3. George Washington, in his personal prayer book entitled *Daily Sacrifice* (1752), consisting of twenty-four pages in his own handwriting, intended for private devotional use. Quoted in Federer, *America's God and Country,* 657.
4. Parting words to Washington from his mother, Mary Washington, in November 1753, as recorded in John N. Norton, *Life of General George Washington* (1870), 34. Quoted in Federer, *America's God and Country,* 636.
5. *Miracles and Other Wonders,* Sun Classic Pictures, CBS Television, 1991.
6. George Bancroft, *Bancroft's History of the United States,* 3rd ed. (Boston: Charles C. Little and James Brown, 1838), 4:190. Quoted in Marshall and Manuel, *The Light and the Glory,* 286.
7. Bancroft, *Bancroft's History,* 190. Quoted in Marshall and Manuel, *The Light and the Glory,* 286.
8. Hart, *Faith and Freedom,* 233–34.
9. This re-creation adapted from Hart, *Faith and Freedom,* 233–34; and Federer, *America's God and Country,* 636–37.

10. George Washington, quoted in Vincent Wilson Jr., *The Book of the Founding Fathers* (Harrisonburg, Va.: R. R. Donnelley & Sons Company, 1985), 74.

11. George Washington, quoted in James Thomas Flexner, *George Washington*, 4 vols. Quoted in Hart, *Faith and Freedom*, 273.

12. George Washington, quoted in Henry Halley, *Halley's Bible Handbook* (Grand Rapids, Mich.: Zondervan, 1927, 1965), 18. Quoted in Federer, *America's God and Country*, 660.

13. W. Herbert Burk, *Washington's Prayers* (Norristown, Pa.; published for the benefit of the Washington Memorial Chapel, 1907), 87–95. Quoted in LaHaye, *Faith of Our Founding Fathers*, 111–13.

14. William J. Johnson, *George Washington, the Christian* (Nashville, Tenn.: Abingdon Press, 1919), 69–70. Quoted in Marshall and Manuel, *The Light and the Glory*, 289.

15. Benjamin Tallmadge, quoted in George F. Scheer and Hugh F. Rankin, *Rebels and Redcoats* (New York: World Publishing Company, 1957), 171. Quoted in Marshall and Manuel, *The Light and the Glory*, 315.

16. Quoted in B. F. Morris, *Christian Life and Character of the Civil Institutions of the United States* (Philadelphia: George W. Childs, 1864), 298–99.

17. Hart, *Faith and Freedom*, 290.

18. Morris, *Christian Life and Character*, 297.

19. Beliles, *America's Providential History*, 141.

20. Morris, *Christian Life and Character*, 299.

21. Marshall and Manuel, *The Light and the Glory*, 322.

22. Bruce Lancaster, *The American Revolution* (Garden City, N.Y.: Garden City Books, 1957), 42. Quoted in Beliles, *America's Providential History*, 157.

23. George Washington, quoted in E. C. M'guire, *The Religious Opinions and Character of Washington* (New York: Harper and Bros., 1836), 162–67. Quoted in Morris, *Christian Life and Character*, 299.

24. Marshall and Manuel, *The Light and the Glory*, 332.

25. Ibid., 332–33.
26. Washington, quoted in Scheer and Rankin, *Rebels and Redcoats,* 504, 506–507. Quoted in Marshall and Manuel, *The Light and the Glory,* 333.
27. Tallmadge, quoted in Scheer and Rankin, *Rebels and Redcoats,* 504, 506–507. Quoted in Marshall and Manuel, *The Light and the Glory,* 334.
28. George Washington, quoted in Scheer and Rankin, *Rebels and Redcoats,* 504, 506–507. Quoted in Marshall and Manuel, *The Light and the Glory,* 335.
29. George Washington's inaugural address, quoted in Charles E. Kistler, *This Nation under God* (Boston: Richard G. Badger, The Gorham Press, 1924), 97; and in Johnson, *George Washington, the Christian,* 161–62. Quoted in Marshall and Manuel, *The Light and the Glory,* 349.
30. *Bible for the Revolution* (New York: Arno Press, 1782, reprinted 1968), cover page. Quoted in Federer, *America's God and Country,* 25.

Chapter 14: Amazing Documents

1. Declaration of Independence. Quoted in *Encyclopedia Britannica,* 15th ed., s.v. "Independence, Declaration of."
2. Vincent Wilson Jr., *The Book of Great American Documents* (Brookville, Md.: American History Research Associates, 1987), 13.
3. John Adams, quoted in W. David Stedman and Lewis G. La-Vaughn, *Our Ageless Constitution* (Asheboro, N.C.: W. David Stedman Associates, 1997), 15.
4. Samuel Adams, quoted in Beliles, *America's Providential History,* 133.
5. William Ellery, quoted in Stedman, *Our Ageless Constitution,* 15.
6. John Quincy Adams, quoted in Stedman, *Our Ageless Constitution,* 15.

7. Thomas McKean, quoted in Stedman, *Our Ageless Constitution*, 16.

8. *Adams Family Correspondence*, L. H. Butterfield, ed. (Cambridge, Mass.: Harvard University Press, 1963), 2:28–31. Quoted in Marshall and Manuel, *The Light and the Glory*, 310–11.

9. Webster, *History of the United States*, 273–74.

10. George Washington, 14 June 1783, in "Circular Letter Addressed to the Governors of all the States on Disbanding the Army," included in Jared Spanks, ed., *The Writings of Washington*, vol. 8 (Boston: American Stationer's Company, 1837). Quoted in Federer, *America's God and Country*, 646.

11. Benjamin Franklin, quoted in Barton, *America: To Pray or Not to Pray*, ix–xi.

12. This re-creation adapted from Barton, *America: To Pray or Not to Pray*, and Federer, *America's God and Country*, 246–50.

13. Barton, *America: To Pray or Not to Pray*, x.

14. Jonathan Dayton, quoted in M'Guire, *The Religious Opinions and Character of Washington*, 152. Quoted in Federer, *America's God and Country*, 250.

15. William C. Rives, *History of the Life and Times of James Madison* (Boston: Little, Brown and Company), 1:33–34. Quoted in LaHaye, *Faith of Our Founding Fathers*, 129–30.

16. James Madison, quoted in James H. Smylie, "Madison and Witherspoon: Theological Roots of American Political Thought," *The Princeton University Library Chronicle* (spring 1961), 125. Quoted in John Eidsmoe, *Christianity and the Constitution* (Grand Rapids, Mich.: Baker Books, 1987), 110.

17. Lewis Henry Boutell, *The Life of Roger Sherman* (Chicago: A. C. McClure and Company, 1896), 272–73. Quoted in LaHaye, *Faith of Our Founding Fathers*, 136–37.

18. Quoted in LaHaye, *Faith of Our Founding Fathers*, 162–65.

19. Alex Garden, *Eulogy of Charles Cotesworth Pinckney* (Charleston, S.C.: Printed by A. E. Miller, 1825), 42–43. Quoted in LaHaye, *Faith of Our Founding Fathers*, 178.

20. Robert Flood, *America: God Shed His Grace on Thee* (Chicago: Moody Press, 1975), 168.
21. Thomas J. Burke, ed., *Man and State: Religion, Society, and the Constitution* (Hillsdale, Mich.: Hillsdale College Press, 1988), 32.
22. Burke, *Man and State,* 32.
23. Taken from the "National Day of Prayer" flyer, 2.

THE REVIVALISTS
Chapter 15: Miraculous Intervention by God

1. J. Edwin Orr, *The Role of Prayer in Spiritual Awakening* (video) (San Bernardino, Calif.: Inspirational Media, 1976).
2. Ibid.
3. Ibid.
4. Jeremiah Hallock, quoted in Bennet Tyler, *New England Revivals as They Existed at the Close of the Eighteenth and the Beginning of the Nineteenth Centuries* (Boston: Massachusetts Sabbath School Society, 1846), 23. Quoted in Edward Charles Lyrene, "The Role of Prayer in American Revival Movements, 1740–1860" (Ph.D. diss., Southern Baptist Theological Seminary, 1985), 83.
5. Samuel Shepard, quoted in *Connecticut Evangelical Magazine,* (October 1801), 2:137. Quoted in Lyrene, "The Role of Prayer," 89.
6. Edward Dorr Griffith, quoted in William B. Sprague, *Lectures on Revivals of Religion* (Edinburgh, 1958). Quoted in Hardman, *Seasons of Refreshing,* 109.
7. Flood, *America,* 110.
8. John H. Wigger, "Holy, Knock-'Em-Down Preachers," *Christian History Magazine,* 45:22.
9. A. Gregory Schneider, "Focus on the Frontier Family," *Christian History Magazine,* 45:38.
10. Lyrene, "The Role of Prayer," 105.
11. Hardman, *Seasons of Refreshing,* 166; Tucker, *From Jerusalem to Irian Jaya,* 122.

12. Orr, *The Role of Prayer.*

13. Peter Marshall and David Manuel, *From Sea to Shining Sea* (Old Tappan, N.J.: Fleming H. Revell, 1986), 116.

14. Charles Finney, *Memoirs* (New York: Fleming H. Revell Company, 1876), 142. Quoted in Lyrene, "The Role of Prayer," 145.

15. Lyrene, "The Role of Prayer," 157.

16. Hardman, *Seasons of Refreshing,* 162.

17. This re-creation adapted from Charles Finney, *How to Experience Revival* (Springdale, Pa.: Whitaker House, 1984), 6–9.

18. Finney, *How to Experience Revival,* 7–8.

19. Hardman, *Seasons of Refreshing,* 167.

Chapter 16: The Prayer Revival

1. James Madison, *Notes of Debates in the Federal Convention of 1787* (1787; reprint New York: W. W. Norton Company, 1987), 504. Quoted in Federer, *America's God and Country,* 423.

2. William A. Arthur, *The Tongue of Fire* (New York: The Methodist Book Concern, 1856), 109. Quoted in Lyrene, "The Role of Prayer," 195.

3. Warren A. Chandler, *Great Revivals and the Great Republic* (Nashville, 1904), 190. Quoted in Hardman, *Seasons of Refreshing,* 172.

4. Hardman, *Seasons of Refreshing,* 174.

5. This re-creation adapted from Hardman, *Seasons of Refreshing,* 172–75.

6. Charles G. Finney, *The Memoirs of Charles G. Finney,* Garth M. Rosell and Richard A. G. Dupuis, eds. (Grand Rapids, Mich.: Zondervan Publishing House, 1989), 563. Quoted in Hardman, *Seasons of Refreshing,* 178.

7. Orr, *The Role of Prayer.*

Chapter 17: The Blue and the Gray

1. Charles Finney, quoted in Tim Stafford, "The Abolitionists," *Christian History Magazine: The Untold Story of Christianity and the Civil War,* 33:25.

2. Terry D. Bilhartz, "Revival in the Army of Northern Virginia" (master's thesis, Emory University, 1973), 25.

3. Gardiner H. Shattuck Jr. "Revivals in the Camp," *Christian History Magazine: The Untold Story of Christianity and the Civil War,* 33:28.

4. William W. Bennet, *A Narrative of the Great Revival Which Prevailed in the Southern Armies* (Harrisonburg, Va.: Sprinkle Publications, 1973), 431.

5. "Did You Know?" *Christian History Magazine: The Untold Story of Christianity and the Civil War,* 33:2.

6. John W. Schildt, quoted in Jeffrey Warren Scott, "Fighters of Faith," *Christian History Magazine: The Untold Story of Christianity and the Civil War,* 33:35.

7. Thomas Jonathan "Stonewall" Jackson, quoted in Beliles, *America's Providential History,* 234.

8. Stonewall Jackson, quoted in James B. Ramsey, *A Discourse Occasioned by the Death of Lieut. Gen. T. J. Jackson* (Lynchburg, Va.: Virginia "Water-Power Presses" Print, 1863), 7.

9. Robert E. Lee, quoted in John William Jones, D.D., *Christ in the Camp* (Richmond, Va.: B. F. Johnson and Company, 1887, 1897; The Martin and Hoyt Company, 1904; Harrisonburg, Va.: Sprinkle Publications, 1986), 58. Quoted in Federer, *America's God and Country,* 365.

10. Robert E. Lee, quoted in Robert Flood, comp., *The Rebirth of America* (Philadelphia: The Arthur S. DeMoss Foundation, 1986), 183. Quoted in Federer, *America's God and Country,* 365.

11. Bilhartz, "Revival in the Army," 63.

12. E. M. Bounds, quoted in a Thanksgiving brochure on prayer published by the National Citizen Action Network, Anaheim, California, 1989.

13. This re-creation adapted from Albert J. Raboteau, "The Secret Religion of the Slaves," *Christian History Magazine,* 33:42–45.

Chapter 18: Let My People Go

1. This re-creation adapted from the CBS television special, *Miracles and Other Wonders,* Sun Classic Pictures, CBS Television, 1991.

2. Abraham Lincoln, quoted in Catherine Millard, *Rewriting of American History* (Camp Hill, Pa.: Horizon House Publishers, 1991), 165.

3. Abraham Lincoln, quoted in William J. Johnson, *Abraham Lincoln the Christian* (Milford, Mich.: Mott Media, 1976), 16. Quoted in Bob and Rose Weiner, *The Forging of Christian Character* (Gainsville, Fla.: Maranatha Publications, 1985), 31.

4. Ibid.

5. Johnson, *Abraham Lincoln the Christian,* 16. Quoted in Weiner, *The Forging of Christian Character,* 31.

6. Johnson, *Abraham Lincoln the Christian,* 61. Quoted in Weiner, *The Forging of Christian Character,* 29.

7. Johnson, *Abraham Lincoln the Christian,* 70. Quoted in Weiner, *The Forging of Christian Character,* 29.

8. Abraham Lincoln, quoted in B. F. Morris, *Christian Life and Character of the Civil Institutions of the United States,* 557.

9. Flood, *America,* 126.

10. William Gladstone, quoted in Flood, *America,* 126.

11. David Elton Trueblood, *Abraham Lincoln: Theologian of American Anguish* (New York: HarperCollins Publishers, Inc., 1973). Quoted in *Abraham Lincoln: The Spiritual Growth of a Public Man* (Burke, Va.: The Trinity Forum, 1993), 23–25.

12. Abraham Lincoln, quoted in Johnson, *Abraham Lincoln the Christian,* 105–106. Quoted in Weiner, *The Forging of Christian Character,* 30.

13. Abraham Lincoln, quoted in Beliles and McDowell, *America's Providential History,* 225–26.

14. This re-creation adapted from Nancy Roberts, *Civil War Ghost Stories and Legends* (Columbia, S.C.: South Carolina University Press, 1992), 60–69.

15. Johnson, *Abraham Lincoln the Christian*, 107–108. Quoted in Beliles and McDowell, *America's Providential History*, 238–39.

16. Vincent Wilson Jr., ed., *The Book of Great American Documents* (Brookeville, Md.: American History Research Associates, 1987), 75.

17. Abraham Lincoln, quoted in Beliles and McDowell, *America's Providential History*, 231.

18. Johnson, *Abraham Lincoln the Christian*, 136–43. Quoted in Weiner, *The Forging of Christian Character*, 33–36.

19. Abraham Lincoln, quoted in Mark A. Noll, "The Puzzling Faith of Abraham Lincoln," *Christian History Magazine: Christianity and the Civil War*, 33:12.

Chapter 19: Igniting the Fires

1. D. L. Moody, quoted in David Maas, "The Life and Times of D. L. Moody," *Christian History Magazine: Dwight L. Moody*, 25:8.

2. D. L. Moody, quoted in J. C. Pollock, *Moody: A Biographical Portrait of the Pacesetter in Modern Mass Evangelism* (MacMillan, 1963). Quoted in Flood, *America*, 142.

3. D. L. Moody, quoted in a treasured, yellowed copy of the *Chicago Times-Herald*, Washburne Collection. Quoted in Richard Ellsworth Day, *Bush Aglow: The Story of Dwight Lyman Moody* (Grand Rapids, Mich.: Baker Books, 1977), 81–84.

4. Day, *Bush Aglow*, 81–84.

5. Flood, *America*, 135.

6. Vinita Hampton and C. J. Wheeler, "Key People in the Life of D. L. Moody," *Christian History Magazine: Dwight L. Moody*, 25:13.

7. Ibid.

8. Allan Fisher, "D. L. Moody's Contribution to Christian Publishing," *Christian History Magazine: Dwight L. Moody*, 25:33.

9. Flood, *America*, 135.

10. This re-creation adapted from Hardman, *Seasons of Refreshing*, 227.

11. Burlington (Iowa) Hawkeye, quoted in Elijah P. Brown, *The Real Billy Sunday* (New York, 1914), 116–21. Quoted in Hardman, *Seasons of Refreshing,* 230.

12. R. A. Torrey, quoted in George T. B. Davis, *Torrey and Alexander: The Story of a World-Wide Revival* (New York, 1905), 37–38. Quoted in Hardman, *Seasons of Refreshing,* 220.

13. Orr, *The Role of Prayer.*

14. Ibid.

15. Ibid.

THE EVANGELICALS
Chapter 20: When God Intervenes

1. Robert S. Alley, quoted in Richard G. Hutcheson, *God in the White House* (New York: Collier Books, 1988), 43.

2. Beverly J. Armuto, Gary B. Nash, Christopher L. Salter, and Karen K. Wixson, *A More Perfect Union* (Boston: Houghton Mifflin Company, 1991), 541.

3. Federer, *America's God and Country,* 698.

4. William Warren Sweet, *The Story of Religion in America* (New York: Harper & Brothers, 1950), 560–63; and Mark A. Noll, *A History of Christianity in the United States and Canada* (Grand Rapids, Mich.: William B. Eerdmans Publishing Company, 1992), 403–405.

5. Robert T. Handy, *A Christian America: Protestant Hopes and Historical Realities* (New York: Oxford University Press, 1971), 185.

6. Handy, *A Christian America,* 196.

7. Tucker, *From Jerusalem to Irian Jaya,* 324.

8. Quoted in Sweet, *The Story of Religion,* 75.

9. Quoted in Betty Lee Skinner, *Daws* (Grand Rapids, Mich.: Zondervan Publishing House, 1974), 195.

10. This re-creation adapted from Skinner, *Daws,* 197–202.

11. Skinner, *Daws,* 201.

12. Sweet, *The Story of Religion,* 436.

13. This re-creation adapted from Paul Aurandt, *Paul Harvey's the Rest of the Story* (New York: Bantam Books, 1977), 170–72.

14. Spencer January, "Covered by the Cloud," *Guideposts* 52, no. 6 (August 1997): 35–36.

15. K. Neil Earle, "D-Day: The Untold Story," *The Plain Truth*, July/August 1984, 31–32.

16. Ibid., 34.

17. Ibid.

18. Ibid., 33.

19. George M. Marsden, *Altered Landscapes: Christianity in America, 1935–1985* (Grand Rapids, Mich.: William B. Eerdmans Publishing Company, 1989), 66.

20. Marsden, *Altered Landscapes,* 67.

Chapter 21: A Spiritual Malaise

1. Timothy K. Beougher, "Student Awakenings in Historical Perspective," *Accounts of a Campus Revival: Wheaton College 1995* (Wheaton, Ill.: Harold Shaw Publishers, 1995), 40.

2. Ibid., 41.

3. J. Edwin Orr, *Good News in Bad Times: Signs of Revival* (Grand Rapids, Mich.: Zondervan Publishing House, 1953), 85. Quoted in Beougher, "Student Awakenings in Historical Perspective," 49.

4. Beougher, "Student Awakenings in Historical Perspective," 42.

5. "Week Ending Friday, July 20, 1979," *Public Papers of the Presidents of the United States: Administration of Jimmy Carter* (Washington, D.C.: Government Printing Office, 1979), 1236–37.

6. Barton, *America: To Pray or Not to Pray,* 19.

7. Hart, *Faith and Freedom,* 346.

8. Barton, *America: To Pray or Not to Pray,* 151–52.

9. Ibid., 151–54.

10. *Family News from Dr. James Dobson,* no. 10 (October 1997), 1.

11. William Murray, speech made at the Miracle Day Rally in Baltimore, Md., 17 June 1993. Videotaped by Religious Freedom Coalition.

12. Barton, *America: To Pray or Not to Pray,* 58–69.

13. George Washington, quoted in Federer, *America's God and Country,* 661.

14. Barton, *America: To Pray or Not to Pray,* 58–69.

15. *Education Week* (13 June 1985), 28; quoted in Barton, *America: To Pray or Not to Pray,* 146.

16. John Adams, quoted in Eidsmoe, *Christianity and the Constitution,* 22.

17. "Violence and Teens in the Home and in the Schools in the 1990s" (George H. Gallup International Institute, 10 March 1994), 2. Quoted in Robert L. Maginnis, "Insight" (Washington, D.C.: Family Research Council, n.d.), 4.

18. Don Oldenburg, "Primal Screen: Kids, TV Violence & Real-life Behavior," *Washington Post* (7 April 1992), E-5. Quoted in "A Closer Look: Key Research on TV's Impact" in *Family Policy* (Washington, D.C.: Family Research Council, August 1994), 4.

19. "Disorder in our Public Schools," United States Department of Education, Office of the Deputy Undersecretary for Planning, Budget, and Evaluation, memorandum for the Cabinet Council on Human Resources (3 January 1984). Quoted in Maginnis, "Insight," 1.

20. "Violence in the Schools: How America's School Boards Are Safeguarding Our Children" (National School Boards Association, 1993), 3. Quoted in Maginnis, "Insight," 3.

21. "Weapon-Carrying among High School Students—United States, 1990," (U.S. Department of Health and Human Services, 1990–1991), 18. Quoted in Maginnis, "Insight," 4.

22. "Violence and Teens," 2. Quoted in Maginnis, "Insight," 4.

23. "Age-Specific Arrest Rates and Race-Specific Arrest Rates for Selected Offenses, 1965–1992," *Uniform Crime Reports* (Washington, D.C.: U.S. Department of Justice, Federal Bureau of Investigation, December 1993), 13, 17. Quoted in "Crime and Its Roots: A Look behind the Numbers" in *Family Policy* (Washington, D.C.: Family Research Council, June 1994), 3.

24. "Births to Unmarried Women: How the States Are Measuring Up" in *In Focus* (Washington, D.C.: Family Research Council, n.d.), 1.

25. Dan Loeffler, *Face on the Twenty-First Century* (LaJolla, Calif.: World Research, 1994).

26. Herbert Kohl, "What Teen Suicide Means," *Nation* (9 May 1987), 603. Quoted in Barton, *America: To Pray or Not to Pray,* 31.

27. *Family News from Dr. James Dobson,* 11.

Chapter 22: Rays of Hope

1. "Remarks at the Annual National Prayer Breakfast," 31 January 1985, *Public Papers of the Presidents of the United States: Administration of Ronald Reagan* (Washington, D.C.: Government Printing Office, 1985), 97.

2. Federer, *America's God and Country,* 174.

3. This re-creation adapted from a personal telephone interview of Susan Sorensen by Joette Whims, Beverly Hills, Michigan, 11 May 1997.

4. Gerald R. Ford, *A Time to Heal* (New York: Harper & Row/Reader's Digest, 1979), 10. Quoted in Richard G. Hutcheson, *God in the White House* (New York: Collier Books, 1988), 93.

5. Ibid., 94.

6. *Public Papers of the Presidents of the United States: Administration of Jimmy Carter* (Washington, D.C.: Government Printing Office, 1977), 24. Quoted in Hutcheson, *God in the White House,* 136.

7. Bill Peterson, "Reagan's Use of Moral Language to Explain Policies Draws Fire," *Washington Post* (23 March 1983), A-15. Quoted in Hutcheson, *God in the White House,* 180.

8. Henry Steele Commager, quoted in Peterson, "Reagan's Use of Moral Language." Quoted in Hutcheson, *God in the White House,* 180.

9. *Public Papers of the Presidents of the United States: Administration of Ronald Reagan* (Washington, D.C.: Government Printing

Office, March 1984), 312–17. Quoted in Hutcheson, *God in the White House,* 181.

10. *Public Papers of the Presidents of the United States: Administration of George Bush* (Washington, D.C.: Government Printing Office, 20 January 1989), 102.

11. "Alabama Governor: Fight Drought with Prayer," *Atlanta Journal and Constitution* (26 June 1988).

12. Governor Guy Hunt, radio address, 25 June 1988. Transcript provided by the Governor's Press Office, State of Alabama, Montgomery, Alabama.

13. Press release, 28 June 1988. Transcript provided by the Governor's Press Office, State of Alabama, Montgomery, Alabama.

14. Ibid.

15. H. Norman Schwarzkopf and Peter Petre, *It Doesn't Take a Hero: The Autobiography of General H. Norman Schwarzkopf* (New York: Bantam Books, 1992), 397–98.

16. Ibid., 398.

17. Ibid., 412–13.

18. Ibid., 413.

19. Evangelical Press News Service (Minneapolis: 4 September 1992), 3–4.

20. Joel Belz, "Don't Believe Gossip about Gospel in the U.S. Military," *World* (22 December 1990), 3.

21. Federer, *America's God and Country,* 589.

22. "Proclamation 4826: National Day of Prayer, 1981," 19 March 1981, *Public Papers of the Presidents of the United States: Administration of Ronald Reagan* (Washington, D.C.: Government Printing Office, 1981).

Chapter 23: Carrying On the Mantle of Prayer

1. William Martin, *A Prophet with Honor: The Billy Graham Story* (New York: William Morrow and Company, Inc., 1991), 113.

2. Ruth Bell Graham, *It's My Turn* (Old Tappan, N.J.: Fleming H. Revell Company, 1982), 17.

3. Bill Bright, *Come Help Change the World* (Orlando, Fla.: NewLife Publications, 1985), 7.

4. Bill Bright, *The Coming Revival: America's Call to Fast, Pray, and "Seek God's Face"* (Orlando, Fla.: NewLife Publications, 1995), 16.

5. Rolf Zettersten, *Dr. Dobson: Turning Hearts toward Home* (Dallas: Word Publishing, 1989), 89.

6. Ibid., 102.

7. Dr. Larry Dossey, *Healing Words: The Power of Prayer and the Practice of Medicine* (San Francisco: HarperCollins Publishers, 1993), xvii.

8. Ronna Casar Harris, M.Ed., M.P.H., and Mary Amanda Dew, Ph.D., "A Surprising Factor in Transplant Success," *Lifetimes,* no. 1 (1997), 34.

9. Ibid.

10. Ibid., 35.

11. This re-creation adapted from the video *Believer's Voice of Victory* (Fort Worth: Kenneth Copeland Ministries, 1997) and from a personal telephone interview of Sandi Frye by David Balsiger, 6 April 1997.

12. This re-creation adapted from a personal interview of Kristen Day by David Balsiger, Loveland, Colorado, 30 March 1997.

Chapter 24: The Power of Ordinary People

1. John Avant, Malcolm McDow, and Alvin Reid, *Revival!* (Nashville: Broadman & Holman, 1996), 143.

2. Statistics taken from The *JESUS* Film Project flyer dated 1 January 1996.

3. William R. Mattox Jr., "Christianity Goes to the Playoffs," *The American Enterprise* (November/December 1995), 40.

4. Bright, *The Coming Revival,* 155.

5. Dan Hayes, *Fireseeds of Spiritual Awakening: Igniting the Flame of Spiritual Renewal* (San Bernardino, Calif.: Here's Life Publishers, 1983), 114.

BIBLIOGRAPHY

Andrews, Charles M. *Our Earliest Colonial Settlements.* Ithaca, N.Y.: Great Seal Books, 1933.

Armuto, Beverly J., Gary B. Nash, Christopher L. Salter, and Karen K. Wixson. *A More Perfect Union.* Boston: Houghton Mifflin Company, 1991.

Aurandt, Paul. *Paul Harvey's the Rest of the Story.* New York: Bantam Books, 1977.

Bakke, Dr. Robert. *The Concert of Prayer: Back to the Future?* Minneapolis, Minn.: Evangelical Free Church of America, 1993.

Barton, David. *America: To Pray or Not to Pray.* Aledo, Tex.: Wallbuilder Press, 1988.

Beliles, Mark A., and Stephen K. McDowell. *America's Providential History.* Charlottesville, Va.: Providence Foundation, 1989.

Belz, Joel. "Don't Believe Gossip about Gospel in U.S. Military." *World* (22 December 1990): 3.

Bennett, William W. *A Narrative of the Great Revival in the Southern Armies.* Harrisonburg, Va.: Sprinkle Publications, 1976.

Bilhartz, Terry D. "Revival in the Army of Northern Virginia." Master's thesis, Emory University, 1973.

Bolton, Herbert Eugene, and Thomas Maitland Marshall. *The Colonization of North America: 1492–1783.* New York: Macmillan, 1920.

Bonfanti, Leo. *The Witchcraft Hysteria.* Burlington, Mass.: Pride Publications, Inc., 1992.

Bounds, E. M. *Complete Works of E. M. Bounds on Prayer.* Grand Rapids, Mich.: Baker Book House, 1990.

Bowen, Catherine Drinker. *Miracle at Philadelphia: The Story of the Constitutional Convention, May to September 1787.* New York: The American Past, 1986.

Bradford, M. E. *A Worthy Company: Brief Lives of the Framers of the United States Constitution.* Marlborough, N.H.: The Plymouth Rock Foundation, 1982.

Bradford, M. E. *Religion & the Framers: The Biographical Evidence.* Marlborough, N.H.: The Plymouth Rock Foundation, 1991.

Bright, Bill. *Come Help Change the World.* Orlando, Fla.: NewLife Publications, 1985.

Bright, Bill. *The Coming Revival: America's Call to Fast, Pray, and "Seek God's Face."* Orlando, Fla.: NewLife Publications, 1995.

Burke, Robby Wray Jr. "Confederate Chaplains, the Great Revival, and the Prolongation of the Civil War." Master's thesis, James Madison University, 1991.

Burke, Thomas J., ed. *Man and State: Religion, Society, and the Constitution.* Hillsdale, Mich.: The Hillsdale College Press, 1988.

Chandler, Russell. *Racing toward Two Thousand One: The Forces Shaping America's Religious Future.* San Francisco: HarperSanFrancisco, 1992.

Christian History Magazine: Dwight L. Moody. (vol. 25).

Christian History Magazine: The Untold Story of Christianity and the Civil War. (vol 33).

Christian History Magazine: Columbus & Christianity. (vol. 35).

Christian History Magazine: George Whitefield. (vol. 38).

Christian History Magazine: The American Puritans. (vol. 41).

Christian History Magazine: Camp Meetings and Circuit Riders. (vol. 45).

Christian History Magazine: The American Revolution. (vol. 50).

Colby, Jean Poindexter. *Plimouth Plantation: Then and Now.* New York: Hastings House Publishers, 1970.

Colman, Robert, and A. Duane Litfin. *Accounts of a Revival: Wheaton College 1995.* Wheaton, Ill.: Harold Shaw Publishers, 1995.

Davies, Horton. *The Worship of the American Puritans, 1629–1730.* New York: Peter Lang Publishing, Inc., 1990.

Day, Richard Ellsworth. *Bush Aglow: The Story of Dwight Lyman Moody.* Grand Rapids, Mich.: Baker Books, 1977.

DeNevi, Don, and Noel Francis Moholy. *Junipero Serra.* San Francisco: Harper & Row Publishers, 1985.

Donovan, Frank R. *The Mayflower Compact.* New York: Grosset & Dunlap Publishers, 1968.

Dossey, Dr. Larry. *Healing Words: The Power of Prayer and the Practice of Medicine.* San Francisco: HarperCollins, 1993.

Dreisbach, Daniel L. *Real Threat and Mere Shadow.* Westchester, Ill.: Crossway Books, 1987.

Earle, K. Neil. "D-Day: The Untold Story." *The Plain Truth* (July/August 1984): 31–32.

Edwards, Jonathan. *A Faithful Narrative of the Surprising Work of God.* Grand Rapids, Mich.: Baker Books, 1979.

Eidsmoe, John. *Christianity and the Constitution: The Faith of Our Founding Fathers.* Grand Rapids, Mich.: Baker Books, 1987.

Eidsmoe, John. *Columbus and Cortez: Conquerors for Christ.* Green Forest, Ark.: New Leaf Press, 1992.

Fan into Flame (video). Colorado Springs, Colo.: Promise Keepers, 1996.

Federer, William J. *America's God and Country Encyclopedia of Quotations.* Coppell, Tex.: FAME Publishing, Inc., 1994.

Finney, Charles G. *How to Experience Revival.* Springdale, Pa.: Whitaker House, 1984.

Flood, Robert. *America: God Shed His Grace on Thee.* Chicago: Moody Press, 1975.

Foster, Marshall, and Mary-Elaine Swanson. *The American Covenant: The Untold Story.* Thousand Oaks, Calif.: Mayflower Institute, 1981.

Frey, Herman S. *Foundations of the Republic.* Nashville, Tenn.: Frey Enterprises, 1976.

Graham, Ruth Bell. *It's My Turn.* Old Tappan, N.J.: Fleming H. Revell Company, 1982.

Grant, George. *The Last Crusader.* Wheaton, Ill.: Crossway Books, 1992.

Hall, Verna M. *The Christian History of the American Revolution:*

Consider and Ponder. San Francisco: Foundation for American Christian Education, 1976.

Handy, Robert T. *A Christian America: Protestant Hopes and Historical Realities.* New York: Oxford University Press, 1971.

Hardman, Keith J. *Seasons of Refreshing: Evangelism and Revivals in America.* Grand Rapids, Mich.: Baker Books, 1994.

Hart, Benjamin. *Faith and Freedom: The Christian Roots of American Liberty.* San Bernardino, Calif.: Here's Life Publishers, 1988.

Hawke, David Freeman. *Everyday Life in Early America.* New York: Harper & Row Publishers, 1988.

Hayes, Dan. *Fireseeds of Spiritual Awakening: Igniting the Flame of Spiritual Renewal.* San Bernardino, Calif.: Here's Life Publishers, 1983.

Hefley, James, and Marti Hefley. *No Time for Tombstones: Life and Death in the Vietnamese Jungle.* Wheaton, Ill.: Tyndale House Publishers, 1974.

Howell Harris: His Own Story. Chepstow, Gwent, England: Bridge Publishing U.K., 1984.

Hutcheson, Richard G. *God in the White House.* New York: Collier Books, 1988.

Jones, Archie P. *America's First Covenant: Christian Principles in the Articles of Confederation.* Marlborough, N.H.: The Plymouth Rock Foundation, 1991.

Kinlaw, Dennis. *A Revival Account: Asbury—1970* (video). Spokane, Wash.: Reel to Reel Ministries, n.d.

Kuiper, B. K. *The Church in History.* Grand Rapids, Mich.: William B. Eerdmans Publishing Company, 1951.

LaHaye, Tim. *Faith of Our Founding Fathers.* Brentwood, Tenn.: Wolgemuth & Hyatt Publishers, Inc., 1987.

Long, A. L. *Personal Memoirs of Robert E. Lee.* Edison, N.J.: The Blue and Grey Press, 1983.

Lotz, David W., Donald W. Shriver Jr., and John F. Wilson, eds. *Altered Landscapes: Christianity in America, 1935–1985.* Grand Rapids, Mich.: William B. Eerdmans Publishing Company, 1989.

Lyrene, Edward Charles. "The Role of Prayer in American Revival

Movements, 1740–1860." Ph.D. diss., Southern Baptist Theological Seminary, 1985.

Marshall, Peter, and David Manuel. *From Sea to Shining Sea.* Old Tappan, N.J.: Fleming H. Revell Company, 1986.

Marshall, Peter, and David Manuel. *The Light and the Glory: Did God Have a Plan for America?.* Old Tappan, N.J.: Fleming H. Revell Company, 1977.

Martin, William. *A Prophet with Honor: The Billy Graham Story.* New York: William Morrow and Company, Inc., 1991.

Marty, Martin E. *Pilgrims in Their Own Land: 500 Years of Religion in America.* Boston: Little, Brown and Company, 1984.

McIntosh, Gary L. *Three Generations: Riding the Waves of Change in Your Church.* Grand Rapids, Mich.: Fleming H. Revell Company, 1995.

Millard, Catherine. *The Rewriting of America's History.* Camp Hill, Pa.: Horizon House Publishers, 1991.

Miller, Basil. *Charles Finney.* Minneapolis: Bethany Fellowship, Inc., 1951.

Miracles and Other Wonders, Sun Classic Pictures, CBS Television, 1991.

Moffatt, Timothy. *The Life and Times of Christopher Columbus.* London: Paragon Books, 1994.

Murray, Iain H. *The Puritan Hope.* London: The Banner of Truth Trust, 1971.

Noll, Mark A. *A History of Christianity in the United States and Canada.* Grand Rapids, Mich.: William B. Eerdmans Publishing Company, 1992.

Noll, Mark A., ed. *Religion & American Politics: From the Colonial Period to the 1980s.* New York: Oxford University Press, 1990.

Orr, Dr. J. Edwin. Revival: Awakening (video series). The U.S. Prayer Track, n.d.

Orr, Dr. J. Edwin. *The Role of Prayer in Spiritual Awakening* (video). San Bernardino, Calif.: Inspirational Media, 1976.

Prince, Derek. *Shaping History through Prayer and Fasting.* Old Tappan, N.J.: Fleming H. Revell Company, 1973.

Ramsey, Rev. James B. *A Discourse Occasioned by the Death of Lieut. Gen. T. J. Jackson.* Lynchburg, Va.: Virginia "Water-Power Presses" Print, 1863.

Rebirth of America. The Arthur S. DeMoss Foundation, 1986.

Roberts, Nancy. *Civil War Ghost Stories & Legends.* Columbia, S.C.: University of South Carolina Press, 1992.

Schwarzkopf, General H. Norman, and Peter Petre. *It Doesn't Take a Hero: The Autobiography of General H. Norman Schwarzkopf.* New York: Bantam Books, 1992.

Sharman, J. Michael, ed. *Faith of the Fathers: Religion and Matters of Faith Contained in the Presidents' Inaugural Addresses from George Washington to Bill Clinton.* Culpeper, Va.: Victory Publishing, 1995.

Skinner, Betty Lee. *Daws: A Man Who Trusted God.* Colorado Springs, Colo.: NavPress Publishing Group, 1974.

Smith, Helen Evertson. *Colonial Days & Ways As Gathered from Family Papers.* New York: Frederick Ungar Publishing Company, 1966.

Sorensen, Susan, and Joette Whims. *Kit Cat and the Whirling Watches: The Story of a Nation Built on Prayer.* San Juan Capistrano, Calif.: Joy Publishing, 1992.

Stedman, W. David, and LaVaughn G. Lewis. *Our Ageless Constitution.* Asheboro, N.C.: W. David Stedman Associates, 1997.

Strange Stories, Amazing Facts: Stories That Are Bizarre, Unusual, Odd, Astonishing, and Often Incredible. Pleasantville, N.Y.: Reader's Digest Association, Inc., 1976.

Sweet, William Warren. *The Story of Religion in America.* New York: Harper & Brothers Publishing, 1950.

Thanksgiving brochure on prayer published by the National Citizen Action Network, Anaheim, California, 1989.

Torrey, R. A. *The Power of Prayer and the Prayer of Power.* New York: Fleming H. Revell Company, 1924.

Tucker, Ruth A. *From Jerusalem to Irian Jaya: A Biographical History of Christian Missions.* Grand Rapids, Mich.: Zondervan Publishing House, 1983.

Waters, Kate. *Sarah Morton's Day: A Day in the Life of a Pilgrim Girl.* New York: Scholastic, Inc., 1989.

Webster, Noah. *History of the United States.* Ann Arbor, Mich.: University Microfilms, 1975.

Weiner, Bob, and Rose Weiner. *The Forging of Christian Character.* Gainesville, Fla.: Maranatha Publications, 1985.

White, Tom. *Between Two Tigers: Testimonies of Vietnamese Christians.* Bartlesville, Okla.: Living Sacrifice Books, 1996.

Wilson, Vincent Jr. *The Book of the Founding Fathers.* Harrisonburg, Va.: R. R. Donnelley & Sons Company, 1985.

Wilson, Vincent Jr., ed. *The Book of Great American Documents.* Brookeville, Md.: American History Research Associates, 1987.

Wright, Louis B. *The Cultural Life of the American Colonies.* New York: Harper & Row Publishers, 1957.

Wyatt-Brown, Bertram. *Yankee Saints and Southern Sinners.* Baton Rouge, La.: Louisiana State University Press, 1985.

Zettersten, Rolf. *Dr. Dobson: Turning Hearts toward Home.* Dallas: Word Publishing, 1989.